T0355960

ESSAYS ANGLICAN AND ANALYTIC

Essays Anglican *and* Analytic

Explorations in Critical Catholicism

Robert MacSwain

WILLIAM B. EERDMANS PUBLISHING COMPANY

GRAND RAPIDS, MICHIGAN

Wm. B. Eerdmans Publishing Co.
2006 44th Street SE, Grand Rapids, MI 49508
www.eerdmans.com

Published 2025

Book design by Leah Luyk

Printed in the United States of America

31 30 29 28 27 26 25   1 2 3 4 5 6 7

ISBN 978-0-8028-8311-7

Library of Congress Cataloging-in-Publication Data

A catalog record for this book is available from the Library of Congress.

This book is dedicated to Eleonore Stump
and in memory of Ann Loades,
both of whom taught me much about
the labor of the mind in the life of faith.

Contents

Preface

When I wrote most of the essays in this volume, it did not occur to me that they might one day be drawn together into a collection. This was partly because several of them were written early in my academic career; partly because they were composed for various occasions and exemplify different rhetorical approaches and genres; and partly because they range over such a wide diversity of topics. But one July in Sewanee, while out for a Sunday afternoon walk, I suddenly realized, rather to my surprise, that several essays focused either on Austin Farrer or David Brown interlocked sufficiently on the twin issues of Anglican identity and philosophical/theological method to form the core of a book, and that the way they often engaged with other figures added to their potential interest for a wider readership. I subsequently realized that including my essay on William Alston (one of those who initially pointed me back to Farrer); the coauthored essay on David Brown, Sarah Coakley, and David Ford; my presentation of the hagiological argument; and a new conclusion on what I had previously dubbed "Critical Catholicism" added up to a plausible volume.

I am thus grateful to the original journals and presses for allowing me to republish the material here; for Ben King and Jason Fout for agreeing to include our coauthored piece; for Eerdmans and the Templeton Religion Trust for working with me on this project; and for Pollyanne Frantz and Connie Patton for administering the Templeton grant on Sewanee's end. However, note that the opinions expressed in this publication are those of the author(s) and do not necessarily reflect the views of the Templeton Religion Trust.

The essays were put in their final shape and the introduction and conclusion written while I was on a 2023–2024 sabbatical (funded partially by Sewanee and partially by the Templeton grant) as a visiting scholar at Vanderbilt Divinity School. I am thus also grateful to that distinguished academic community for its hospitality, and in particular for stimulating conversations with Bruce Morrill, SJ, and Paul DeHart. And I am deeply indebted for all that I have learned from both the writings and the persons of Eleonore Stump and the late Ann Loades, which is why this volume is codedicated to them. I hope that it bears witness to their equally remarkable but quite different ways of bringing philosophy and theology together in the context of Christian faith and discipleship.

Robert MacSwain, OGS
Nashville, Tennessee
The Feast of George Herbert, 2024

Introduction

Since beginning my academic career almost twenty years ago, my primary research interests have been in both philosophy of religion and Anglican theology.[1] I was of course aware that a Venn diagram would display considerable overlap between these two areas, in that many distinguished philosophers of religion were also Anglicans. However, at some point it occurred to me that this familiar combination of discipline and denomination was not a coincidence. That is, I realized not only that (1) the Anglican tradition is hospitable to philosophical reflection, which was obvious enough, but also that (2) at least some *philosophical* work by Anglicans might also be considered as specifically *Anglican* thought and perhaps even as a form of Anglican *theology*. And while both of these points are worth further reflection, the second one seems to need more emphasis at the present moment.[2]

---

1. In this volume I use the term "Anglican" (the Latinized form of "English") to refer to the global Christian tradition derived historically from the Church of England and collectively forming the Anglican Communion and various other ecclesial bodies. Some Anglican churches also describe themselves as "Episcopal" due to their retention of the office of bishop after the Reformation, and in the United States "Episcopal" and "Anglican" are overlapping but not equivalent terms. I am thus not using the term "Anglican" specifically to refer to those who left the Episcopal Church to form alternative jurisdictions such as the Anglican Church in North America (ACNA).

2. In addition to the selected essays in this volume, for a monograph poised at the intersection of philosophical and Anglican theology, see Robert MacSwain, *Solved by Sacrifice: Austin Farrer, Fideism, and the Evidence of Faith* (Leuven: Peeters, 2013). And for a monograph more in the genre of philosophy of religion that draws heavily on Anglican figures, see Robert MacSwain, *Saints as Divine Evidence: The Hagiological Argument for the Existence of God* (Cambridge: Cambridge University Press, forthcoming).

I. Between Anglican Theology and Analytic Philosophy

To begin with the first point, Anglicans have historically valued human reason as a divine gift to be celebrated and used with a degree of confidence that may surprise and even dismay Christians of other affiliations. Leading representatives of this tendency include Richard Hooker, the Cambridge Platonists, John Locke, Joseph Butler, and John Henry Newman before his conversion to Roman Catholicism.[3] While Anglicans certainly do not deny human sinfulness or the doctrine of the "Fall" of humanity, or the need for divine revelation through authoritative Scripture, when it comes to our mental capacities they have tended to side with their optimistic Catholic inheritance rather than the more pessimistic followers of Martin Luther, John Calvin, and Karl Barth. Reason in the Anglican tradition is often understood as participation in the divine image, the *imago Dei* (Gen. 1:27); as "the candle of the LORD" in the soul (Prov. 20:27); or even as the very *logos* of Christ, the light which "enlightens everyone" (John 1:9).

This Anglican cognitive confidence has implications for both moral and natural theology, and thus for both secular ethics and epistemology, and it has had significant consequences when it comes to the critical study of the Bible and the dialogue between religion and science. But it is also true that, unlike many Roman Catholics (especially among previous generations), Anglicans have tended to avoid embracing specific metaphysical systems, theories, or conclusions as constitutive of what it means to be an Anglican. So while Anglicans are happy to employ philosophical methods within theological reflection, they normally do so with a degree of reverent agnosticism about the deliverances of such methods. It has also been argued that Anglicans tend toward inductive rather than deductive modes of thought, and emphasize probabilistic cumulative arguments rather than formal demonstrations leading to cognitive certainty. In thus treading a line between Catholic optimism and Protestant pessimism, Anglicanism may be understood as an epistemological *via media* as well as an ecclesial one.[4]

3. For a general survey, see A. S. McGrade, "Reason," in *The Study of Anglicanism*, ed. Stephen Sykes, John Booty, and Jonathan Knight, 2nd ed. (London: SPCK; Minneapolis: Fortress, 1998), 115–28; for a more focused study, E. J. Newey, "The Form of Reason: Participation in the Work of Richard Hooker, Benjamin Whichcote, Ralph Cudworth and Jeremy Taylor," *Modern Theology* 18 (2002): 1–26.

4. See William J. Abraham, *Canon and Criterion in Christian Theology: From the Fathers to*

In regard to the second point above, the field of "Anglican studies" is fairly new and still organizing itself in regard to method and content.[5] While both Anglican and non-Anglican scholars have of course explored aspects of the Anglican tradition for centuries, these studies have tended to focus on privileged national churches such as the Church of England or the Episcopal Church in the United States, classic figures such as Lancelot Andrewes or Jeremy Taylor, definitive texts such as the Book of Common Prayer and its variants, and have been largely historical in nature. By contrast, "Anglican studies" seeks to be more thematically inclusive and methodologically interdisciplinary. Anglican studies takes a broader view of what counts as worth investigating, endorses a more global perspective on the Anglican diaspora, and employs a wider range of academic techniques than most previous approaches, up to and including the social sciences. Inevitably, Anglican studies is much interested in the postcolonial legacy of the British Empire and how churches of the Anglican Communion in Africa, Asia, Australasia, and the Americas both reflect and refract that problematic heritage. Furthermore, intersectional analyses have finally brought to the fore long-neglected issues of class, race, gender, and sexual orientation.[6]

I will return to Anglican studies in a moment, but first, what about Anglican theology? Anglican theology as such has mostly been studied by other Anglicans, and mainly by those preparing for ordained ministry, which means that its details are basically unknown and thus uninfluential outside the clergy

Feminism (Oxford: Oxford University Press, 1998), in the chapter "Canonical Synthesis: The Anglican *Via Media*," 188–214, and esp. the representative list in note 50 on 212. For the concern that American Episcopalians might be reneging on their historic Anglican commitment to reason, see Charles Hefling, "On Being Reasonably Theological," in *A New Conversation: Essays on the Future of Theology and the Episcopal Church*, ed. Robert Boak Slocum (New York: Church Publishing, 1999), 48–59.

5. Thus, while journals such as *Anglican Theological Review* (*ATR*) and *Anglican and Episcopal History* have existed for many decades, with *ATR* even recently celebrating its centenary, the *Journal of Anglican Studies* was only founded in 2003, and the representative *Oxford Handbook of Anglican Studies*, edited by Mark D. Chapman, Sathianathan Clarke, and Martyn Percy, was only published in 2015. While more traditional in its topics and methodology, the Sykes, Booty, and Knight volume cited in note 3 was a landmark text and remains an important point of reference.

6. For a recent example of these concerns, see Kwok Pui-lan, *The Anglican Tradition from a Postcolonial Perspective* (New York: Seabury, 2023).

of the tradition.[7] However, and speaking as one myself, Anglican clerics tend to be notoriously insouciant on doctrinal matters. This characteristic conceptual vagueness ("woolly" is our preferred if rueful term for it) may be partly explained by a pervasive distaste for making up one's mind, or latitudinarian indifference, or even skeptical doubt, but is also partly because many Anglicans are self-consciously committed to holding the doctrines of what they call "the undivided Church." By this they mean the beliefs of the "orthodox" Christian community of the first five centuries AD as articulated in the early ecumenical creeds and councils, before the "Great Schism" between East and West in 1054. Such Anglicans are therefore less interested in engaging explicitly with important postpatristic developments such as Scholasticism, the Renaissance, the Reformation, the Enlightenment, Romanticism, and the rise of modern science. Indeed, in the early nineteenth century the history of doctrine as taught at Oxford ended with the Council of Chalcedon in 451! Please note: the idea that Anglicanism is committed solely to "patristic consensus" is the story that many Anglicans like to tell themselves, even if the historical reality was rather different. For instance, Anglicans in the sixteenth and seventeenth centuries were arguably more Protestant than patristic.[8]

Partly as a result of this common self-understanding, Anglicans have been remarkably reluctant—almost on principle—to practice what other traditions call "systematic" theology, or to engage in creative "constructive" doctrinal projects. Scholarly energies within Anglicanism have rather focused on biblical studies, church history (especially the patristic period), and liturgy, and in these fields Anglican have long produced scholars of international renown and

7. For some helpful introductions, see Mark Chapman, *Anglican Theology* (London: T&T Clark, 2012), which is historical in nature; Ralph McMichael, ed., *The Vocation of Anglican Theology* (London: SCM, 2014), which is arranged by doctrine; and Stephen Burns, Bryan Cones, and James Tengatenga, eds., *Twentieth Century Anglican Theologians: From Evelyn Underhill to Esther Mombo* (Chichester, UK: Wiley-Blackwell, 2021), which is arranged by individual figures of that specific century.

8. For the fairly recent development of this familiar story, see Benjamin J. King, "Anglican Theology and the History of Doctrine: From the Oxford Movement to the Second World War," in *The Oxford Handbook of the Reception History of Doctrine*, ed. Sarah Coakley, Richard Cross, and Jonathan Teubner (Oxford: Oxford University Press, forthcoming). Rightly or wrongly, those who affirm this story see Anglicanism as more akin to Eastern Orthodoxy than any form of Western Christianity, at least when it comes to doctrinal development and theological reflection.

major influence. But there is no single defining figure of Anglican theology such as Thomas Aquinas, Martin Luther, John Calvin, or John Wesley, and only rarely have Anglicans in any period or region fielded practitioners of the sort of normative theological reflection that is common within Roman Catholicism, Lutheranism, Calvinism, and other Christian traditions. As mentioned above, scholars in these other traditions therefore rarely engage with Anglican theology, as in their view there is little Anglican theology to engage with.[9]

Furthermore, aside from the ancient English universities of Oxford and Cambridge, along with important later centers such as Durham University and King's College, London, Anglicans have rarely established research-oriented universities in which theological scholarship can flourish and be passed along to doctoral students. In the United States, for instance, there is no Anglican research university to be compared with Catholic institutions such as Georgetown or Notre Dame, Methodist institutions such as Duke or Emory, or Presbyterian institutions such as Princeton Theological Seminary (which is not a university but which has a respected PhD program). Consequently, the only Anglican graduate schools of theology in the United States are a handful of comparatively small denominational seminaries (such as the one where I teach) whose primary raison d'être is training clergy rather than forming doctoral students. Such seminaries offer a range of master's degrees and perhaps the professional doctor of ministry, but not a PhD or ThD. Aspiring Anglican theologians in the United States often study at one of these Episcopal seminaries but must then look elsewhere for their doctoral formation, either at home or abroad (I, for example, followed a common path and went to Great Britain). In short, aside from some notable exceptions, Anglican theology largely lacks both clear exemplars and strong institutions.[10]

9. For a very helpful analysis of this situation and discussion of some recent counterexamples such as Sarah Coakley, Graham Ward, Katherine Sonderegger, and Ralph McMichael, see Scott MacDougall, *The Shape of Anglican Theology: Faith Seeking Wisdom* (Leiden: Brill, 2022). More briefly, see also Peter Sedgwick, "Anglican Theology," in *The Modern Theologians: An Introduction to Christian Theology Since 1918*, ed. David F. Ford with Rachel Muers (Malden, MA: Blackwell, 2005), 178–93. But during the early nineteenth century, "The English universities taught that scripture and the Anglican formularies said the same thing, and that systematic theology was unnecessary" (King, "Anglican Theology").

10. I mention some individual exceptions to this general assessment below, but a partial institutional exception in the United States might be Berkeley Divinity School (BDS) at Yale,

It is precisely in the midst of this comparatively weak conceptual and institutional context that I now return to my proposal in the second point mentioned above, namely, that at least some *philosophical* work by Anglicans might also fall under the broader rubric of Anglican thought or even theology. Or, put differently, among the genres that the new field of Anglican studies recognizes as constitutive of Anglicanism and among the methods that it employs to explore the Anglican tradition should also be included philosophy. If so, then to the standard list of distinguished "Anglican divines" could be added not just those from the recent past and present whose academic appointments were or are in seminaries and university departments of theology, such as Michael Ramsey, John Macquarrie, Stephen Sykes, Rowan Williams, David Ford, Kathryn Tanner, Mark McIntosh, Ellen Charry, Katherine Sonderegger, and Kelly Brown Douglas, but those whose teaching and research are more specifically philosophical in nature.[11] Such names would include Donald MacKinnon, Basil Mitchell, George Grant, William Alston, Marilyn McCord Adams, William Wainwright, Peter van Inwagen, Douglas Hedley, and Charles Taliaferro, among others, as well as those who perhaps more equally fuse both philosophy and theology such as Austin Farrer, Eric Mascall, Helen Oppenheimer, Brian Hebblethwaite, Keith Ward, Ann Loades, David Brown, and Sarah Coakley. For here, in striking contrast to the general situation in systematic and constructive theology described above, philosophically minded Anglicans have made very substantial contributions over the past several decades.[12]

---

a once-separate Episcopal seminary that gradually affiliated more and more closely with Yale Divinity School (YDS), a historically Congregationalist but now nondenominational Christian graduate school of theology within Yale University. At this point, BDS is effectively merged with YDS while retaining some distinctive instruction and formation for students who are registered specifically for Berkeley certificates. But Yale University itself is not an Anglican nor even a Christian institution, and Yale doctorates in theology are granted by the Graduate Program in Religious Studies rather than the Divinity School. There are also important Episcopal/Anglican programs at Duke and Emory, but the same caveats apply.

11. See John Booty, "Standard Divines," in Sykes, Booty, and Knight, *The Study of Anglicanism*, 176–87, for the main historical figures and some suggestions about their more recent successors.

12. There is no hard-and-fast distinction between these two groupings of "philosophers of religion" and "philosophical theologians," but only a matter of emphasis, especially as some moved back and forth across the disciplines in regard to their formal academic appointments. For a helpful survey, see Brian Hebblethwaite, "The Anglican Tradition," in *A Companion to the*

Such a proposal immediately raises the question, "But what kind of philosophy are we talking about?" The aforementioned Peter van Inwagen, one of the world's leading metaphysicians and philosophers of religion, once sagely observed: "Philosophers do not agree about anything to speak of."[13] This lack of agreement includes the very nature of philosophy itself and how to go about doing it. In addition to the main schools of Anglo-American philosophy—namely, the broad analytic tradition, various forms of pragmatism, and the powerful lingering influence of Ludwig Wittgenstein—there are multiple strands of Continental thought emanating from France, Germany, and Italy: phenomenology, structuralism, deconstructionism, critical theory, and so on. Roman Catholic and Orthodox philosophers still look to classic figures in their own traditions such as Augustine, Anselm, Aquinas, Gregory of Nyssa, Maximus the Confessor, and Gregory Palamas, but often put them into conversation with more recent schools of thought mentioned above. Furthermore, the same postcolonial and intersectional lenses that focused their critique on the Anglican tradition have also turned their gaze to Western philosophy, assessing it as exclusively Eurocentric, masculinist, and oppressively hegemonic in its sources, methods, and assumptions. Academic philosophy must, such critics urge, expand its conceptual horizons to include African, Chinese, Indian, Japanese, and other intellectual traditions such as various indigenous cultures, along with the voices of women, persons of color, and other minorities, including sexual ones.

Such ferment in the field notwithstanding, and to the chagrin of some observers, philosophers in the Anglican tradition since the mid-twentieth century have largely but not exclusively still positioned themselves in relation to the changing currents of specifically *English* philosophy. The Hegelian metaphysical idealism of the late nineteenth and early twentieth century exemplified by T. H. Green and F. H. Bradley gave way to the severely logical and empirical

---

Philosophy of Religion, ed. Philip Quinn and Charles Taliaferro (Cambridge, MA: Blackwell, 1997), 171–78. More broadly, but with substantial attention to Anglican figures, see Daniel W. Hardy, "Theology through Philosophy," in *The Modern Theologians: An Introduction to Christian Theology in the Twentieth Century*, ed. David F. Ford, 2nd ed. (Oxford: Blackwell, 1997), 252–85, and Ann Loades, "Philosophy of Religion: Its Relation to Theology," in *Faith and Philosophical Analysis: The Impact of Analytical Philosophy on the Philosophy of Religion*, ed. Harriet A. Harris and Christopher J. Insole (Aldershot, UK: Ashgate, 2005), 136–47.

13. Peter van Inwagen, "Quam Dilecta," in *God and the Philosophers: The Reconciliation of Faith and Reason*, ed. Thomas V. Morris (New York: Oxford University Press, 1994), 41.

approach of figures such as Bertrand Russell, G. E. Moore, A. J. Ayer, and the early Wittgenstein (an Austrian based at Cambridge), and then to the ordinary language philosophers partly inspired by the later Wittgenstein such as J. L. Austin, Gilbert Ryle, H. P. Grice, and Peter Strawson. The initial "positivist" phase of this revolutionary development was equally hostile to metaphysics, ethics, *and* theology, as was famously proclaimed by Ayer's *Language, Truth, and Logic* in 1936.[14] However, toward the end of the twentieth century all three of these discourses were gradually if grudgingly allowed back into the philosophical conversation, and what counts as "analytic" has become increasingly diffuse. Furthermore, recent studies have emphasized the previously neglected but essential work of Elizabeth Anscombe, Iris Murdoch, Philippa Foot, and Mary Midgley.[15] But for better or worse, those who came to be known as analytic philosophers set the tone and agenda of what counted as "philosophy" in the United Kingdom during this period, and then eventually in the United States, Canada, and other parts of the Anglophone world as well.

However, by contrast, many British theologians in the twentieth century rejected decisively these strictures and looked instead to the Continent for both theological and philosophical inspiration. Among them are important contemporary Anglican figures such as John Milbank, Graham Ward, and Catherine Pickstock, who collectively founded the movement known as Radical Orthodoxy in the late 1990s, and I will return to them at the conclusion of this volume. But as the main title of this book indicates, I am here interested primarily in exploring the ways in which some Anglican philosophers and philosophical theologians rather chose to work *within* the conceptual parameters of analytic philosophy, whether explicitly or implicitly, in either basic agreement or disagreement. Put differently, what they mean by "philosophy" in its current mode is analytic philosophy. Not all of the essays collected here are purely philosophical in nature, but they all deal with Anglicans who wrestled

---

14. A. J. Ayer, *Language, Truth, and Logic* (London: Victor Gollancz, 1936; 2nd ed. 1946). See, in particular, chapter 6, "Critique of Ethics and Theology."

15. See Benjamin J. B. Lipscomb, *The Women Are Up to Something: How Elizabeth Anscombe, Philippa Foot, Mary Midgley, and Iris Murdoch Revolutionized Ethics* (New York: Oxford University Press, 2022), and Clare Mac Cumhaill and Rachael Wiseman, *Metaphysical Animals: How Four Women Brought Philosophy Back to Life* (New York: Doubleday, 2022). These books developed independently of each other, although the respective authors were aware of the others' work.

with how to respond to the powerful challenge that analytic philosophy presented to traditional Christian belief and practice.[16] And to that extent this volume stands squarely within the tradition begun by a group known as the Metaphysicals and exemplified in their book *Faith and Logic: Oxford Essays in Philosophical Theology*, edited by Basil Mitchell (London: Allen & Unwin, 1957). My own title, however, alludes more specifically to an earlier volume, *Essays Catholic and Critical: By Members of the Anglican Communion*, edited by Edward Gordon Selwyn (London: SPCK, originally published in 1926, with the third edition appearing in 1929). As I explain further below, I endorse a renewed "Critical Catholicism" (or "post–Liberal Catholicism") as an ecumenical theological project that cuts across various Christian traditions, not just Anglicanism.

Before looking at the essays themselves, let me address a significant divide within contemporary analytic philosophy that has also manifested itself within philosophy of religion and philosophical theology. As alluded to above, rather than monolithic, analytic philosophy is internally diverse, and there are lively debates about what precisely its defining methods and canonical figures consist of, as well as just what makes it different from other approaches. The recent movement known as "Analytic Theology" has been drawn to a vision of analytic philosophy that—as William J. Abraham put it—values "clarity, precision, logical dexterity, probability lattices, and no metaphors please." It employs formal logic and confirmation theory and is often written in a highly technical style that seeks to exclude ambiguity to the greatest extent possible. Abraham locates this approach primarily within North America and associates it with philosophers in the Reformed tradition such as Alvin Plantinga and Nicholas Wolterstorff and their many students, but a British figure such as Richard Swinburne (originally Anglican, now Orthodox) belongs very much in this group as well. Because of Plantinga's immense influence in shaping this school of thought,

16. For helpful study, see the essays gathered in Harriet A. Harris and Christopher J. Insole, eds., *Faith and Philosophical Analysis: The Impact of Analytical Philosophy on the Philosophy of Religion* (Aldershot, UK: Ashgate, 2005). A more recent movement is Analytic Theology, launched by Oliver D. Crisp and Michael C. Rea, eds., *Analytic Theology: New Essays in the Philosophy of Theology* (Oxford: Oxford University Press, 2009), which I reviewed along with Andrew Davison, ed., *Imaginative Apologetics: Theology, Philosophy, and the Catholic Tradition* (London: SCM, 2011) in *Sewanee Theological Review* 56 (2013): 399–401, with the second volume being more influenced by Radical Orthodoxy.

Abraham humorously dubs it "the strand of St. Alvin," and it is currently the dominant approach in Analytic Theology.[17]

However, Abraham observes that a rather different type of analytic philosophy of religion originated in the book *Faith and Logic* mentioned above, which he dubs "the strand of St. Basil," after its editor. And of this strand he observes:

> The canon of exemplars is different: Basil Mitchell, John Lucas, I. M. Crombie, M. B. Foster, and Austin Farrer, for starters. The site of operations is different: Oxbridge and various outposts. The theological heritage in which it originates is different: Anglo-Catholic Anglican, and Arminian. The canon of literature is different: start with *Faith and Logic* and the material subsequently published by the authors included. So too are the methodological strategies and the prized intellectual virtues. Consider the following laundry list of maxims: Pay attention to the historical etiology of our concepts, allow for the possibility of open as opposed to closed concepts, be especially aware of essentially contested concepts, make ample use of parable and apt metaphor, avoid convoluted imaginary examples, write in a way that allows access to those interested in the big questions that motivate philosophical inquiry, cultivate wisdom and other informal intellectual virtues, and allow elbow room for growth in insight and spiritual perception.[18]

I will say more about Analytic Theology in the conclusion of this volume, but note that while my opening chapter on William Alston as an "analytic Anglican" predated the arrival of this movement by several years, Alston may be regarded not simply as a prime exemplar of the first approach but also as a

---

17. In addition to the works cited in note 16, see also my review of Michael C. Rea, *Essays in Analytic Theology*, vols. 1 and 2, *Journal of Analytic Theology* 10 (2022): 730–34, available online at https://tinyurl.com/w4xh8zsc, and my "Analyzing the Analysts: A Review Essay on Recent Work in Analytic Theology," *Anglican Theological Review* 105 (2023): 510–14.

18. William J. Abraham, "Turning Philosophical Water into Theological Wine," *Journal of Analytic Theology* 1 (2013): 1–16, with the citations in both this and the previous paragraph quoting from 7–8. Available online at https://tinyurl.com/3ekjkyhr. For his description of the more formal "St. Alvin" approach, he is drawing primarily on Michael Rea's introduction to *Analytic Theology* (cited in n. 16 above). Rea was one of Plantinga's PhD students at the University of Notre Dame.

mediating figure between these two strands, as indicated by his stated appreciation of Crombie, Farrer, and Mitchell.[19] However, the subsequent essays on
Farrer and Brown, and my own methodological preferences, belong very much
in Abraham's second group. In these collected essays I look primarily to the
United Kingdom and Anglo-Catholicism for both philosophical and theological insight, and so this book may be regarded as contributing to the strand of St.
Basil.[20] Due to the postcolonial and intersectional concerns mentioned above,
this avowedly Anglophile approach is both risky and controversial, which I will
discuss further in the conclusion.

II. Anglican and Analytic Essays

In turning then to the chapters themselves, let me comment on their origin and
place within the context of this current volume. They are arranged in rough
chronological order of publication but are also sequenced to move from a primary focus on Austin Farrer (1904–1968) to David Brown (1948–), in many
ways Farrer's natural successor in representing a particular kind of Anglican
philosophical theology I call "Critical Catholicism." Brown, like Farrer, studied both philosophy and theology at Oxford, was ordained in the Church of
England, and held a joint position as chaplain, tutor, and fellow of an Oxford
college. More significantly, however, Brown follows closely in Farrer's footsteps
by seeking to integrate the three major intellectual tasks of biblical interpretation, philosophical analysis, and theological reflection in the context of Anglo-
Catholic doctrine and devotion, and in so doing exemplifies at least one form
of Critical Catholicism.[21]

---

19. See, for example, the acknowledgments in William P. Alston, *Divine Nature and Human Language: Essays in Philosophical Theology* (Ithaca, NY: Cornell University Press, 1989), x.

20. Given that Austin Farrer was Basil Mitchell's acknowledged mentor and inspiration,
the strand of "St. Austin" might be more appropriate, but Mitchell was undoubtedly more
successful than Farrer in gaining a hearing for their general approach within the philosophical
guild. Both David Brown and William Abraham studied with Mitchell in Oxford during the
1970s, and their work thus exemplifies the Basilian strand as well.

21. In *Twentieth Century Anglican Theologians*, ed. Burns, Cones, and Tengatenga, I wrote
the chapter on Farrer (54–64) and Christopher R. Brewer wrote the chapter on Brown (185–
94). For Brown's direct engagement with Farrer, see his "God and Symbolic Action," in *Divine*

The first chapter is one of the earliest pieces in this collection and began its life as a review essay in *Anglican Theological Review*, published in 2006. It is the only essay focused entirely on an American figure; and given Anglicanism's strongly clerical nature, it is noteworthy that Alston was a lay member of the Episcopal Church rather than a deacon, priest, or bishop. While it accomplished my primary goals of telling Alston's story and presenting his distinctive analytic/Anglican methodology, the word limit imposed on the review essay format required me to then simply list the theological topics on which he had written and provide the references rather than go into the doctrinal substance of his work in any more detail. I regretted this, as I particularly wanted to draw further attention to his interesting proposed *via media* between the classical theism of Thomas Aquinas and the process theology of Charles Hartshorne (Alston's doctoral supervisor at the University of Chicago). Most adherents of either school assume them to be "package deals" in which, when it comes to the standard list of divine attributes, one must go entirely with Aquinas's "classical" traditionalism or with Hartshorne's "neoclassical" revisionism (in which God is temporal, changing, of limited power and knowledge, must create the universe, and so on). Alston, however, argues that it is possible to take a more nuanced perspective, finding value in selected aspects of each thinker's system.

To achieve this goal, he first divides the standard list of divine attributes into two groups, which he naturally designates "1" and "2." As he summarizes his subsequent argument at the conclusion of the essay:

> Group 1 contains such classical attributes as absoluteness (construed as absence of internal relatedness), total necessity, pure actuality, and simplicity—along with their neoclassical counterparts, relativity, contingency, etc. Group 2 contains such classical attributes as creation ex nihilo, omnipotence, incorporeality, nontemporality, and absolute unsurpassability, along with their neoclassical counterparts. The neoclassical position on Group 1

Action: Studies Inspired by the Philosophical Theology of Austin Farrer, ed. Brian Hebblethwaite and Edward Henderson (Edinburgh: T&T Clark, 1990), 103–22, reprinted in *Scripture, Metaphysics, and Poetry: Austin Farrer's* The Glass of Vision *with Critical Commentary*, ed. Robert MacSwain (Farnham, UK: Ashgate, 2013; London: Routledge, 2016), 133–47, and "The Role of Images in Theological Reflection," in *The Human Person in God's World: Studies to Commemorate the Austin Farrer Centenary*, ed. Douglas Hedley and Brian Hebblethwaite (London: SCM, 2006), 85–105.

does not entail the neoclassical position on Group 2, though it is, of course, consistent with it. On the contrary, the neoclassical Group 1 attributes can be combined with the classical Group 2 attributes into a consistent and coherent conception that captures the experience, belief, and practice of the high theistic religions better than either of Hartshorne's total packages [that is, his interpretation of Aquinas and his own counterproposal].[22]

In other words, it is at least possible to conceive of God's nature as exemplifying some classical attributes and some neoclassical attributes. While Alston does not here explicitly argue for the truth of this "middle way" between Aquinas and Hartshorne, he clearly finds it attractive and worth further consideration. Because of the considerable passage of time, which has sadly included Alston's death, the text of this essay has been revised to bring it up to date.[23]

While also originally published in 2006, chapter 2 is the earliest essay in this collection, beginning its life in a course with Timothy Sedgwick at Virginia Theological Seminary during a year of Anglican studies in 1999–2000. I had been introduced to the work of Austin Farrer several years earlier by Diogenes Allen at Princeton Theological Seminary, and then later wrote on Farrer and Wittgenstein in a paper for Fergus Kerr, OP, at New College, Edinburgh, but this essay was my initial attempt to grapple with Farrer as a paradigmatic Anglican theologian. Tim encouraged me to publish it, and several years later when I was a PhD student at Durham University and chaplain at St. Chad's College, I finally decided to submit a revised version to the newly founded *Journal of Anglican Studies*.

My location in Durham during this time allowed me to share a draft of the essay with Stephen Sykes (1939–2014), then principal of St. John's College, and the author of the highly influential volume *The Integrity of Anglicanism* (London: Mowbray, 1978). Conversation with him was helpful as I continued

22. See "Hartshorne and Aquinas: A Via Media," in Alston, *Divine Nature and Human Language*, 142. The grouped list of both sets of divine attributes, classical and neoclassical, may be found on 123–24.

23. I am grateful to Daniel Howard-Snyder, professor of philosophy at Western Washington University and one of Alston's former PhD students, for reading the original version of this essay in 2006 and then providing helpful suggestions in this recent revision process. Some of the other essays in this volume have also had some minor revision to the main text, but aside from chapter 1, most updating has been kept to the footnotes.

to wrestle with the problem of Anglican identity as formulated by Paul Avis: That is, is Anglican distinctiveness a matter of method (how Anglicans *do* theology, which Avis defends) or content (the material *positions* that Anglicans take, which Sykes preferred)? That is, what makes Anglicanism *Anglican* and different from other forms of Christianity—if indeed it is? Here we encounter a pervasive tension between the Anglican self-understanding mentioned earlier about supposedly *not* holding any distinctive doctrines not shared by other Christians and the more complicated historical reality—although, to be precise, Sykes suggests that we should speak of what is *characteristically* Anglican rather than what is *distinctively* Anglican. In the conclusion of the essay I avoid the Avis/Sykes dilemma by arguing that Anglican identity is not an either/or but must rather involve *both* method *and* content, and that in particular it was *how* Farrer put the various material ingredients together that made him a distinctively (or at least characteristically) Anglican theologian. As Scott MacDougall later put it, "it is in examining the *combination* of [material ingredients], the way that they *interact* . . . that allows one to perceive whether a typically Anglican theological imagination is at work or not."[24] Anglican identity might thus best be understood as a "particular sensibility, an ethos" as much as anything else.[25] MacDougall's generative proposal expresses my attempted point more clearly than I did in 2006 and is worth further investigation.

Chapter 3 emerged as a historical/biographical side project while doing a PhD in philosophical theology. As I will explain further below, I had gone to Durham in 2004 to work with David Brown on Austin Farrer as a doctrinal theologian in the Anglican tradition, although my research eventually took an unexpected detour into religious epistemology. But in reading Philip Curtis's biography of Farrer, *A Hawk among Sparrows* (London: SPCK, 1985), I became intrigued by a subtle but apparent lacuna: not just the specific date and location of Farrer's baptism in the Church of England during his first year as an Oxford undergraduate, but Austin's whole side of the correspondence with his Baptist parents during this difficult period was missing from Curtis's account. In working through the Farrer papers held in the Bodleian Library of Oxford University, I was thus surprised and delighted to discover Austin's unpublished letters tucked away in a box of uncatalogued material. Why Curtis did not have

24. MacDougall, *Shape of Anglican Theology*, 82 (emphasis added).
25. MacDougall, *Shape of Anglican Theology*, 20.

access to them is unclear, but presumably they were either lost or kept separately until after he finished his biography.

However, Farrer's baptismal record remained frustratingly elusive until an experienced archivist suggested that I look at his ordination materials. These were kept in Wakefield, Yorkshire, and I might have never managed to visit them had I not been stranded in England after a conference in Manchester due to the eruption of the Icelandic volcano Eyjafjallajökull on April 14, 2010. Taking advantage of the unanticipated time and proximity, I went to Wakefield and discovered the surprising and ironic facts of the case. In terms of genre, note that this essay mostly consists of the transcribed letters between Austin and his parents. Because the initial research in the Bodleian was supported by a grant from the Historical Society of the Episcopal Church in 2008, the article was eventually published in their journal, *Anglican and Episcopal History*.

Chapter 4 was the result of an invitation to give a paper at the Oxford University C. S. Lewis Society on April 29, 2008. At this point I was still at Durham as both college chaplain and doctoral student, but another side project during this time was coediting *The Cambridge Companion to C. S. Lewis* (eventually published in 2010) with Michael Ward, then chaplain at Peterhouse, Cambridge. Michael had recently completed a doctorate at St. Andrews that was soon to appear as *Planet Narnia: The Seven Heavens in the Imagination of C. S. Lewis.*[26] Like many others, I had read, enjoyed, and benefited greatly from Lewis's voluminous writings across multiple genres since I was a child, but unlike Michael, I was not a professional Lewis scholar. How this volume thus came to be is a story for another occasion,[27] but it is relevant to note that as a matter of fact I had, like most people, first heard of Farrer through his close friendship with Lewis, his involvement with Lewis's Socratic Club, his ministrations to Joy Lewis at the end of her life, and his posthumous tributes to Lewis. These details are included in the standard Lewis biographies, but when asked to present a paper to the Oxford society because of my involvement with the forthcoming *Cambridge Companion*, I realized that no one had yet looked more closely at

26. Michael Ward, *Planet Narnia: The Seven Heavens in the Imagination of C. S. Lewis* (New York: Oxford University Press, 2008), and see also the shorter version written for a more popular audience: *The Narnia Code: C. S. Lewis and the Secret of the Seven Heavens* (Carol Stream, IL: Tyndale House, 2010).

27. I tell it in "The Continuing (Ir)Relevance of C. S. Lewis," *Sehnsucht: The C. S. Lewis Journal* 7/8 (2013–14): 11–22.

the Lewis/Farrer relationship. The paper was published in the society's journal, which later became the *Journal of Inklings Studies.*

Chapter 5 came from an invitation to contribute to a Festschrift for Ann Loades, who sadly passed away on December 6, 2022. As noted above, I went to Durham to work with David Brown, but a wonderful side benefit was getting to know Ann as well. She had retired from full-time teaching the year before I arrived but remained a major intellectual presence and a formidable (yet also kind and generous) force to be reckoned with. Among her many areas of expertise she was also a Farrer scholar, and conversations with her greatly enriched my research and thinking about these matters, as well as far more broadly, which is why this current book is codedicated to her.[28] As soon as I was asked by Natalie Watson if I would contribute to a volume in Ann's honor, I immediately knew what I wanted to write about and the personal anecdote I would begin with. This essay also enabled me to perhaps incongruously bring together Austin Farrer with Stanley Hauerwas, another contributor to Ann's Festschrift, who had also been a mentor and friend since I met him in the summer of 1992, just before beginning my MDiv at Princeton Seminary. While different in many respects, especially in regard to thinking about those with cognitive disabilities, Hauerwas has always declared his deep appreciation for and indebtedness to Farrer.[29]

Chapter 6 was the result of an invitation from Stephen Platten to contribute to an interdisciplinary volume on Farrer that he coedited with Richard Harries, published in 2020. Here I decided to summarize for a different audience the basic argument of my doctoral thesis, published as *Solved by Sacrifice: Austin Farrer, Fideism, and the Evidence of Faith* (Leuven: Peeters, 2013). As stated

---

28. Just before her death, Ann had compiled a collection of her essays in philosophical theology, two of which are on Lewis, as it happens, and two on Farrer: see Ann Loades, *Explorations in Twentieth-Century Theology and Philosophy: People Preoccupied with God*, ed. Stephen Burns (Melbourne: Anthem, 2023). I was privileged to write the afterword: "The Passionate Intellect of Ann Loades," 215–18. See also Burns's chapter on her in Burns, Cones, and Tengatenga, *Twentieth Century Anglican Theologians*, 157–66.

29. See, for example, his brief comments in his autobiography, *Hannah's Child: A Theologian's Memoir* (Grand Rapids: Eerdmans, 2010), 51–52. Hauerwas also has a close relationship with Anglicanism: while brought up in the Methodist tradition, and for many years a professor at Duke Divinity School (a Methodist institution), he now attends an Episcopalian congregation in Chapel Hill, North Carolina.

above, my initial plan was to present a synoptic vision of Farrer as an Anglican theologian by integrating his various writings in philosophy, theology, biblical studies, sermons, and other devotional works in order to present him as something like an Anglican systematic theologian. However, I soon discovered an important gap in the secondary literature, and so moved in a more philosophical direction in order to address it.[30] Primarily this was to consider the neglected epistemological implications of Farrer's thought rather than the more common focus on his metaphysics, and to do so from a developmental angle.[31] More specifically, as one part of that account, I had realized that an important influence on Farrer's last book, *Faith and Speculation: An Essay in Philosophical Theology* (London: Black, 1967), had gone largely unrecognized, namely, that of the young Diogenes Allen. I tell that story in *Solved by Sacrifice*, chapter 4, but in this essay I also wanted to rectify another and more general way in which Allen's contribution had been neglected, which was in developing a theory of faith and reason that was remarkably similar to the hugely influential "Reformed epistemology" presented by Alvin Plantinga and Nicholas Wolterstorff almost twenty years later. This is in no way to denigrate their immense achievement, as it was made entirely independently of Allen's, but it is to draw attention to his practically unnoticed earlier defense of an analogous position.

Continuing this focus on religious epistemology, chapter 7 was my own contribution to an issue of *Sewanee Theological Review* that I guest-edited, focused on voices in contemporary Anglican/Episcopal theology, and it summarizes the main argument of my second monograph, *Saints as Divine Evidence: The Hagiological Argument for the Existence of God* (forthcoming). It is the only

---

30. For a study that later performed a rather similar task to what I originally had in mind, see Robert Boak Slocum, *Light in a Burning-Glass: A Systematic Presentation of Austin Farrer's Theology* (Columbia: University of South Carolina Press, 2007).

31. The metaphysical focus on Farrer is manifest in earlier secondary works such as Jeffrey C. Eaton, *The Logic of Theism: An Analysis of the Thought of Austin Farrer* (Lanham, MD: University Press of America, 1980); Brian Hebblethwaite and Edward Henderson, eds., *Divine Action: Studies Inspired by the Philosophical Theology of Austin Farrer* (Edinburgh: T&T Clark, 1990); and Charles Conti, *Metaphysical Personalism: An Analysis of Austin Farrer's Theistic Metaphysics* (Oxford: Clarendon, 1995). My developmental approach in this study was inspired by Bruce McCormack's magisterial *Karl Barth's Critically Realistic Dialectical Theology: Its Genesis and Development, 1909–1936* (Oxford: Clarendon, 1995), which taught me the value of a historical-genetic, rather than a synchronic-systematic, approach to a given figure.

previously published essay in this volume that is thematic in nature rather than primarily concerned with a specific individual or individuals, but the crucial claim about the evidential value of human holiness is drawn from Farrer, and I explicate it from his writings among others, both Anglican and otherwise.

Chapter 8 came from an invitation from Tim Sedgwick to contribute to a series of essays in *Anglican Theological Review* on the broad topic of exemplary Anglican identity. The three coauthors each wrote about their own teachers, and it was a pleasure to work with Jason Fout and Ben King in paying tribute to and summarizing the work of David Ford, David Brown, and Sarah Coakley. Jason is the academic dean and associate professor of Anglican theology at Bexley Seabury, and Ben is the Duncalf-Villavoso Professor of Church History at the Seminary of the Southwest. This collection is enriched by these other two authorial voices and the expanded treatment of figures covered. This essay also marks the transition in the volume away from the initial primary focus on Farrer to the concluding chapters on Brown. As already noted above, in 2004 I went to Durham University to work with Brown on a Farrer-related doctoral thesis. But in 2007 he moved from being Van Mildert Canon Professor of Divinity—a joint appointment at both Durham University and Durham Cathedral—to St. Mary's College, the School of Divinity at the University of St. Andrews, as Wardlaw Professor of Theology, Aesthetics, and Culture, and professorial fellow at the Institute for Theology, Imagination, and the Arts (ITIA). I thus transferred from Durham to St. Andrews to complete the doctorate with him, finishing in 2010. Partly as a result of Brown's move to St. Andrews, I coorganized an ITIA conference there on his later work, the expanded proceedings of which were eventually published as Robert MacSwain and Taylor Worley, eds., *Theology, Aesthetics, and Culture: Responses to the Work of David Brown* (Oxford: Oxford University Press, 2012).

Chapters 9 and 10 were the results of invitations from Chris Brewer to contribute to two additional volumes focused on Brown, the first being a Festschrift and the second dealing more specifically with the implications of his work for biblical interpretation. As with the Festschrift for Ann Loades, I immediately knew what I wanted to write about as soon as I received each of these invitations. The Festschrift genre encourages contextual reflection related to the figure being honored, so my introduction to chapter 9 does not need repeating here, other than to say that the eighteenth-century bishop Joseph Butler is another historically important but currently neglected Anglican philosopher that I had considered writing a doctoral thesis on with Brown, so this was a good opportunity to finally produce something on him.

Chapter 10 has a longer and more complicated origin. When I was a philosophy undergraduate at Liberty University, Eleonore Stump was still teaching at Virginia Polytechnic Institute and State University.[32] Late in the fall semester of 1990 she drove across the Blue Ridge Mountains from Blacksburg to Lynchburg to deliver two lectures, one in the morning and one in the afternoon. The first had already appeared as "Dante's Hell, Aquinas's Moral Theory, and the Love of God," *Canadian Journal of Philosophy* 16 (1986): 181–98, but the second was then unpublished: "Betrayal of Trust: Philosophy of Religion and Biblical Exegesis." Stump continued working on it for two decades, and it finally reached its definitive form as a chapter in her *Wandering in Darkness: Narrative and the Problem of Suffering* (Oxford: Oxford University Press, 2010). I was profoundly impressed by both of these lectures as well as by Stump's intellectual and spiritual presence, and have greatly benefited from her wisdom and encouragement over the years since then, which is why this book is dedicated to her along with Ann Loades. After her visit to Liberty, I began corresponding with Eleonore and reading her work, including her appreciative yet critical review of Brown's *The Divine Trinity*, which was how I first heard about him as well.[33] When I received Chris's second invitation, I knew that I needed to write a compare-and-contrast essay on Brown's and Stump's respective approaches to biblical interpretation. This allowed me to pay tribute to Eleonore as well as David.[34]

32. Like *The Cambridge Companion to C. S. Lewis*, my undergraduate studies at Liberty are another story for another occasion, but for some critical reflections on this controversial Christian university's past and present, see Robert MacSwain, "An Inevitable Fall from Grace? Falwell, Liberty, and Where It All Went Wrong" (2020), an essay published on the University of Virginia's "Religion and Its Publics" website (https://tinyurl.com/3b5znt2u).

33. Eleonore Stump, review of *The Divine Trinity*, by David Brown, *Faith and Philosophy* 3 (1986): 463–68. There is thus a direct connection between Stump's visit to Liberty in 1990 and my doctoral studies with Brown at Durham and St. Andrews from 2004 to 2010. We rarely recognize the significance of such apparently minor events until well after the fact, but our lives are shaped decisively by them.

34. Comparing and contrasting their CVs is also fascinating, as they approach the Bible with remarkably similar academic backgrounds, received in exactly the same period, albeit in different cultural contexts—Stump in the United States and Brown in the United Kingdom. Thus, both began their higher education with degrees in classics—Stump at Grinnell College (1969) and Brown at Edinburgh (1970). Both earned second degrees dealing with biblical stud-

As the introduction to chapter 11 explains, it was the result of an invitation to deliver a paper at the 2014 annual meeting of the Society of Anglican and Lutheran Theologians (SALT). Given the stated focus on sacramental theology, I was at first inclined politely to say no, as I had not previously published anything in this field or done the necessary research to speak authoritatively on it. But I then realized that this topic was a major focus of Brown's and that I could indeed plausibly address it through his work, especially given the way the invitation had been framed. This also enabled me to draw on both the recent conference and the published version of *Theology, Aesthetics, and Culture*, as well as a colleague's review in response to it. Including this essay in the collection allows me to bring in Brown's major interest in the arts, and thus the sacramental significance of paintings, architecture, music, and literature. This chapter thus widens the perspective considerably beyond the topics normally considered by most philosophers and theologians. It was published in *International Journal of the Study of the Christian Church*, which, like the *Journal of Anglican Studies*, is still a fairly new enterprise.

Finally, the seed of the conclusion was initially published as my editor's introduction to a collection of Brown's essays in philosophical theology that I coedited with Chris Brewer: *God in a Single Vision: Integrating Philosophy and Theology* (London: Routledge, 2016).[35] This was where I first floated the description of Critical Catholicism, which I here develop in some more detail, and which will be the topic of a forthcoming monograph. In this book I will seek to articulate such Critical Catholicism as methodological stance that could possibly take its place alongside "Yale School" postliberalism, Radical

---

ies—Stump at Harvard (1971) and Brown at Oxford (1972). Both then received doctorates in philosophy—Stump with a focus on medieval Christian philosophy and logic at Cornell (1975), and Brown with a focus on ancient Greek philosophy and ethics at Cambridge (1976). When it comes to philosophy itself, both were trained in the analytic tradition and acknowledge their indebtedness to it, although both have also raised questions about its various limitations, as I explain in more detail in chapter 10. For a Festschrift for Stump, see Kevin Timpe, ed., *Metaphysics and God: Essays in Honor of Eleonore Stump* (London: Routledge, 2009).

35. We also coedited a companion volume of Brown's essays in theology and the arts, for which Chris wrote the introduction: *Divine Generosity and Human Creativity: Theology through Symbol, Painting, and Architecture* (London: Routledge, 2017). As it happens, the main title of this volume is an intentional *hommage* to Alston's *Divine Nature and Human Language*, cited above and discussed in the first chapter.

Orthodoxy, Analytic Theology, Canonical Theism, and other more contextual theological projects, including those that emphasize the vital postcolonial and intersectional concerns with race and gender noted above. This is work for the future, but a future rooted in the past, including these "essays Anglican and analytic." For now, I hope that bringing them together in this current volume will assist ongoing discussions of not only Anglican identity but of philosophical argument, theological method, Christian doctrine, denominational affiliation, formative friendship, cognitive disability, religious epistemology, human holiness, divine hiddenness, biblical interpretation, sacramental presence, and engagement with the work of important but often neglected Anglican philosophical theologians such as Austin Farrer and David Brown.[36]

36. For comments on earlier drafts of this introduction, I am grateful to David Brown, Mark Chapman, Richard Cogill, Stanley Hauerwas, Kelli Joyce, Ben King, Scott MacDougall, Eleonore Stump, Charles Taliaferro, and James Tengatenga.

An Analytic Anglican:
The Philosophical Theology of William P. Alston

Observers of Anglicanism have often remarked on the tradition's relative dearth of theologians. Biblical scholars, patristic scholars, and liturgical scholars, yes— but systematic theologians, not so much. This is particularly true in the United States.[1] In past generations, figures such as Paul Tillich (Lutheran), Karl Barth (Reformed), and the Niebuhr brothers (Reformed) dominated the thinking of American Episcopal theologians, and the present is hardly different from the past. Today, Episcopalians still mostly look to Lutherans, Presbyterians, Methodists, Roman Catholics, Anabaptists, the Orthodox, and of course, Anglicans from other provinces such as the Church of England to provide the substance of our theological training. Thus, despite a cadre of talented professors of theology in the seminaries of the Episcopal Church, as well as those based in other academic institutions, one is hard pressed to think of a contemporary Episcopal theologian who has exercised a significant, formative influence on the discipline as a whole.[2]

1. See, for example, the comments of David L. Holmes in *A Brief History of the Episcopal Church* (Harrisburg, PA: Trinity Press International, 1993), 159–62.

2. As noted in the introduction, this essay has been revised slightly to reflect the passage of time. When it was first published in 2006, the original version of this footnote said that the exception to this claim that proves the rule would be the late Hans W. Frei (1922–1988), but I would now add Kathryn Tanner. To be clear, by "Episcopal theologians" I mean only those scholars who formally belong to the Episcopal Church, and so major British figures such as Rowan Williams and Sarah Coakley are ruled out. I should also make it clear that I am in no way denigrating the excellent work of my fellow Episcopal theologians, both now and in the past. My observation here is not meant to be catty, contentious, or controversial, but simply matter-of-fact (cf. Holmes in n. 1). I take it as agreed that, aside from important exceptions

Originally published in *Anglican Theological Review* 88, no. 3 (Summer 2006): 421–32.

By contrast, over the past several decades the field of philosophy of religion has been strongly influenced by Episcopalians, one or two ordained, but mostly lay. Whereas their theological counterparts have been educated within seminaries, divinity schools, and departments of theology or religion, these scholars have been formed primarily by secular departments of philosophy, giving their writing and thinking style a particular sharpness. Rather than grand system-building, they are concerned with basic issues of conceptual analysis and clarification.[3] Nevertheless, such Episcopal philosophers are often surprisingly forthcoming about their theological convictions and ecclesial identity as Anglicans. Several are converts to the Episcopal Church who care deeply about the doctrinal integrity and intellectual substance of their adopted denomination. Thus, among the most important and influential philosophers of religion in the world during this period, one must include—at the very least—Marilyn McCord Adams (formerly of the University of Michigan, UCLA, and Yale, then Regius Professor of Divinity at Oxford before taking up research posts at UNC–Chapel Hill and Rutgers), Peter van Inwagen (Notre Dame and Duke), and William P. Alston (Syracuse). There is also a wider penumbra of significant Episcopal philosophers who, while not necessarily at the discipline-shaping level of these three, have still made considerable contributions.[4]

---

such as Frei and Tanner, even those Episcopal theologians who have won respect and recognition from the wider academic guild have not exercised influence either inside or outside the Episcopal Church comparable to those such as Tillich, Barth, or the Niebuhrs.

3. See *God, Philosophy, and Academic Culture: A Discussion between Scholars in the AAR and the APA*, ed. William J. Wainwright (Atlanta: Scholars Press, 1996), for a fascinating dialogue between the different intellectual mind-sets exemplified by philosophers of religion in the AAR (American Academy of Religion)—usually trained in departments of religion—and those in the APA (American Philosophical Association)—usually trained in departments of philosophy.

4. Two collections of spiritual autobiographies by philosophers contain a number of Anglicans or Episcopalians, and in particular a number of converts to the Episcopal Church. See Kelly James Clark, ed., *Philosophers Who Believe: The Spiritual Journeys of 11 Leading Thinkers* (Downers Grove, IL: InterVarsity Press, 1993), and Thomas V. Morris, ed., *God and the Philosophers: The Reconciliation of Faith and Reason* (Oxford: Oxford University Press, 1994). Adams, Inwagen, and Alston all tell their stories in the Morris volume, as does William Wainwright, the editor of the book mentioned in note 3: he converted to the Episcopal Church partly due to his undergraduate experience at Kenyon College. Since the original version of this essay was published, Adams (1943–2017), Alston (1921–2009), and Wainwright (1935–2020) have passed away.

Of these Episcopal philosophers, William Alston was notable both for his immense influence on the field and for his articulation of explicit Anglican commitment. In this review article, I will sketch the outline of his career, summarize the salient features of his work, and highlight its significance for Episcopal theological reflection. In so doing, I hope to draw attention to a neglected intellectual resource that is both *for* and *of* the Episcopal Church—namely, its philosophical lay members.

I. An Analytic Anglican

If they are close readers, many Episcopalians will have already come across Alston's name in the widely used reference volume *The Study of Anglicanism*. In A. S. McGrade's survey of the historic Anglican commitment to reason, only two Americans are mentioned: Hans Frei and William Alston. Near the end of the chapter—and thus at the culmination of his discussion of contemporary developments—McGrade references Alston's work in the epistemology of religious experience by observing that "an analytic philosophy not compelled to identify intelligence with scepticism can argue for the cognitive value of 'Christian mystical perceptual practice.'"[5] Likewise, in a chapter titled "The Anglican Tradition" in the first edition of Blackwell's *A Companion to Philosophy of Religion*, Alston is the only American mentioned by name. The author, Brian Hebblethwaite, writes that "within the remarkable Society of Christian Philosophers in the United States . . . there are to be found a number of Episcopalians, some of whose names will feature elsewhere in this volume, most notably that of William Alston (b. 1921), whose major study in the epistemology of religion, *Perceiving God* (1991), exemplifies a quintessentially Anglican penchant for unashamed natural theology."[6] Both McGrade and Hebblethwaite single out Alston's book *Perceiving God* for special consideration. While I will discuss this book briefly toward the end of the essay, let me here pause to observe that

5. A. S. McGrade, "Reason," in *The Study of Anglicanism*, ed. Stephen Sykes, John Booty, and Jonathan Knight, 2nd ed. (London: SPCK; Minneapolis: Fortress, 1998), citing page 126 and footnote 9 on page 128.

6. Brian Hebblethwaite, "The Anglican Tradition," in *A Companion to Philosophy of Religion*, ed. Philip L. Quinn and Charles Taliaferro (Cambridge, MA: Blackwell, 1997), 178.

Alston's endorsement of natural theology is rather more nuanced than Hebblethwaite's comment might suggest.

William Payne Alston was born in 1921 in Shreveport, Louisiana. Although brought up as a Methodist, he writes that his "undoubtedly imperfect recollection of this particular religious ambiance was that it was perfunctory and lacking in warmth of conviction."[7] This noncompelling early religious experience combined with a certain rationalist outlook led him to "abandon ship" as an adolescent. He studied music at Centenary College in Shreveport with a primary focus on the piano. While his professional interests gradually shifted from music to philosophy, his love of music remained, and in fact contributed to his eventual (re)conversion to Christianity in general and Anglicanism in particular.

During his doctoral studies in philosophy at the University of Chicago, one of Alston's primary teachers was the great Charles Hartshorne (1897–2000). Hartshorne's "process theology" is, of course, one of the most important schools in twentieth-century American theology and is considered an important alternative to the so-called classical theism of Thomas Aquinas. One of Alston's signal achievements is a rapprochement between these two competing systems—a rapprochement he attributes, somewhat facetiously, to his preference for the Anglican *via media*.[8]

Alston received his PhD in 1951, and his first appointment was at the University of Michigan, where he taught from 1949 to 1971. According to Daniel Howard-Snyder, "There his eyes were opened to contemporary English analytic philosophy and he underwent a fundamental shift, accelerated by trying to teach Hegel."[9] From this point onward, Alston became a practitioner of the

7. William P. Alston, "A Philosopher's Way Back to the Faith," in Morris, *God and the Philosophers*, 19.

8. See "Hartshorne and Aquinas: A Via Media," in William P. Alston, *Divine Nature and Human Language: Essays in Philosophical Theology* (Ithaca, NY: Cornell University Press, 1989), 121–43. For his comments on the *via media* of the title, see page 10 in the volume's introduction. This essay was originally published in *Existence and Actuality: Conversations with Charles Hartshorne*, ed. John B. Cobb Jr. and Franklin I. Gamwell (Chicago: University of Chicago Press, 1984), 78–98.

9. This sentence is quoted from Daniel Howard-Snyder, "Alston, William Payne (1921–)," an online PDF essay that may now be found linked to one of the references to Alston's Wikipedia page (https://tinyurl.com/34zx6nv5, last edited April 12, 2024). Much of the basic

analytic method, and it was as an analytic philosopher that he continued to teach at Rutgers (1971–1976), the University of Illinois at Urbana-Champaign (1976–1980), and Syracuse (1980–1992), where he retired as professor emeritus. It was also as an analytic philosopher that he made his mark on the discipline, providing some of the most distinguished contributions to epistemology, metaphysics, philosophical psychology, and philosophy of language in the mid to late twentieth century. These contributions led to numerous honors, including presidencies of (what is now) the Central Division of the American Philosophical Association and the Society for Philosophy and Psychology, becoming the founding editor of the *Journal of Philosophical Research*, and receiving a fellowship in the American Academy of Arts and Sciences.[10]

But under the surface of his gleaming academic career, Alston was engaged in a fitful spiritual search. During his first year of teaching at Michigan, he joined St. Andrew's Episcopal Church in Ann Arbor, and was confirmed in 1950. In an autobiographical essay, he writes, "[I] chose Episcopalianism over Methodism, Presbyterianism, and so on, partly because I was drawn to the liturgy and partly because I found the intellectual climate of Anglican thought congenial."[11] As Alston makes clear, however, this apparently positive development did not last. For one thing, he was still not convinced of the *truth* of Christianity, and so there was a pervasive element of cognitive disconnect. For another, he says that at this point he was "seeking to use the church and the Christian faith as a refuge from life" (21). When Alston realized that he was practicing a dead religion, he left the church for a second time. And so for the next fifteen years he resumed his secular stance and continued on with his philosophical career.

In 1974–1975, however, while he was teaching at Rutgers University, Alston and his wife, Valerie, spent a sabbatical year in Oxford. Alston says that he had never been a convinced atheist, and the question of Christian faith decisively re-presented itself during this time. At the suggestion of their daughter—once a nonbeliever herself, now an Episcopal priest—William and Valerie attended a service at Christ Church Cathedral. He writes: "This was literally the first

biographical information on Alston was derived from this essay, a slightly shorter version of which was then published in John R. Shook, ed., *The Dictionary of Modern American Philosophers*, vol. 1 (Bristol, UK: Thoemmes Continuum, 2005), 56–60.

10. Howard-Snyder, "Alston, William Payne (1921–)."

11. Alston, "A Philosopher's Way Back to the Faith," 20. Hereafter, page references from this work will be given in parentheses in the text.

religious service, apart from weddings and funerals, that I had attended in about fifteen years. Something happened, which I still find it difficult to put my finger on. But I definitely made a positive response to the proclamation of the gospel and to the sacramental presence of our Lord, and we began attending services regularly." He adds, "Oxford is a marvelous place for being drawn back into the church if music plays a large role in one's communication with the divine, as is true in my case" (23).

On returning to New Jersey, Alston continued to explore Christianity with this newfound freedom and openness. But the cognitive disconnect remained, and so, he says, "Insofar as I had any expectations of my religious future, I supposed I would adopt some sort of watered-down Christianity in which I would participate in the services of worship, supposing the doctrinal elements to be symbolic of some ineffable supreme reality" (23). But two elements conspired to alter this prediction: attendance at All Saints' Episcopal Church in Princeton, and a subsequent exposure to the charismatic movement.

At All Saints' the Alstons encountered the rector during that time, the Reverend Doctor A. Orley Swartzentruber (1926–2019). Alston credits Swartzentruber's example of pastoral care, wisdom, scholarship, faith, and—in particular—his remarkable sermons with finally making Christianity credible to Valerie and himself. In these sermons, he says, one "not only heard the gospel being interpreted in a way that had direct application to one's situation then and there, but one could, as it were, literally see the gospel being lived out in front of one" (24). Swartzentruber—a parish priest— profoundly shaped Alston's perception of Christianity, including its doctrines, as an intellectually substantial interpretation of reality that could and should be taken with utmost seriousness.

The second aspect of All Saints' that influenced Alston was his first encounter with the charismatic movement. This was in early 1976, and charismatic elements were beginning to percolate through various Episcopal and Roman Catholic congregations. While his initial response to the charismatic members of the parish was dubious, Alston was gradually drawn to share their basic perspective. He assures us that this "was a very muted and proper Anglican-style charismatic group," with less focus on dramatic manifestations such as speaking in tongues and more on private and corporate prayer, but "clearly, something was happening there" (24). He writes, "I began to see that these people were really in touch with God as a more or less continual living presence in their lives, and that this influenced, to a greater or lesser degree, every facet of their existence" (24).

In short, these various strands from Oxford and Princeton combined to provide Alston with an intellectually and experientially integrated vision of Christianity. He soon reengaged for the first time in twenty years with questions in philosophy of religion, and Alston's return to these topics was to have momentous implications for the field. But I have deliberately spent much of this essay on Alston's spiritual journey in order to emphasize an important fact worth further reflection, namely, that the most significant influences on his theological development—aside from reading classical figures such as Aquinas—were a parish priest, worshiping communities, and the living example of "ordinary" Christians. While I will consider some of his scholarly contributions in a moment, let me here mention some more broadly institutional accomplishments.

In 1977, soon after his return to both Christian faith and the Episcopal Church, Alston initiated the founding of the Society of Christian Philosophers and was then in 1978 elected its first president. This society has several hundred members and has been instrumental in spearheading a renaissance of interest in philosophical issues raised by Christian doctrine. In 1981 Alston also became the founding editor of the Society's journal, *Faith and Philosophy*, which is one of the leading journals in philosophy of religion.[12] He was also the founding editor of an important monograph series published by Cornell University Press: Cornell Studies in the Philosophy of Religion. In all three of these initiatives, Alston exercised an enormous, if sometimes indirect, influence on the shape, health, and direction of the discipline. It would be difficult to imagine what has occurred during this period without his involvement.

Alston's final teaching position was at Syracuse University, where he retired as professor emeritus. Since his Syracuse period began soon after his return to faith—and at the height of his academic career—a number of younger Christian philosophers went to Syracuse to study with him and receive their doctorates under his supervision. In addition to university commitments, he also wrote, "[Since] coming to Syracuse in 1980 I have, God help me, become increasingly involved in ecclesiastical affairs in both St. Paul's Cathedral, where we are mem-

12. See William P. Alston, "Some Reflections on the Early Days of the Society of Christian Philosophers" (141–43); Arthur F. Holmes, "Reflections on Divine Providence" (147–50); Alvin Plantinga, "Twenty Years Worth of the SCP" (151–55); and Michael L. Peterson, "A Long and Faithful Journey" (156–59), all in *Faith and Philosophy* 15 (1998).

bers of the congregation, and the Diocese of Central New York."[13] According to his obituary, these activities included serving on the cathedral vestry and the diocesan standing committee. After officially retiring from the university in 1992, he continued to teach until 2000. With his final book published in 2005, he remained a vibrant philosophical presence up until his death on September 13, 2009, at the age of eighty-seven.[14]

II. Alston's Manifesto

Twenty years earlier, in 1989, Alston published two collections of his most important papers to date, one in epistemology and one in philosophy of religion.[15] The volume in philosophy of religion—*Divine Nature and Human Language*—begins with an introductory essay that functions as a convenient manifesto of Alston's basic convictions and methodology in this field. While he denies being a systematic thinker, in the sense that he is not concerned to develop an overarching structure in which all the doctrines of Christianity fit together in a particular shape or according to certain criteria, he does acknowledge having a "fundamental religious and philosophical orientation." He thus provides his readers a fairly detailed description of that orientation, which is key to understanding his relevance not only for philosophy of religion but also for contemporary discussions in Episcopal/Anglican theology.

Rather unusually for a philosopher, Alston begins with a frank expression of faith:

> I am a Christian of a relatively conservative cast, by current standards outside evangelical and fundamentalist circles. I am not a fundamentalist about the Bible, and I am alive to the need of each age to rethink the substance of the faith. But I take the Christian tradition very seriously; I don't feel free to ig-

13. Alston, "A Philosopher's Way Back to the Faith," 25.

14. See William P. Alston, *Beyond "Justification": Dimensions of Epistemic Evaluation* (Ithaca, NY: Cornell University Press, 2005). For a memorial tribute, see Alvin Plantinga, "In Memoriam: William P. Alston, 1921–2009," *Faith and Philosophy* 26 (2009): 359–60. For Alston's obituary, see https://tinyurl.com/5e9vmw2r.

15. See William P. Alston, *Epistemic Justification: Essays in the Theory of Knowledge* (Ithaca, NY: Cornell University Press, 1989), and Alston, *Divine Nature and Human Language*.

nore it whenever it doesn't jibe with my own personal predilections. Hence the interest, displayed in these essays, in exploring, partly refashioning, and defending a fairly traditional conception of God and His work in the world, a conception that owes a great deal to medieval philosophical theology. This enterprise involves the use of much up-to-date philosophical equipment.[16]

He further observes that this "blend of fairly traditional Christianity, heavy borrowings from medieval philosophical theology, and the employment of contemporary analytical philosophy is typical of much recent work in philosophical theology" (6).

Coming from one of its most influential practitioners, this statement is an important expression of an intellectual strategy that—for better or worse—sets Christian analytic philosophy of religion apart from other current modes of theological discourse such as process theology, liberation theology, feminist theology, postliberal theology, postmodern theology, the existentialism of a John Macquarrie, the antirealism of a Don Cupitt, or the revisionism of a Maurice Wiles. Although Alston is being descriptive rather than prescriptive at this point, it is partly due to the impact of his own work that his observation is so accurate. His example has helped create the school which he describes and to which others have subsequently contributed.

Having stated his basic starting point and methodology, Alston further elaborates his views under three headings: (A) "Anti-positivism, Anti-scientism, Anti-naturalism"; (B) "Realism"; and (C) "Multiple Sources of Religious Knowledge." In positive terms, (A) declares that his approach to philosophy is not in principle closed off to the theoretical (i.e., both metaphysical and epistemological) possibility of the supernatural. In this regard, he maintains the right *as a philosopher* to take religious claims seriously, although not uncritically. Thus, Alston's work represents a sea change from the unremittingly hostile methodological naturalism that characterized most Anglo-American philosophy in the middle of the twentieth century.

In outlining his commitment to (B)—*realism*—Alston identifies disagreement on this issue "as perhaps the deepest divide in current religious thought" (7). He says: "I find myself at odds with most contemporary liberal

16. William P. Alston, introduction to *Divine Nature and Human Language*, 5. Hereafter, page references from this work will be given in parentheses in the text.

theologians and religious thinkers (outside the ranks of 'analytic philosophy') in accepting an uncompromisingly realistic interpretation of religious belief. I take it that when someone believes that God created the heavens and the earth, then, assuming that the belief is sufficiently determinate, that belief is true or false depending on whether things are as asserted" (6).

In other words, "There is a truth of the matter that is independent of us, our 'conceptual schemes,' our social institutions and associations, our conventions and values." Specifically addressing the guild of theologians, he adds: "I note, to my dismay, that many colleagues in theology and religious studies find it unutterably quaint that serious thinkers still take this realistic stance." Alston is not naïve: he recognizes the enormous difficulties involved in seeking to obtain sufficient clarity on a particular religious belief to determine whether it is, in fact, true or false. But he still maintains that *truth* and *falsity* are relevant categories in dealing with religious doctrine.

Finally, under (C), Alston takes a firmly Anglican view on religious epistemology: "In opposition to exclusivists of all stripes—Biblical fundamentalists, 'traditionalists,' rationalists—I hold that there are multiple sources of religious knowledge and/or rational (justified) belief" (7). While he does not pause to acknowledge it, it is interesting to note that in listing those three "exclusivist" positions he has in fact reproduced the familiar (if contested) Anglican triad of Scripture, tradition, and reason, although in their disconnected (and hence problematic) condition. He then describes the character of these various multiple sources and defends his right to take account of them all:

> I take very seriously the idea that people are experientially aware of God, that God presents Himself to their experience in various ways and thereby provides them with an empirical basis for beliefs about His presence and activity.... But I also take seriously the idea that God has revealed Himself, facts about His nature and character, and some of His purposes and intentions, through certain selected recipients and, more generally, through the religious community and its traditions. The traditions of the community thus serve as another avenue of religious truth, not to be taken uncritically, but not to be rejected out of hand either. Finally, I do not reject the enterprise of natural theology, the attempt to establish basic truths concerning the existence and nature of God by reasoning that does not rely in any way on data or convictions taken from the religious life. I do not think that

natural theology can live up to the expectations of its more enthusiastic advocates, but nor do I take it to be worthless. (7)

In making these latter claims about natural theology, Alston seems to set himself at a slight distance from the "more enthusiastic" portrait suggested earlier by Brian Hebblethwaite, who cited Alston as an example of Anglicanism's alleged "penchant for unashamed natural theology." Nevertheless, Alston certainly includes such philosophical reasoning as one of his various sources of religious knowledge.

Contrary to the stereotype of the abstract, *a priori* character of philosophy of religion, Alston insists that it must be rooted in the lives of actual religious individuals and communities. He also maintains that philosophers must adopt an appropriate degree of humility before the mysteries they investigate and not set too high expectations for themselves. In short, although he is a contemporary analytic philosopher using cutting-edge techniques and developments, Alston views his work as simply contributing to the classic project of faith seeking understanding. He says, "I seek to bring rational intelligibility and order into a system of belief and thought within a religious tradition, rather than examine the system's credentials from without" (8).

III. Conclusion

From this analytic perspective, Alston goes on to consider a number of theological issues. I have already mentioned his important work in developing a *via media* between the rival concepts of God provided by Hartshorne and Aquinas. Other theological topics he has investigated philosophically include the nature and limits of religious language,[17] God's action in the world,[18] divine command

---

17. See the five essays in part 1 of *Divine Nature and Human Language*, 17–117.

18. See "God's Action in the World," in *Divine Nature and Human Language*, 197–222; "How to Think about Divine Action: Twenty-Five Years of Travail for Biblical Language," in *Divine Action: Studies Inspired by the Philosophical Theology of Austin Farrer*, ed. Brian Hebblethwaite and Edward Henderson (Edinburgh: T&T Clark, 1990), 51–70; and "Divine Action: Shadow or Substance?" in *The God Who Acts: Philosophical and Theological Explorations*, ed. Thomas F. Tracy (University Park, PA: Penn State University Press, 1994), 41–62.

ethics,[19] the Trinity,[20] the Holy Spirit,[21] the nature of religious faith,[22] and biblical interpretation.[23] And his major work on the epistemology of religious experience—*Perceiving God*—concludes with a sustained discussion of religious pluralism and the place of experience within the general grounds for religious belief.[24] All of this material is well worth careful attention from theologians, even if they disagree with Alston's conclusions or methodology.

Aside from its inherent interest, Alston's work is also indicative of a significant shift in the philosophical and theological landscape. Much of his work is explicitly critical of figures who were highly influential among previous generations of Episcopal theologians, such as Paul Tillich, John Macquarrie, Langdon Gilkey, Gordon Kaufmann, Maurice Wiles, and of course, the process theology of Charles Hartshorne and his followers. *Pace* such "revisionist" thinkers, Alston is impressed by the coherence and resilience of classical Christian doctrine, although he finds it needs tweaking here and there. Although they are not normally included in such company, I suggest that Alston and his fellow analysts may thus be placed within the broad trend of *ressourcement*, which looks primarily to traditional sources for inspiration rather than contemporary culture, praxis, or innovatory insights. Unlike the currently dominant influence

19. See "Some Suggestions for Divine Command Theorists," in *Divine Nature and Human Language*, 253–73.

20. See "The Holy Spirit and the Trinity," in *Philosophy and Theological Discourse*, ed. Stephen T. Davis (London: Macmillan, 1997), 102–23, and "Substance and the Trinity," in *The Trinity: An Interdisciplinary Symposium on the Doctrine of the Trinity*, ed. Stephen T. Davis, Daniel Kendall, SJ, and Gerald O'Collins, SJ (Oxford: Oxford University Press, 1999), 179–201.

21. In addition to the first article in note 20, see also "The Indwelling of the Holy Spirit," in *Divine Nature and Human Language*, 223–52.

22. See "Christian Experience and Christian Belief," in *Faith and Rationality: Reason and Belief in God*, ed. Alvin Plantinga and Nicholas Wolterstorff (Notre Dame, IN: University of Notre Dame Press, 1983), 103–34, and "Belief, Acceptance, and Religious Faith," in *Faith, Freedom, and Rationality: Philosophy of Religion Today*, ed. Jeff Jordan and Daniel Howard-Snyder (Lanham, MD: Rowman & Littlefield, 1996), 3–27.

23. See "Biblical Criticism and the Resurrection," in *The Resurrection: An Interdisciplinary Symposium on the Resurrection of Jesus*, ed. Stephen T. Davis, Daniel Kendall, SJ, and Gerald O'Collins, SJ (Oxford: Oxford University Press, 1997), 148–83, and "Historical Criticism of the Synoptic Gospels," in *"Behind" the Text: History and Biblical Interpretation*, ed. C. Bartholomew et al. (Grand Rapids: Zondervan, 203), 151–80.

24. See *Perceiving God: The Epistemology of Religious Experience* (Ithaca, NY: Cornell University Press, 1991), chapter 8.

of much Barthian thought, however, Alston's stance follows Aquinas in being more theocentric than Christocentric (although he does accept a Chalcedonian model of Christ's two natures).

Alston's work across a wide range of interdisciplinary topics has generated a considerable body of commentary, both critical and appreciative, positive and negative: symposia, conference discussions, numerous citations throughout the literature, and at least two Festschriften.[25] Very many questions could be posed to him. To name just two concerns relevant to this review essay, James Kellenberger has asked if the genuine insights expressed in Alston's spiritual autobiography are in fact fully integrated into his academic work; and Sarah Coakley raises a question mark over what she sees as the overly individualistic nature of his methodology.[26] Here I am primarily interested in presenting his journey into the Episcopal Church and the analytic methodology underlying his work. I am not seeking to commend the *results* of his work to the readers of this volume, but rather to recommend that we take him and it seriously. Not simply as a philosopher, but also as a dedicated lay member of the Episcopal Church and as a builder of a substantial intellectual community, Alston is perhaps the most influential recent American Episcopalian in the overlapping disciplines of philosophy, theology, and religious studies. If Episcopalians pride themselves on their commitment to "reason," it might behoove them actually to listen to those who have made reason their life's study.[27]

25. See Thomas D. Senor, ed., *The Rationality of Belief and the Plurality of Faith: Essays in Honor of William P. Alston* (Ithaca, NY: Cornell University Press, 1995), and Heather D. Battaly and Michael P. Lynch, eds., *Perspectives on the Philosophy of William P. Alston* (Lanham, MD: Rowman & Littlefield, 2005).

26. See James Kellenberger, "The Fool of the Psalms and Religious Epistemology," *International Journal for Philosophy of Religion* 45 (1999): 99–113, and Sarah Coakley, "Response" to William Alston, "Biblical Criticism and the Resurrection," in Davis, Kendall, and O'Collins, *The Resurrection*, 184–90. At this point I could add my own concerns about Alston's stout defense of literal language in relation to God against Aquinas's contrary insistence that we always speak analogically when referring to the divine nature.

27. I wish to thank Daniel Howard-Snyder and Peter van Inwagen for their help in establishing certain points of detail; and also David Brown, the late Joe Cassidy, and Paul Murray for their comments on an earlier version of this essay. Special thanks to the late William Alston for kindly reading it for accuracy back in 2006.

CHAPTER 2

Above, Beside, Within:
The Anglican Theology of Austin Farrer

Austin Farrer suffers from a surfeit of praise and a deficit of attention. According to Rowan Williams, he is "possibly the greatest Anglican mind of the 20th century."[1] In 1987 Richard Harries published a set of readings from Farrer titled *The One Genius*, for "it has been said of him that he is the one genius that the Church of England has produced during this century."[2] In a similar vein, Diogenes Allen once remarked that "Oxford had only produced one great theologian since Newman, and that was Farrer."[3] Less dramatically, perhaps, Brian Hebblethwaite argues that he provides the best twentieth-century example of "the Anglican tradition's ability to marry natural theology, rational theology, and the theology of revelation."[4] Nearing the end of a comprehensive essay on the historic Anglican commitment to reason, A. S. McGrade claims that "Farrer's work is a particularly attractive recent example of the qualities we have encountered in earlier authors," such as Hooker, Locke, Butler, and Coleridge.[5]

---

1. Rowan Williams, "Debate on *The Gift of Authority*—Archbishop of Canterbury's Remarks," Dr. Rowan Williams, February 13, 2004, https://tinyurl.com/bdf8kzka. In a later address in 2011, he was less guarded and described Farrer without qualification as "the greatest Anglican intellect of the last century": see https://tinyurl.com/pnmtjexy.

2. Richard Harries, introduction to *The One Genius: Readings through the Year with Austin Farrer*, ed. Richard Harries (London: SPCK, 1987), ix.

3. Cited by Eric Springsted in his introduction to *Spirituality and Theology: Essays in Honor of Diogenes Allen*, ed. Eric O. Springsted (Louisville: Westminster John Knox, 1998), 3.

4. Brian Hebblethwaite, "The Anglican Tradition," in *A Companion to the Philosophy of Religion*, ed. Philip Quinn and Charles Taliaferro (Cambridge, MA: Blackwell, 1997), 175.

5. A. S. McGrade, "Reason," in *The Study of Anglicanism*, ed. Stephen Sykes, John Booty, and Jonathan Knight, rev. ed. (London: SPCK; Minneapolis: Fortress, 1998), 124. In this

Originally published in *Journal of Anglican Studies* 4, no. 1 (June 2006): 33–57.

In a survey of religion in Oxford from 1914 to 1970, F. M. Turner says, "More than any figure of his generation in the University, Farrer embodied the highest ideal of the college chaplain-theologian."[6] And Susan Howatch says that he "deserves to be read today by all those interested in truth, tradition, and twentieth-century spirituality."[7]

With that array of endorsements, one would expect that Austin Farrer would be—if not a household name—at least regarded as a major figure in current Anglican theological discussions. One would expect a steady stream of books and articles and doctoral dissertations investigating his achievements. One would expect a considerable amount of citations scattered throughout the primary and secondary literature relating to the areas on which he himself wrote. One would expect several significant contemporary figures to publicly avow themselves as "Farrerians" in some form or fashion. One would expect a "school" built up around his writings and a consequent "presence" that influenced our present understandings of religious epistemology or biblical interpretation or Anglican identity or spiritual practice. One would expect Farrer to stand as an authority among other authorities like Karl Barth or Paul Tillich or Karl Rahner or Hans Urs von Balthasar. One would expect for most, if not all, of Farrer's works to still be in print.

But all that one would expect—if, that is, Williams, Harries, Allen, Hebblethwaite, McGrade, Turner, and Howatch are correct—is in fact far from the case. Rather than being a major figure, Farrer's impact on contemporary discussions in theology, philosophy, Anglican studies, and spirituality is insignificant. This is not to say that Farrer has *no* impact or presence on the contemporary

---

volume, Farrer is also mentioned in John Booty's chapter, "Standard Divines," as a potential inheritor of that title (184), and in A. M. Allchin's chapter, "Anglican Spirituality," as an example—along with Richard Hooker, Lancelot Andrewes, Jeremy Taylor, Thomas Traherne, William Law, Samuel Taylor Coleridge, John Henry Newman, and C. S. Lewis—of the Anglican tradition of great theological prose writers (353).

6. F. M. Turner, "Religion," in *The History of the University of Oxford*, vol. 8, *The Twentieth Century*, ed. Brian Harrison (Oxford: Clarendon, 1994), 309.

7. Susan Howatch, introduction to Austin Farrer, *Saving Belief: A Discussion of Essentials* (London: Mowbray; Harrisburg, PA: Morehouse, 1994), xi. This book was originally published in 1964 by Hodder & Stoughton in the UK. Howatch included it in her Library of Anglican Spirituality series, which is an encouraging sign that Farrer has not been (and will not be) entirely forgotten.

scene. There is a small but interesting secondary literature; there have been several doctoral dissertations; there is the occasional conference; citations of his work do appear.[8] A flurry of activity on both sides of the Atlantic greeted the centenary of his birth in 2004, and it may be that a renewal of interest is pending.[9] But, in general, Farrer's actual impact is not nearly in proportion to the litany of enthusiasm collated above.

Farrer died in December 1968, twenty days after Karl Barth, but it is no exaggeration to say that more books, articles, and dissertations have been written on Barth in the past five years than have been written on Farrer in the past five decades. Barth, of course, deserves the attention. But if Rowan Williams thinks that Austin Farrer was "possibly the greatest Anglican mind of the 20th century," then surely he ought to be regarded with more respect than he is and have more influence than he does. Anglicans, at least, should be reading him to discover what their (possibly) greatest mind of the last century thought.

Of course, there are *reasons* why Farrer does not have the audience he deserves. And some of them, it must be said, are Farrer's own fault. While his relative obscurity is puzzling, it is not as though there has been an active conspiracy to erase his accomplishment. Cultural and academic trends have in many ways made Farrer seem old-fashioned or irrelevant, but Farrer's idiosyncrasies and difficulties have not helped his reputation. In this article, I hope to provide an introductory sketch of Farrer's specifically Anglican accomplishments, a sketch that will perhaps encourage others to seek out his writing with renewed curiosity.[10]

8. See the very useful "Bibliography of Writings about Austin Farrer with Other Research Aids," in *Captured by the Crucified: The Practical Theology of Austin Farrer*, ed. David Hein and Edward Hugh Henderson (New York: T&T Clark International, 2004), 197–208.

9. Specifically, two international centenary conferences were held in 2004: "The Human Person in God's World" at Oriel College, Oxford, in September; and "Captured by the Crucified—the Legacy of Austin Farrer: A Conference and Spiritual Life Workshop Celebrating the Centenary Year of His Birth" at the St. James Center for Spiritual Formation, Baton Rouge, Louisiana, in November. The second conference was associated with and preceded by the book of the same title, mentioned in note 8; the papers of the Oxford conference were published as Douglas Hedley and Brian Hebblethwaite, eds., *The Human Person in God's World: Studies to Commemorate the Austin Farrer Centenary* (London: SCM, 2006).

10. Rowan Williams points out that not only Farrer but his whole generation was forgotten by John A. T. Robinson and others in the 1950s and '60s. He writes, "Looking back, it is plain that the postwar period was not nearly such a wilderness from the point of view of robust doctrinal exposition and exploration as [*Honest to God*] might suggest. Gregory Dix, Austin Farrer, and

The renewal of such curiosity is necessary if Anglicanism is to continue to exist as a coherent and distinctive *intellectual* and *theological* tradition. That is, attention is currently focused on the sustainability of the Anglican Communion as an *institution* (or set of institutions). But institutional futures cannot be separated from conceptual ones. Unless and until those charged with the task of teaching theology in Anglican churches have their intellectual imagination *reengaged* with their own tradition, questions of institutional sustainability are moot. While certainly not the only—or even the most obvious—choice, I would argue that Farrer is an important figure for contemporary Anglicans to learn from as we grapple with present debates over our heritage and identity.[11]

I. A Brief Sketch of Farrer's Life and Work

Austin Farrer (1904–1968) was born in Hampstead, England, to Baptist parents.[12] His father was in fact an ordained lecturer at Regent's Park College,

---

Eric Mascall had all produced work that represented an amazingly creative reworking of classical themes.... But if the immediate postwar period witnessed such an explosion of first-class Anglican doctrinal reflection, still fresh and suggestive more than fifty years later, it rather looks as though the 1950s had forgotten why any of this mattered." See "*Honest to God* and the 1960s," in Rowan Williams, *Anglican Identities* (London: Darton, Longman & Todd, 2003), 103–20, esp. 109–11.

11. In addition to Williams's positive comments about Farrer cited in notes 1 and 10, it is interesting to observe that his name has appeared several times in *Anglican Theological Review*'s occasional "Essential Reading" feature. Describing "ten books from among the most helpful and influential I have read," Arthur A. Vogel first lists Farrer's *The Glass of Vision* and concludes with Farrer's *The Freedom of the Will* (*ATR* 81 [1999]: 767–68). Mark McIntosh discusses twelve authors: St. Gregory of Nyssa, St. John of the Cross, John Donne, John Henry Newman, Austin Farrer, Étienne Gilson, Herbert McCabe, Karl Barth, Hans Urs von Balthasar, Simone Weil, Rowan Williams, and James Alison (*ATR* 83 [2001]: 189–90). Like Vogel, Richard A. Norris Jr. also begins his list with Farrer, whom he describes as "surely the finest Anglican theologian of his generation." After discussing several of Farrer's works, Norris comments: "In a time when everyone is busy talking about the heart or soul or spirit of Anglicanism, it is odd that the great fashioners and interpreters of that tradition—not just Farrer, but Hooker, Pearson (author of *On the Creed* [1640], probably the most widely employed introduction to Christian doctrine in the history of Anglicanism), Maurice, Gore, Westcott, Scott-Holland, DuBose, Temple, and others of that ilk, should be almost uniformly out of print and unavailable, as far as I know, even for downloading" (*ATR* 82 [2000]: 631–34, quoting from 631).

12. For the general information in this section, see in particular the one biography of Farrer:

a Baptist theological college once located in London, now a permanent private hall in the University of Oxford. After a rigorous education at St. Paul's School in London, Farrer went up to Balliol College, Oxford, where he distinguished himself with two first-class efforts, in "Mods" (Classical Moderations) and "Greats" (Literae Humaniores). During his undergraduate studies, he felt a gentle but inexorable pull toward the Church of England and a consequent call to its priesthood. His conversion to Anglicanism was carried out with intense self-awareness, theological consideration, and in constant dialogue with his parents. With their (somewhat reluctant) blessing, he was baptized at St. Peter-le-Bailey (now the chapel of St. Peter's College) and then confirmed at Christ Church Cathedral in Oxford in May 1924.[13] Farrer proceeded to Cuddesdon for his theological studies (for which he was also awarded a first) and was ordained in Wakefield Cathedral in 1928.

After a curacy in Yorkshire, Farrer returned to Oxford, where he spent the rest of his life in teaching, preaching, pastoral ministry, writing, and administration. His first university position was as chaplain and tutor at St. Edmund Hall (1931–1935), followed by a long period as chaplain and fellow of Trinity College (1935–1960), and he culminated his career as warden of Keble College

---

Philip Curtis, *A Hawk among Sparrows: A Biography of Austin Farrer* (London: SPCK, 1985), and "Farrer, Austin Marsden (1904–1968)," by I. M Crombie, rev., in *Oxford Dictionary of National Biography: From the Earliest Times to the Year 2000*, vol. 19, *Fane–Flatman*, ed. H. C. G. Matthew and Brian Harrison (Oxford: Oxford University Press, 2004), 121–23. Other important sources are Susan Howatch's introduction to her edition of *Saving Belief* (cited in note 7); Ann Loades, "Farrer, Austin Marsden," in *The SPCK Handbook of Anglican Theologians*, ed. Alister E. McGrath (London: SPCK, 1998), 120–23; Robert B. Slocum, "Light in a Burning-Glass: The Theological Witness of Austin Farrer," *Anglican Theological Review* 85 (2003): 365–73; and the editors' introduction to *Captured by the Crucified* (cited in note 8).

13. In *A Hawk among Sparrows*, Curtis observes that Farrer had not been baptized in the Baptist denomination (20) but was eventually confirmed in the Church of England in the Latin Chapel of Christ Church (23–24). From this, J. Barry Vaughn draws the natural conclusion that Farrer was both baptized and confirmed in the cathedral ("Resurrection and Grace: The Sermons of Austin Farrer," *Preaching* 9 [1994]: 61–63). In fact, Curtis never mentions when or where Farrer was baptized. But according to Farrer's ordination certificate in the West Yorkshire Archive Service, he was baptized on May 14, 1924, in St. Peter-le-Bailey. For more detail, see Robert MacSwain, "Correspondence and Documentation Related to Austin Farrer's Baptism in the Church of England on 14 May 1924," *Anglican and Episcopal History* 81 (2012): 241–76, now republished under a different title as chapter 3 in this volume.

from 1960 until his early death in 1968. To the surprise of many, he was never appointed to a university professorship, but this lack of recognition was typical and (as indicated above) continues in the contemporary scene.

In addition to several posthumous collections of essays and sermons, Farrer published fifteen books of philosophy, biblical studies, doctrinal theology, and sermons. His major works are *Finite and Infinite* (1943), *The Glass of Vision* (1948), *A Rebirth of Images: The Making of St. John's Apocalypse* (1949), *The Freedom of the Will* (1958), *St. Matthew and St. Mark* (1954), *Love Almighty and Ills Unlimited* (1961), and *Faith and Speculation* (1967). Farrer spent his academic career cutting against the grain in various disciplines. He practiced metaphysical natural theology during the reign of logical positivism and found complex typologies and literary structures in Scripture during the period of rigid historical criticism. He embraced a creative and sophisticated Trinitarian orthodoxy in a time of theological uncertainty, and preached literary and doctrinal sermons in a time of turmoil and innovation. He was, in sum, traditional but fiercely independent. In many ways, he was thus far ahead of his time, and his work prefigured certain trends in contemporary analytic philosophy of religion, postliberal theology, and the renewal of spirituality and Trinitarian reflection.[14]

It is important to mention Farrer's *style*. For a theologian, Farrer's writing and preaching manifested an unusually imaginative poetic voice. Leslie Houlden states that Farrer was "a giant of a preacher" and comments that his sermons had "a certain literary quality which . . . was certainly becoming unusual in the

14. For monographs on Farrer that explore some of these themes, see Charles C. Hefling Jr., *Jacob's Ladder: Theology and Spirituality in the Thought of Austin Farrer* (Cambridge, MA: Cowley, 1979); Jeffrey C. Eaton, *The Logic of Theism: An Analysis of the Thought of Austin Farrer* (Lanham, MD: University Press of America, 1980); and Charles Conti, *Metaphysical Personalism: An Analysis of Austin Farrer's Theistic Metaphysics* (Oxford: Clarendon, 1995). In addition to the centenary volumes cited in notes 8 and 9, two important essay collections are Jeffrey C. Eaton and Ann Loades, eds., *For God and Clarity: New Essays in Honor of Austin Farrer* (Allison Park, PA: Pickwick, 1983), and Brian Hebblethwaite and Edward Henderson, eds., *Divine Action: Studies Inspired by the Philosophical Theology of Austin Farrer* (Edinburgh: T&T Clark, 1990). Two more recent collections associated with the fiftieth anniversary of his death are Markus Bockmuehl, Stephen Platten, and Nevsky Everett, eds., *Austin Farrer: Oxford Warden, Scholar, Preacher* (London: SCM, 2020), and Richard Harries and Stephen Platten, eds., *Austin Farrer for Today: A Prophetic Legacy* (London: SCM, 2020).

pulpit of his day (now it has virtually vanished)."[15] John Austin Baker claims Farrer "developed a new kind of rhetoric" in his preaching: "His style was concrete, articulate, often beautiful, but above all acceptable, because it was suffused at its best with a delicacy that could be sensitive or light-hearted as the time required. It was a quiet, sometimes self-mocking rhetoric; but a rhetoric none the less. . . . He aimed to move his hearers, to play upon them, not for any false effects, but so that they might see and perceive, hear and understand, and turn again and be healed."[16] Both Leslie Houlden and Charles Taliaferro compare Farrer's sermons to those of John Henry Newman.[17]

Richard Harries argues that Farrer's "captivating prose style" is in fact the key element of his genius, allowing him to fuse together his immense (but otherwise separate) gifts of intellect, imagination, and spirituality.[18] He says, "What gives the unity of Farrer, so apparent in all his work, its remarkable distinction, is the sheer quality of his prose; the product of a poetic imagination, honed by the study of ancient literature and put to the service of divine truth."[19] But perhaps the best way to convey the power of Farrer's style is to hear a firsthand description of its effects. In a spiritual autobiography, Basil Mitchell—a distinguished philosopher of religion—recounts a key moment in his journey to Christian faith:

15. Leslie Houlden, introduction to *Austin Farrer: The Essential Sermons*, ed. Leslie Houlden (London: SPCK; Cambridge, MA: Cowley, 1991), ix.

16. John Austin Baker, introduction to Austin Farrer, *The End of Man* (London: SPCK, 1973), ix. For further considerations of Farrer's preaching, see Vaughn, "Resurrection and Grace"; Robert B. Slocum, "Farrer in the Pulpit: A Systematic Introduction to His Sermons," *Anglican Theological Review* 86 (2004): 493–503; and O. C. Edwards and David Hein, "Farrer's Preaching: 'Some Taste of the Things We Describe,'" in Hein and Henderson, *Captured by the Crucified*, 173–95.

17. Houlden: Farrer "invites comparison with J. H. Newman or, more remotely, George Herbert," in *Austin Farrer*, ix. Taliaferro: "I do not think it exaggerated to compare his sermons in terms of literary merit and religious illumination to the mature sermons of Cardinal John Henry Newman," from his review of Hebblethwaite and Henderson, *Divine Action*, in *Faith and Philosophy* 10 (1993): 119–23.

18. Harries, "'We Know on Our Knees . . .': Intellectual, Imaginative and Spiritual Unity in the Theology of Austin Farrer," in Hebblethwaite and Henderson, *Divine Action*, 30.

19. Harries, "'We Know on Our Knees . . . ,'" 33. See also A. M. Allchin's comments in "Anglican Spirituality," 353–54.

If there was a moment in my new life at Oxford at which I experienced a conversion, or rather realized that a conversion had occurred, it was while listening to Austin Farrer's Bampton Lectures, given in St. Mary's Church for the Michaelmas term 1948 and published under the title *The Glass of Vision*. The restrained delivery, the precision of utterance, the controlled imagination, together with the capacity, without apparent alteration of pace or emphasis, to raise the discourse to the most intense level of religious contemplation without loss of philosophical substance, were unlike anything I have ever experienced before or since.[20]

Mitchell concludes, "Here at last was the mystical vision . . . but a vision that acknowledged and enhanced the reality of the created order and the significance of human history and was intimately involved in the lives and loves of individual persons."[21]

Within the wide spectrum of Anglicanism, Farrer has been described as "a Prayer-Book Anglican in the Tractarian tradition," "a quintessential Anglican Catholic,"[22] and "a 'Catholic' and robustly confident and critical member of the Church of England."[23] Houlden says that Farrer's sermons were marked by "a Catholic hue which might seem sectional in its appeal, especially as it was a very special Catholic hue—firmly non-Roman, even anti-Roman, unmistakably Anglican and Oxford Anglican at that; yet there was no better spokesman for universal, deep-rooted mature Christian orthodoxy."[24] But while Farrer embodied the Tractarian priest-don, he did so without abandoning the virtues of his Baptist background. He could easily identify himself as both Catholic *and* Reformed—and despite his strong Anglo-Catholic credentials, he still re-

20. Basil Mitchell, "War and Friendship," in *Philosophers Who Believe: The Spiritual Journeys of 11 Leading Thinkers*, ed. Kelly James Clark (Downers Grove, IL: InterVarsity Press, 1993), 38–39.

21. Mitchell, "War and Friendship," 39. Writing forty-five years after the event, Mitchell misplaced the date of Farrer's Bamptons, which occurred in the spring rather than the autumn of 1948. For a critical edition of these seminal lectures, see Robert MacSwain, ed., *Scripture, Metaphysics, and Poetry: Austin Farrer's* The Glass of Vision *with Critical Commentary* (Farnham, UK: Ashgate, 2013; London: Routledge, 2016).

22. Both quotations from Howatch, introduction to *Saving Belief*, viii.

23. Loades, "Farrer, Austin Marsden," 122.

24. Houlden, *Austin Farrer*, ix.

tained a touch of Nonconformity in his personal devotion and expression of faith. J. Barry Vaughn says rightly that he "was a High Church Anglican with the warm-hearted piety of an Evangelical or Methodist,"[25] and Stephen Platten states that "the evangelical side of his Baptist heritage was an important formative influence" in Farrer's emphasis on preaching.[26]

As indicated above and stated explicitly by Houlden, Farrer's Anglicanism was wedded to traditional Christian doctrine. Susan Howatch states that he was "classically orthodox, a theologian utterly committed to the doctrine of the Trinity and supremely adept at expounding it."[27] Ann Loades says Farrer was "a Trinitarian theologian, unsurprisingly for one who lived liturgically, whilst giving full weight to the particularity of the incarnation."[28] Over and over again, Farrer presents himself as one who lives within the tradition of the church, seeking to believe that he may understand. And yet, over and over again, his commentators remark that his orthodoxy was neither sterile nor reactionary, but living and creative. Concluding a brief overview of his life and works, Jeffrey Eaton and Ann Loades suggest that we may "understand Farrer best if we think of him as one whose primary vocation was that of a priest dedicated to the care of souls, whether through the preaching of the Christian faith, the administration of the sacraments, or the writing of books for learned specialists and interested laity. He humbly employed his considerable gifts toward the end of making the love of God explicit. The legacy of those labors are some splendid volumes which exhibit on nearly every page Farrer's passion for God and clarity."[29]

II. Austin Farrer: Anglican Theologian

In this section I will look at three different texts that exemplify Farrer's Anglican theology: a sermon, a set of meditations, and a lecture series. Most scholars

25. Vaughn, "Resurrection and Grace," 62.

26. Stephen Platten, "Diaphanous Thought: Spirituality and Theology in the Work of Austin Farrer," *Anglican Theological Review* 69 (1987): 46.

27. Howatch, introduction to *Saving Belief*, viii. However, as we will see below, Farrer's orthodox Trinitarian devotion was not always in harness with his speculative Trinitarian exposition.

28. Loades, "Farrer, Austin Marsden," 122.

29. Jeffrey C. Eaton and Ann Loades, "Austin Marsden Farrer (1904–1968)," in Eaton and Loades, *For God and Clarity*, xiii.

working on Farrer have focused on his major academic writings, but here I am more interested in what Ann Loades describes as "the Farrer of the sermons, the Lent books, the paragraphs for use at the Eucharist; even the Farrer who taught the use of the rosary."[30] In drawing attention to this aspect of his work, I want to highlight the Anglican elements of Farrer's thought and, thus, his potential contribution to current questions of Anglican identity. In the following section I will pull back from the texts for questions and analysis.

A. "On Being an Anglican"

The sermon "On Being an Anglican" was preached in Pusey House, Oxford, in 1960—the year Farrer was appointed warden of Keble College. This confluence of institutions named for two founders of the Oxford Movement gives a clear indication of the sermon's audience. This sermon is valuable as a rare direct and public expression of Farrer's commitment to Anglicanism, and so provides an excellent starting place for our investigation.

Farrer delves into the center of ecclesiological controversy—what is the nature of the church?—and begins by distinguishing between "the Church of God" and the various divided bodies of Christendom. "Did not Christ establish sacraments, and an apostolic ministry, and a visible company of faithful men?" he asks, and the clear answer he expects at all three questions is yes.[31] The function of the church on earth is "to incorporate men into the life of Incarnate God, and the Church is itself the means and the form of such an incorporation."[32] But, he instantly admits, "The Church of England is not *the* Church; there is

---

30. Ann Loades, "Austin Farrer on *Love Almighty*," in Eaton and Loades, *For God and Clarity*, 93. This essay was recently reprinted in Ann Loades, *Explorations in Twentieth-Century Theology and Philosophy: People Preoccupied with God*, ed. Stephen Burns (Melbourne: Anthem, 2023), 89–103.

31. Austin Farrer, "On Being an Anglican," in *The End of Man*, ed. Charles Conti (London: SPCK, 1973), 48–52, quoting from 49 (hereafter cited as *EOM*). Farrer regularly uses noninclusive language, and I will not modify quotations. Some of the Farrer texts cited below are reprinted in Ann Loades and Robert MacSwain, eds., *The Truth-Seeking Heart: Austin Farrer and His Writings* (Norwich, UK: Canterbury, 2006), with this quotation on 144, and when they are included I will also cite from this edition (hereafter cited as *TSH*).

32. *EOM*, 49; *TSH*, 144.

only one Church, as there is only one Christ. The centre of the Church is neither Rome nor Canterbury; it is the heart of heaven."[33] Tragically, however, on
earth this essential unity is "scattered" and "divided" in a state of "warfare": "The
Church feels herself to be one, and groans to find herself divided, but there is
no easy way to heal all her divisions."[34]

Does it matter, then, whether one belongs to the Church of England, or
Rome, or Constantinople, or any number of Protestant denominations? Farrer is convinced that it does matter. His conviction is built on two principles:
(1) his Catholic belief in the reality of apostolic succession and consequent role
of the sacraments, and (2) his Reformed belief that Scripture is the touchstone
of doctrine. He thus produces a standard textbook defense of the Church of
England as a *via media* of Reformed Catholicism:

> It is not for me to admire or embrace, or even prefer, a sect called Anglican-
> ism. What is it then? There are two overriding considerations. I dare not dis-
> sociate myself from the apostolic ministry, and the continuous sacramental
> life of the Church extending unbroken from the first days until now. That
> is the first point, and the second is this: I dare not profess belief in the great
> Papal error. Christ did not found a Papacy. . . . I cannot desert the apostolic
> ministry, I cannot submit to the Pope. And I was not born a Greek or Slavic
> Christian. I was born in this English-speaking world, where God's merciful
> providence has preserved the form and substance of the Catholic Church,
> and freed it from papal usurpation.[35]

In making this claim, Farrer is careful to stress its doctrinal integrity. The
Church of England is truly Catholic *and* truly Reformed. Consequently, it is
the only place where Farrer, *in his specific context*, can "truly and with a good
conscience, abide in the Church of God."[36] He "dare" not go elsewhere. He thus
rejects any vestige of aesthetic or English sentimentality as a valid reason to be
Anglican: "we are not Anglicans . . . because of George Herbert, or Dr. Donne,
or Isaac Walton, or Bishop Ken, or John Wesley, or John Keble—because of

---

33. *EOM*, 50; *TSH*, 145.
34. *EOM*, 50; *TSH*, 145.
35. *EOM*, 50–51; *TSH*, 145–46.
36. *EOM*, 50; *TSH*, 145.

Prayer-Book English, or Cathedral psalmody, or Cambridge theology, or Oxford piety. No, we are Anglicans because we can obey Christ in this Church, by abiding in the stock and root of his planting, and in the sacramental life."[37]

Despite his strong claims on behalf of Anglicanism and against Rome, Farrer is hardly triumphalist. As noted above, he denies the simple identity of the Church of England with the church of God, and insists that Canterbury has no special prominence. Farrer also warns against preoccupying ourselves with the church to the extent that we lose sight of Christ, and in this regard he compares the church to a telescope. The instrument itself may interest us at first, but its purpose is "to eliminate itself and leave us face to face with the object of vision."[38] Anglicanism instantiates Christ's one, holy, catholic, and apostolic church only inasmuch as it provides access to that vision. Only then can Anglicans claim to belong to "the Church of God."[39]

B. Lord I Believe

In "On Being an Anglican," Farrer sets out an uncharacteristically direct statement of his underlying ecclesial convictions. To see how those convictions are played out in practice, we need to look at two other texts: *Lord I Believe* and *Saving Belief*. We will begin with *Lord I Believe*.

In 1955, Farrer wrote a series of meditations on the Apostles' Creed for the Church Union, "an Anglican association which exists 'to uphold the doctrine and discipline of the Church; to extend the knowledge of Catholic Faith and

37. *EOM*, 51–52; *TSH*, 146.
38. *EOM*, 52; *TSH*, 146–47.
39. Jeremy Morris describes this sermon as "harsh and polemical" and maintains that "Farrer's position [in] 'On Being an Anglican,' for all its force of language and argument, was already outmoded in tone, almost before the ink was dry"—and since its ink was dry in 1960, it is certainly unsuitable for today. I cannot engage further with Morris's position here, but I think he overemphasizes the negative anti-Roman element in the sermon and does not acknowledge Farrer's critique of *all* ecclesial pretensions, whether Roman, Orthodox, Anglican, or Protestant. Clearly, however, Farrer's words do not fit well in the current ecumenical climate, no matter how cool it may be. See Jeremy Morris, "'An Infallible Fact-Factory Going Full Blast': Austin Farrer, Marian Doctrine, and the Travails of Anglo-Catholicism," in *The Church and Mary: Papers Read at the 2001 Summer Meeting and the 2002 Winter Meeting of the Ecclesiastical History Society*, ed. R. N. Swanson (Suffolk, UK: Boydell, 2004), 358–67, quotations from 358 and 367.

practice at home and beyond the seas; and so bring everyone to worship the Lord as Saviour and King.'"[40] Thus, once again, he is addressing a predominantly Anglo-Catholic audience. In the second edition of the book, however, Farrer deliberately attempted to make the text more accessible to "a less specialized public."[41]

The first thing to note is the character of the book: a commentary on the Apostles' Creed. This alone speaks volumes. While Farrer wrote abstract metaphysical arguments, detailed exegetical studies, and lecture-style treatises, his first specifically doctrinal composition takes up the classic task of commenting on the creed. His first purely theological book begins with tradition, within the "circle of faith,"[42] with the ancient baptismal creed of Western Christendom hallowed by centuries of liturgical and catechetical use.

The second thing to note is the book's subtitle: *Suggestions for Turning the Creed into Prayer*. This, even more than the genre of the book, reveals Farrer's intentions. Rather than simply explaining what each article of the creed "means" in some detached objective external sense, Farrer wants his readers to engage doctrine on a subjective interior level. Thus, to say that the book is "doctrinal" theology is in one sense quite misleading, and to call it "ascetic" or "spiritual" theology might be more accurate. In many ways, *Lord I Believe* is thus a prime example of Charles Hefling's claim that Farrer's theology "bridges the gulf between ascetic and speculative or academic theory."[43]

---

40. See the entry on "Church Union" in *The Oxford Dictionary of the Christian Church*, ed. F. L. Cross and E. A. Livingstone, 3rd ed. (Oxford: Oxford University Press, 1997), 352, from which this quotation was taken. The entry goes on to say that the Church Union was "formed in 1934 under the presidency of the second Lord Halifax by the amalgamation of the English Church Union and the Anglo-Catholic Congress." The first version of *Lord I Believe* was published in 1955 by the Church Union Church Literature Association, as number 10 in their series of Beacon Books.

41. Austin Farrer, *Lord I Believe: Suggestions for Turning the Creed into Prayer*, 2nd ed., revised and enlarged (London: SPCK, 1958), 5. This edition of *Lord I Believe* was reprinted by Cowley Publications in 1989. The contents and pagination of the Cowley version are identical to the SPCK version, except that the brief foreword on page 5—from which this quote is taken—has been omitted from the Cowley reprint (hereafter cited as *LIB*).

42. See Timothy F. Sedgwick, *The Christian Moral Life: Practices of Piety* (Grand Rapids: Eerdmans, 1999), 148, for a current Anglican use and description of the common phrase "circle of faith."

43. Charles C. Hefling, "Farrer, Austin Marsden," in *A Dictionary of Christian Spirituality*,

The book begins with a ringing declaration: "Prayer and dogma are inseparable," then adds immediately, "They alone can explain each other. Either without the other is meaningless and dead."[44] In these three brief sentences (nineteen words total) Farrer outlines his entire theological project. He clarifies and intensifies it further by asserting, "No dogma deserves its place unless it is prayable, and no Christian deserves his dogmas who does not pray them."[45] Here we have a vision in which theology and spirituality intimately intertwine. It is important to stress, however, that Farrer's claim here is not necessarily equivalent to the *lex orandi lex credendi* principle—or, as Leonel Mitchell explains it, "more accurately *legem credendi lex statuat supplicandi*, which means that the way we pray determines the way we believe."[46] Farrer would of course agree with that, but he would also insist that it works the other way around as well: the way we believe determines the way we pray. Belief (dogma) and prayer are neither identical nor independent. They cannot be collapsed into each other, but neither does one (prayer) have precedence over the other (belief). Rather, they exist in a symbiotic relation in which each mutually and equally informs the other. "Prayer," says Farrer, "is the active use or exercise of faith; and the creed defines the contours of that world on which faith trains her eyes."[47]

Given the connection he makes between prayer and dogma, Farrer is thus confronted with the high mystical claim that true prayer moves by the *via negativa* beyond any specific beliefs about the divine. That is, "The sublime doctrines of our faith cannot affect our lives except through prayer, and yet, if we are to take the maxims of the saints at face value, must not we make it our whole endeavour to forget the doctrines when we pray?"[48] Farrer takes the maxims of the saints at face value, but his answer to this dilemma is simple: "The high

---

ed. Gordon S. Wakefield (London: SCM, 1983), 146. For further considerations along these lines, see Hefling, *Jacob's Ladder*; Platten, "Diaphanous Thought"; and Diogenes Allen, "Farrer's Spirituality," in Hein and Henderson, *Captured by the Crucified*, 47–65.

44. *LIB*, 9.

45. *LIB*, 10.

46. Leonel L. Mitchell, *Praying Shapes Believing: A Theological Commentary on the Book of Common Prayer* (Harrisburg, PA: Morehouse, 1985), 1. This book was published in a revised second edition updated by Ruth A. Myers (New York: Seabury, 2016).

47. *LIB*, 10.

48. *LIB*, 11.

instruction of the saints is not for beginners."[49] Only through many years of meditating on the doctrines of the creed, and so incorporating them into one's inner life, may one possibly rise to the height of the saints and simply rest in the interiorized knowledge of God. In contrast to the saints, Farrer says, most of us "are still plotting the circle of our faith, or have not even properly begun. If so, let us not leave off at the call of a false mysticism which mistakes the end for the beginning, moves inward from the tracings of thought and imagination before anything has either been imagined or thought, and dwells in a centre which is as yet the centre of nothing."[50]

Farrer upholds the importance of a set framework to direct our prayer, a framework derived from something beyond ourselves: "Though God be in me, yet without the creed to guide me I should know neither how to call upon God, nor on what God to call."[51] Farrer does not abandon mystic prayer, but he is suspicious of a natural, innate mysticism or religious experience that operates apart from revealed doctrine. In a striking image, he compares the creed to a name cut into the living wood of a tree—the name of God. We are like trees, Farrer says, and the life of God flows like sap through us. However, "the tree has grown so crooked and is so deformed and cankered in its parts, that I should be at a loss to distinguish the divine power among the misuses of the powers given."[52] So, he says, "I take refuge in that image of God which we have described as branded from outside upon the bark. Here is a token I can trust, for he branded it there himself; he branded it upon the stock of man when he stretched out his hands and feet and shed his precious blood. The pattern of the brand was traced on me by those who gave the creed to me; God will deepen it and burn it into me, as I submit my thoughts to him in meditation."[53] Here we see a mystical theology informed (restrained?) by the particularity of the incarnation and the tradition of Christian doctrine encapsulated in the Apostles' Creed.

Having laid the foundation of his method, Farrer then proceeds to offer meditations on the articles of the creed; I will focus on his discussion of the

---

49. *LIB*, 11.
50. *LIB*, 12.
51. *LIB*, 14.
52. *LIB*, 14.
53. *LIB*, 14.

Trinity. He writes, "The Trinity cannot be explored except from the centre. And what is the centre? It is the Love of God."[54] But by the love of God Farrer does not mean, first and foremost, God's love for us. "If God's love for us were all the love there was," Farrer says, "then divine love would never have been. It is only because divine love has a natural object that it overflows to embrace an adopted object. We are the children of God by adoption, the eternal Son of God is Son by nature."[55] Here we find the heart of Farrer's understanding of God, the church, and salvation.

As he said in his sermon on Anglicanism, the function of the church on earth is "to incorporate [humanity] into the life of Incarnate God." This function effects our salvation because of the relation between the Son ("Incarnate God") and the Father: by being incorporated into the Son we share that relation. Farrer tells us that the "love whereby our divine Father loves us is an actual part of the one love with which he loves his eternal Son, for God is love and his love is one piece."[56] The benefit of union with Christ is that the "heavenly sonship . . . overflows from him to us" such that "we have in part and by adoption [what] he has by nature and in fullness."[57]

A classic mystical image is the face of Moses shining with light after the theophany on Mount Sinai. Farrer picks this up and extends it to our understanding of the Trinity. He says:

> What a narrow glass is the up-turned face of Moses to reflect the glory of the Light that warms the world! Only the face of God reflects the face of God, there alone is converse in true equality, and eyes that answer eyes with a perfect intelligence. St. Paul, interpreting for us the shining of Moses' face, says that the God who inflows as light on Moses is the Holy Ghost. . . . But how little is there in us for the divine Spirit to inspire! The Holy Ghost is measured in us by the narrowness of our vessel, to the Eternal Son he gives himself without measure. The Son does not measure the Spirit by limiting him, he perfectly expresses him by perfectly receiving him. Holy Ghost means the divine life communicated or bestowed. Holy Ghost has no being

54. *LIB*, 17; *TSH*, 149.
55. *LIB*, 19; *TSH*, 151.
56. *LIB*, 20; *TSH*, 151.
57. *LIB*, 20; *TSH*, 151–52.

except in another; the first and proper being of the Holy Ghost is in the Eternal Son.[58]

Farrer's understanding of the Trinity is summed up by saying, "Here there are not three Gods; here is one Godhead which can be what it essentially is, a society of Love, only through distribution in three Persons."[59]

And so what? How does this relate to the quotidian life of ordinary Christians? Here again, only an extended sample of Farrer's text can do justice to the richness of his thought and language:

> The Trinity is both the meaning and the setting of that love which the Father has actually bestowed upon us. We need have nothing to do with the Trinity as a cool speculation about the necessary nature of the Godhead; it would be idiocy to place such confidence in theological reasonings as to evolve it by rational argument. The Trinity is revealed to Christians because they are taken into the Trinity, because the threefold love of God wraps them round, because it is in the Trinity they have their Christian being. Every time I worship or pray or make the least motion of the heart toward God, I stand with the divine Son in the face of the divine Father, the mantle of his sonship spread around me, and the love of the Father overflowing from him to me in the grace of the Holy Ghost.[60]

This chapter ends with a remarkable prayer that is apparently original to Farrer and yet reminiscent of ancient Celtic intercessions:

> God above me, Father from whom my being descends, on whom my existence hangs, to whom I turn up my face, to whom I stretch out my hands:
> God beside me, God in a man like me, Jesus Christ in the world with me, whose hand lays hold of me, presenting me with yourself, to God:

58. *LIB*, 21–22; *TSH*, 152–53.
59. *LIB*, 22–23; *TSH*, 153.
60. *LIB*, 23; *TSH*, 153–54.

God within me, soul of my soul, root of my will, inexhaustible fountain, Holy Ghost:
Threefold Love, one in yourself, unite your forces in me, come
together in the citadel of my conquered heart.

You have loved me with an everlasting love. Teach me to care.[61]

C. Saving Belief

Whereas "On Being an Anglican" and *Lord I Believe* are examples of Farrer
"preaching to the choir," *Saving Belief* is written for a distinctly different audience for a distinctly different purpose.[62] Rather than addressing Anglo-
Catholics or even fellow Christians, Farrer here presents a set of six lectures
to undergraduates at the University of Oxford in 1963, explaining to them
the essentials of Christian faith. Unlike in *Lord I Believe* (also concerned with
the essentials of Christian faith), Farrer does not begin with the assertion that
"prayer and dogma are inseparable." Instead, he begins with a leading question,
"Can reasonable minds still think theologically?"[63] This is followed by the first
lecture, titled "Faith and Evidence." Clearly, then, Farrer is here engaged in
the time-honored project of *apologetic* theology: he is seeking to articulate a
version of Christian doctrine that will appeal to and captivate the minds of his
young listeners.

The theme of the first lecture is the interaction of faith and evidence in
regard to belief in the existence of God, and here Farrer slips momentarily
into his persona of austere philosopher. Should those attending Farrer's lectures even believe in God at all? We should do so, Farrer claims, only if we
are convinced by the evidence. He says, "Faith implies genuine persuasion;

61. *LIB*, 23; *TSH*, 154.
62. As mentioned in note 7, *Saving Belief: A Discussion of Essentials* was first published
by Hodder & Stoughton in 1964 (hereafter cited as *SB*). An American edition published by
Morehouse-Barlow followed in 1965, and a new edition with different pagination was published in Susan Howatch's Library of Anglican Spirituality series by Mowbray and Morehouse
in 1994. I will cite from the original edition, along with *TSH* when possible.
63. *SB*, 5.

and persuasion is not genuine unless it comes from the thing which persuades us"—that is, from evidence.[64]

But evidence alone is not enough: one also needs faith, which Farrer defines as "a subjective condition favourable to the reception of the evidence."[65] More precisely, this is what Farrer calls "initial faith," in distinction from the full-blown "saving faith" of Christian commitment. Thus, Farrer rejects both *fideism* (which denies any place for reason and evidence in religious belief) and *rationalism* (a narrow epistemology that limits our knowledge of God to human cognition alone without any appeal to revelation or even religious experience). What is distinctive and appealing about Farrer's apologetic is the intimacy with which he intertwines faith and evidence: the attitude of faith is required to subjectively interpret the evidence that is objectively present and compelling.

To illustrate what he means by initial faith, Farrer asks us to consider a child brought up as an orphan who suddenly wonders if his mother is still alive. This unexpected possibility produces a reaction in the child; he "alternates between hope and resignation."[66] Farrer says, "The suggestion that there might be a mother is not an isolated factual hypothesis; it is a picture of the world, with an attitude built in; it is filial existence in place of orphan existence."[67] And the same situation obtains, Farrer insists, when human beings consider the existence of God.

In an acute and sensitive manner, Farrer argues that fideism and rationalism are both inadequate responses to the possibility of God's existence. To the cool rationalist, he says, "We are too much inclined to think of a disputed idea as a drawing over there on the blackboard, a bloodless diagram about which you and I are calmly deliberating whether to fill it in with the colours of real existence, or not. Such an account is always misleading, but not always equally misleading. It is supremely misleading in cases like those we are considering."[68] That is, the question of God's existence is not an abstract intellectual puzzle but is analogous to the orphan's personal interest in the possibility of a living parent: "For the child, to think of a possible mother is to experiment in having a mother; to try

64. *SB*, 14; *TSH*, 170.
65. *SB*, 22; *TSH*, 176.
66. *SB*, 17; *TSH*, 173.
67. *SB*, 17; *TSH*, 173.
68. *SB*, 17–18; *TSH*, 173.

filial existence. The experiment takes place in the realms of imagination, but it is real enough to the heart. And similarly to think of a possible God is to experiment in having God. The attitude of creature to Creator, of doomed mortal to immortal saviour, is built into the very idea. The heart goes out to God, even to a possible God; whether we should call the attitude 'faith' or something else, is a question of little consequence."[69]

Farrer acknowledges that this "experiment in having God," even if it does result in a longing of the heart for the reality of God, even if it does evoke the "deeply felt personal attitude" of openness to the existence of God, does not as yet *justify* such belief. We may be like orphans who try filial existence and like it—and yet are truly orphaned. As Farrer says bluntly, "The orphan's painful interest in the idea of a possible mother is no evidence that he has a mother."[70]

Thus, after laying the groundwork in "initial faith," the next step in Farrer's argument for religious belief is to apply this faith to the evidence. That is, after insisting on the necessity of faith to the rationalist, Farrer then turns to the fideist and insists on the necessity of evidence. So, Farrer asks, "How can an attitude of trustfulness, evidently appropriate to God if he exists, be appropriate to a decision if he exists or not? I can trust him if he exists, how can I trust him to exist?"[71] Farrer's response is that we cannot simply trust God to exist—we need evidence. But God does not disappoint us in providing such evidence: "A God could show himself through his creation, and it is the simple conviction of believers that God does."[72] But even here faith is required, for God "shows through the evidence more than hard-headed calculation could build out of the evidence; and the readiness to accept that 'more' will be faith, or the effect of faith."[73]

Farrer's final step, however, is to say that simply *believing* in God (or not) is not the actual issue. It is no good to conclude that God exists and then pretend that it makes no difference. What we must do, Farrer tells us, is to "honour our belief in God by giving God his due; and God's due is our life. Indeed we shall

69. *SB*, 18; *TSH*, 173.
70. *SB*, 19; *TSH*, 174.
71. *SB*, 15; *TSH*, 171.
72. *SB*, 22; *TSH*, 176.
73. *SB*, 22; *TSH*, 176.

not achieve full intellectual belief unless we live by it. Who can go on believing in a supreme Good which he makes no motion towards embracing?"[74]

The following five lectures take off from this point and explore what it means to believe in and embrace the Supreme Good: "Providence and Evil," "Creed and History," "Sin and Redemption," "Law and Spirit," and "Heaven and Hell." Once again, I will focus on Farrer's discussion of the Trinity. He begins by eschewing any pretense of philosophical reserve and assumes the mantle of a Christian theologian: "I will take it as agreed that we are talking about the revelation of Christ."[75] Such a stance, however, does not mean abandoning what we believe on the basis of reason, and what we believe on the basis of reason is that Christian theology depends on what Farrer calls "cosmic personalism." That is, on "the reasonableness, and indeed the necessity, of accepting our personal being, our mind or will, as the clue to the supreme cause of the world."[76] To this intuition, Farrer adds "the grand rule of theology": "nothing can be denied of God, which we see to be the highest and best in creaturely existence."[77]

These pieces give Farrer what he needs to help his hearers begin to grasp the Trinity. "Mind," he says, "is a social reality."[78] He acknowledges that "personal reality exists in individual centres, or foci, alone," but he denies that "we know of such a thing as a mind in *isolation*."[79] Farrer argues that we develop as individual persons and thinkers only through conversation with other persons and thinkers, and that such external conversation necessarily precedes the interior dialogue with ourselves that we call thought. He concludes that "mentality, as we know it, is *plurifocal*."[80]

Given the "grand rule of theology," Farrer is able to ask, "Are we then to say that the mind of Godhead is plurifocal too?" He answers with a resounding yes. "How can we deny mutual relation in the Godhead?" he asks. "God is love; not

74. *SB*, 31–32; *TSH*, 183.

75. *SB*, 61.

76. *SB*, 63.

77. *SB*, 65. This "grand rule of theology" bears some resemblance to Anselm's axiom that God is "that than which nothing greater can be conceived." Farrer is usually classed as a type of Thomist, but his similarities to Anselm bear further consideration.

78. *SB*, 63.

79. *SB*, 64 and 63, respectively; emphasis added to the quotation from 63.

80. *SB*, 65.

only loving to ants like us, but related by relations of love on his own level."[81]
He goes on to say:

> The doctrine of the Trinity does not pretend to make God intelligible. It lays
> down certain requirements. It says that if God is to be God, the Godhead
> must be at once more perfectly one than any one of us, and allow also for a
> mutual love more outgoing than is found in any two of us. We do not know
> how these seemingly opposed requirements are fulfilled and reconciled in
> the Godhead; we only know that they must be. If we wish, we may define
> the divine level of being as that level, above all our conceiving, where unity
> of life and discourse of mutual love most perfectly combine.[82]

Farrer allows that it is "abstractly conceivable" that we might have reasoned
our way to these bare assertions about the divine nature—that it must somehow combine unity and diversity—but insists that we did not. "We would
not have known the Trinity," Farrer says, "if one of the Divine Persons had not
become present with us in Jesus Christ."[83] Christ revealed the Trinity by living
the divine life among us; through his life, teaching, death, and resurrection. In
particular, he did this by showing us in visible form the relation between the
Son and the Father.

Farrer discusses the Holy Spirit later on, toward the end of the book, and
here he lays peculiar stress on the Father-Son relation in the life of the Trinity.
"The revealed parable of the Godhead is a story about two characters, Father
and Son."[84] "The Holy Ghost is God," Farrer says, "yet the Trinity is not (in human terms) a society of three, but a society of two, inspiring and inspired."[85] This
seems to be a fairly radical statement of the so-called Augustinian theory of the
Trinity, which (actually endorsed by Augustine or not) sees the Holy Spirit less
as a third Person in its own right, and more as the relation of love between the
first and second Persons. It also seems at odds with Farrer's view of the Trinity
articulated a decade earlier in *Lord I Believe*. But here Farrer claims, "The Spirit

81. *SB*, 65.
82. *SB*, 66.
83. *SB*, 63.
84. *SB*, 128.
85. *SB*, 129.

is the divine life, is God, God the self-bestowing or indwelling, God finding scope of action in the being or action of another; the first other in whom he finds such scope being the eternal Son, himself also God."[86] The "inspiration" of the Son by the Father then finds an echo in the Spirit's inspiration of individual Christians and the church. This "opens up the whole subject of the Church, and of the sacraments," Farrer says, "into which I do not propose to enter"—and I will follow his example.[87]

III. Analysis

Having considered three texts by Austin Farrer, we are now in a position to begin to draw some conclusions. The first thing to notice is how different Farrer can sound given a different audience. The sermon "On Being an Anglican" is written in a simple yet graceful homiletical style. Farrer comes across as a straightforward, clear-thinking man of conviction. *Lord I Believe*, however, is a densely compact web of words, poetic in its cadences and repetitions, mystical in its content. Farrer comes across more as a monastic retreat-leader (he was in fact a husband and father) drawing upon a lifetime of contemplative devotion. And, finally, *Saving Belief* is written in clear but ordinary prose, peppered with colloquial asides and embellished with witty (often self-effacing) comments. Here is Farrer as university lecturer and academic theologian.

So much for the character of the texts—what of their content? As stated above, Farrer's defense of the *via media* in "On Being an Anglican" is standard,

---

86. *SB*, 129. For some later engagements with Farrer's almost binitarian formulation of the Trinity here, see Brian Hebblethwaite, "The Doctrine of the Trinity," in his *The Philosophical Theology of Austin Farrer* (Leuven: Peeters, 2007), 107–18, and Rowan Williams, "'A Society of Two'? Austin Farrer on the Trinity," in Harries and Platten, *Austin Farrer for Today*, 141–53. For a different approach that puts Farrer into conversation with the work of Sarah Coakley, see Jeffrey Vogel, "A Little While in the Son of God: Austin Farrer on the Trinitarian Nature of Prayer," *Scottish Journal of Theology* 64 (2011): 410–24.

87. *SB*, 131. For two somewhat different interpretations of Farrer's Christology, see Brian Hebblethwaite, "The Doctrine of the Incarnation in the Thought of Austin Farrer," in his *The Incarnation: Collected Essays in Christology* (Cambridge: Cambridge University Press, 1987), 112–25, and M. P. Wilson, "Austin Farrer and the Paradox of Christology," *Scottish Journal of Theology* 35 (1982): 145–63.

and *Lord I Believe* and *Saving Belief* both exemplify classic strains of Anglican thought: the ascetic and the apologetic. While each has a different slant—the church (ecclesiology), the Apostles' Creed (doctrine), the reasonableness of faith (prolegomena)—Farrer points us to salvation in all three texts. And salvation in all three texts is articulated according to a common vision.

In "On Being an Anglican," Farrer says that the function of the church is "to incorporate [humanity] into the life of Incarnate God, and the Church is itself the means and the form of such an incorporation."[88] In *Lord I Believe*, Farrer tells us what such incorporation into Christ means: the "heavenly sonship . . . overflows from [Christ] to us," so that we stand "with the divine Son in the face of the divine Father, the mantle of his sonship spread around [us], and the love of the Father overflowing from him to [us] in the grace of the Holy Ghost."[89] And in *Saving Belief* this Trinitarian-ecclesial soteriology comes full circle with the statement that the Holy Ghost is the one who creates both the church and the sacraments that make our incorporation into Christ possible in the first place. It is thus "God above [us]," "God beside [us]," and "God within [us]" who accomplishes our salvation.

In presenting his Reformed Catholic understanding of salvation, Farrer tells us that sin is both personal and ontological. We need more than simple forgiveness; we need to participate in the life of God. According to the classic Thomistic pattern, grace perfects nature instead of destroying it, and revelation completes reason instead of contradicting it. Creation finds its consummation as it is drawn ever more fully into the life of the Trinity.[90]

Farrer's theological vision is both impressive and beautiful. It combines classic doctrine with keen intelligence and deep devotion. A fair question to ask, however, is how well Farrer's thought meets the needs of today, and in particular the current debates within the Anglican Communion regarding doctrine, identity, and ethics. He himself was well aware that his theology was not addressed to current events. In the preface to *Saving Belief*, published in 1964, he writes, "There is nothing in these pages about nuclear bombs, artificial

88. *EOM*, 49; *TSH*, 144.
89. *LIB*, 23; *TSH*, 153–54.
90. In this paper I have focused on the Trinitarian aspects of Farrer's soteriology, but there is a strong Christological element as well. For further Christological considerations with some attention to atonement, see the essays by Hebblethwaite and Wilson cited in note 87.

insemination, free love, world government, Church reunion, or the restyling of public worship. Those who seek after news may save their pains."[91] Farrer's task was to clarify and commend the core of Christian belief rather than radically reinterpret it in a new context.

But Leslie Houlden wonders if Farrer's thought is "too elevated to suit a mood of Christian realism," and notes that there is little in Farrer "to attract the Christian fired with zeal for liberationism and social justice."[92] Houlden suggests, however, that Farrer's thought can be easily turned into "applied theology," and at least one of his commentators has attempted to do just that, although in the area of liberation theology rather than Anglican identity. In a compelling essay, Jeffrey Eaton argues that—while Farrer himself never used it in this direction—something like his understanding of divine action in the world must be true if God really *does* act to liberate the oppressed. Eaton writes: "Sharing as I do with liberation theologians the belief that liberation is the vocation of one who wishes to become *co-operator Dei*, I shall attempt to show that far from requiring a retreat from the God of theism, the liberation theologies actually depend upon the intelligibility of God's agency for their theological integrity."[93] Such a perspective adds needed balance to the view of, for example, Carter Heyward and Margaret C. Huff, whose God (it seems) cannot act or take initiative *apart* from human participation. But Farrer's understanding of "double agency" avoids such reductions by simultaneously maintaining the integrity of *both* agents, human and divine, in the liberating work. Eaton concludes: "The liberation theologies teach us the meaning and implications of our dependence on one another in the struggle against human oppression; Farrer's work enables us to see that it is God's creative activity with which we have to do when we are engaged in the cause of liberating love."[94] In this way, Farrer *via* Eaton has contributed to the better understanding and support of liberation theology.

91. *SB*, 6.

92. Houlden, *Austin Farrer*, ix.

93. Jeffrey C. Eaton, "Divine Action and Human Liberation," in Hebblethwaite and Henderson, *Divine Action*, 214.

94. Eaton, "Divine Action and Human Liberation," 229. For Heyward and Huff, see their essay, "Foundations for Anglican Ecclesiology," in *No Easy Peace: Liberating Anglicanism*, ed. Carter Heyward and Sue Phillips (Lanham, MD: University Press of America, 1992), 3–21.

IV. Conclusion

I began this paper with the claim that Farrer was neglected in contemporary Anglican thought, and that a closer attention to his work would benefit both the project of Anglican theology and current discussions of Anglican identity. I will conclude, therefore, with some brief comments on these issues.

Throughout the paper I have emphasized the Anglican character of Farrer's thought: his context as a priest in the Church of England; his commitment to orthodox creedal Christianity; his practice of Anglo-Catholic spirituality; and his careful attention to "scripture, tradition, and reason." But defining Farrer as an Anglican for those reasons is problematic if we cannot agree on what it means to be "Anglican." Paul Avis claims that Anglicans have typically defined themselves in one of two ways: "those that focus on the material ingredients of the Anglican synthesis . . . and those that claim a distinctive method, ethos, or praxis for the Anglican way."[95]

A prominent defender of the "material ingredients" approach is Stephen Sykes, most notably in *The Integrity of Anglicanism*.[96] Here Sykes argues that (appearances to the contrary notwithstanding) Anglican theology *does* have definite doctrinal content and specific doctrinal commitments. Without denying this entirely, Avis himself inclines toward the second approach and suggests that "the distinctive identity of Anglicanism is located in the sphere of theological method and the understanding of authority that informs it, rather than in terms of liturgy, spirituality or polity."[97]

But do we really need to choose between these two options? Farrer, I would argue, fits under *both* definitions of Anglicanism—the "material ingredients" as well as the "distinctive method." In so doing he provides a salutary reminder that even the "traditional" package of Anglicanism has much to offer today. We could do much worse than to have a few dozen prominent and active Farrer types preaching, teaching, writing, and leading throughout the Anglican Communion. Despite the riches of our tradition, we seem to have lost confidence in

95. Paul Avis, "What Is 'Anglicanism'?" in Sykes, Booty, and Knight, *The Study of Anglicanism*, 464.

96. Stephen Sykes, *The Integrity of Anglicanism* (London: Mowbray, 1978).

97. Avis, "What Is 'Anglicanism'?," 475.

the attractiveness and coherence and imaginative appeal of such an approach to Anglicanism.

But if Avis is right and the second definition is key, then Farrer can function as a model for contemporary Anglican theologians only to the extent that he exemplifies a distinctively Anglican theological method. Again, I would argue that he does. It has been well remarked that there is nothing distinctively "Anglican" about Scripture, tradition, and reason: they are the common property of all Christians. And yet, Farrer's creative fusion of Trinitarian, incarnational, sacramental, scriptural, rational, poetic, and mystical themes in the matrix of Christian liturgy and personal spirituality—a fusion that, without being artificial or forced, can be simultaneously Catholic *and* Reformed—seems a paradigm of Anglican theological method. Such elements are the common property of all Christians, but the way Farrer puts them together is distinctively Anglican. Or, put differently, if one mark of genius is to create new patterns, then one may say that Farrer's accomplishment both exemplifies and further develops a distinctively Anglican theological method.[98]

98. Or, at least, a characteristically Anglican theological method. In comments on an earlier draft of this paper, Stephen Sykes wrote that, in relation to my contrast between his view and Paul Avis's, "One should carefully distinguish between what is characteristic and what is distinctive about Anglicanism," and then references his chapter, "The Anglican Character," in *Celebrating the Anglican Way*, ed. Ian Bunting (London: Hodder & Stoughton, 1996), 21–32. Sykes's written comments continued: "What I emphatically rebut is that there is nothing distinctive. But what is characteristic of Anglicanism can easily be shared with other churches." This parallels a statement from his cited chapter, in which he says, "No Anglican should want or need to claim absolute distinctiveness for the various features of the Anglican way" (23). This distinction between what is characteristic and what is distinctive may provide more breathing room in fraught discussions of Anglican identity. But, *pace* Avis, surely a "distinctive method" will result in distinctive "material ingredients"? Rather than being opposed categories, the one should lead naturally to the other. So it is *because* Anglican theology proceeds according to a distinctive (or characteristic) method that it *results* in its distinctive (or characteristic) ingredients. For it would be extremely odd if a distinctive (or characteristic) methodology did not lead to a distinctive (or characteristic) set of material convictions. The notorious difficulty that remains, however, is pinning down what, exactly, are the material convictions of Anglicanism. For what Avis identifies as the classic set of such convictions—including, for example, the basic Protestantism of the Church of England—may well have been denied by a Prayer Book Catholic like Farrer. Avis could thus

Timothy Sedgwick tells us that "following Hooker the three greatest apologists in Anglicanism are arguably Joseph Butler, Frederick Denison Maurice, and William Temple."[99] While I will not venture to name the *fourth* after Hooker, I would only add that, if a fifth were named, it should be Austin Farrer.[100]

---

argue that Farrer therefore does not fit under the second category, after all. See Avis, "What Is 'Anglicanism'?," 464–65.

99. Sedgwick, *The Christian Moral Life*, 38.

100. I was first introduced to the work of Austin Farrer by Diogenes Allen in his Farrer seminar at Princeton Theological Seminary in the spring of 1994. This particular essay began life in Timothy Sedgwick's seminar on Anglican thought at Virginia Theological Seminary in the autumn of 1999. I am grateful to the late Diogenes Allen, Paul Avis, David Brown, George Carey, the late Joseph Cassidy, Stanley Hauerwas, Edward Henderson, the late Ann Loades, David Marshall, Paul Murray, Timothy Sedgwick, the late Stephen Sykes, and an anonymous reader for *Journal of Anglican Studies* for comments, criticism, and encouragement on this paper. As noted in the introduction of this volume, I also commend Scott MacDougall, *The Shape of Anglican Theology: Faith Seeking Wisdom* (Leiden: Brill, 2022), esp. 20 and 82, for a helpful contribution to the debate about Anglican identity summarized above.

Austin Farrer's Baptism in the Church of England: Correspondence and Documentation

Widely recognized as—in the words of Rowan Williams—"possibly the greatest Anglican mind of the twentieth century," Austin Marsden Farrer belongs to the long list of important Anglican divines who began their lives in another ecclesial tradition.[1] This list includes John Donne (Roman Catholic), Joseph Butler (English Presbyterian), F. D. Maurice (Unitarian), A. M. Ramsey (Congregationalist), John Macquarrie (Church of Scotland), Hans Frei (originally German Lutheran, then American Baptist), and Williams himself (Welsh Presbyterian). Achieving equal distinction as a philosopher, biblical scholar, theologian, and preacher, Farrer was a leading member of the Anglo-Catholic wing of the Church of England in the mid-twentieth century. He died as the seventh warden of Keble College, Oxford, on December 29, 1968, at the age of sixty-four.[2]

However, he was born on October 1, 1904, as the second child and only son of Augustine J. D. Farrer (1872–1954), an English Baptist minister who variously taught church history, the history of religion, Hebrew, and New Testament at Regent's Park College (a distinguished Baptist institution), first in its original location in London and then later when it moved to Oxford. Augustine and

---

1. Rowan Williams, "Debate on *The Gift of Authority*—Archbishop of Canterbury's Remarks," February 13, 2004, https://tinyurl.com/bdf8kzka.

2. For his obituary notice for the British Academy, written by Eric Mascall, see *Proceedings of the British Academy* 54, 1968 (London, 1970), 435–42. For an analysis of the Anglican character of Farrer's thought, see Robert MacSwain, "Above, Beside, Within: The Anglican Theology of Austin Farrer," *Journal of Anglican Studies* 4 (2006): 33–57, now reprinted as chapter 2 in this volume.

Originally published in *Anglican and Episcopal History* 81, no. 3 (September 2012): 241–76.

Evangeline Farrer had three children, including the two girls, Joyce (1903) and Eleanor (1907).[3] They were a serious and devout Nonconformist family, and yet Augustine was "neither an emotional evangelical nor a biblical fundamentalist. He moved in circles which had early come to terms with biblical criticism."[4] Consequently, it was difficult for the Farrers to find a home in the rather more conservative Baptist community of London at that time. Young Austin's experience of several congregational schisms and awareness of his father's intellectual isolation from his coreligionists made him reluctant to be baptized into this tradition, and eventually led to his baptism in the Church of England instead.

Augustine was educated at the nonsectarian City of London School and then, as a Nonconformist, at University College London and Regent's Park, finishing his theological studies in 1898. However, the Farrers ambitiously and deliberately sent their brilliant son to more elite institutions, which were, of course, given English society, historically Anglican foundations.[5] From 1917 to 1923 Austin was a day pupil at St. Paul's School in London, and in 1923 he went up to Balliol College, Oxford, as a classical scholar. In his first year at Oxford he found the pull of Anglicanism inexorable and was both baptized and confirmed in May 1924, at the age of nineteen. Although he and his parents had long anticipated a career in law (his middle name, Marsden, was after John Marsden, a Blackburn solicitor, family friend, and benefactor), this shift in religious allegiance gradually led to a sense of call to ordained ministry—but of course, now in the Church of England rather than in the Baptist tradition. Thus, after finishing his undergraduate "Greats" course, a further year of theological study at Balliol, and formation at Cuddesdon Theological College (just outside

3. For these details, see Philip Curtis, *A Hawk among Sparrows: A Biography of Austin Farrer* (London: SPCK, 1985), 1–4. Curtis says that Farrer was born on October 11, and that his father's name was "Augustus," but these must be typographical errors. Farrer's birth certificate, a copy of which may be found in Box 10 of the Farrer papers in the Bodleian, gives the date and name as provided above. See also the revised entry by I. M. Crombie, "Farrer, Austin Marsden (1904–1968)," in *The Oxford Dictionary of National Biography*, ed. Brian Harrison, vol. 19 (Oxford: Oxford University Press, 2004), 121–23, which agrees with the birth certificate rather than Curtis on both counts (subsequent references to this reference work will be abbreviated *ODNB*, followed by volume and page numbers).

4. Curtis, *A Hawk among Sparrows*, 3.

5. The letters below from both Augustine and Evangeline admit that in allowing and even encouraging Austin to study at these institutions they were making a calculated risk in regard to his ultimate religious affiliation.

Oxford), Austin went to the Diocese of Wakefield in Yorkshire, where he was ordained deacon in 1928 and priest in 1929.[6]

The only biography of Farrer is *A Hawk among Sparrows* by the late Philip Curtis.[7] While it provides an invaluable portrait by one who knew him personally (Curtis was a student of Farrer's in the late 1930s) and contains much currently unattainable and irreplaceable information from other firsthand accounts, it also suffers from several serious deficits. Readers familiar with the biography may be especially puzzled by what Curtis describes as the "crucial months" leading up to Farrer's baptism (January–May 1924) and the event of the baptism itself.[8]

As for the months leading up to the baptism, Curtis uncharacteristically relies entirely on letters from Farrer's parents to their son in order to reconstruct what Austin was thinking at this time: he clearly did not have Austin's actual letters on this topic to hand. Curtis writes, "Two letters from his mother and father, both written on the same day in January [the 26th, 1924], appear to come in reply to an announcement from Austin that he was moving in the direction of Anglicanism and confirmation."[9] Curtis also prefaces a citation from Augustine's letter by stating, "The integrity which was characteristic of the family comes out in his father's answers to points which Austin must have raised," and continues on the next page by observing that Augustine's letter "goes on, taking up Austin point by point."[10]

As for the baptism itself, it is completely omitted. Curtis writes that after this exchange between his parents and some further correspondence from Austin expressing concern that his joining the Church of England might distress his sisters, "we have no further letters until May 1924 when the decision has been taken and [Austin] writes to describe his confirmation."[11] This occurred

6. For this period see Curtis, *A Hawk among Sparrows*, 16–57.

7. Cited in note 3 above. According to *Crockford's Clerical Directory*, Curtis was born in 1917 and died in 1994. He was chaplain of Giggleswick School in North Yorkshire from 1955 to his retirement in 1982.

8. Curtis, *A Hawk among Sparrows*, 20–24. Among the "several serious deficits," consider that this volume gets Farrer's birth date and his father's name wrong!

9. Curtis, *A Hawk among Sparrows*, 21. These are Letters B and C below, and the letter from Austin to which they both respond is Letter A.

10. Curtis, *A Hawk among Sparrows*, 22 and 23.

11. Curtis, *A Hawk among Sparrows*, 23–24. Curtis's note on what I designate below as

in the Latin Chapel of Christ Church Cathedral at the hands of H. M. Burge (1862–1925, bishop of Oxford from 1919).[12] Curtis continues that we "do not know who prepared Austin for confirmation, but it may well have been the Chaplain of Balliol, the Reverend Henry Hensman Gibbon, who began his Balliol career in 1902."[13] But of the baptism itself, he knows and says nothing. It is thus natural to assume that Farrer was baptized and confirmed on the same day at the same place—a conclusion drawn, for example, by J. Barry Vaughn.[14] As it turns out, this is a mistake. However, while Vaughn's conclusion is wrong, Curtis's guess about Gibbon is correct, and ironically it was Gibbon himself who was partly responsible for this confusion about Farrer's baptism, as I will demonstrate in due course.

Seeking clarity on the date and location of Farrer's baptism, I turned first to the Farrer Papers in the Bodleian Libraries, University of Oxford, and then later (at the suggestion of a wise and experienced archivist) to the documents related to Farrer's subsequent ordination in the Diocese of Wakefield, now held in the West Yorkshire Archive Service. The Farrer Papers in the Bodleian consist of two sets of foliated correspondence (MS Eng. Lett. c. 270 and c. 272) and twelve boxes of unfoliated material. The vast majority of the correspondence cited by Curtis is in the two foliated sets. However, for some reason the three letters from Farrer's parents related to Austin's baptism (Letters B, C, and E below) were not included in MS Eng. Lett c. 270 along with the other correspondence from that period, but are found instead in Box 1. Greatly to my surprise, I also found the "missing" letters from Austin himself (to which Letters B, C, and E reply) in Box 10. They are designated as Letters A, D, and F below.

While these letters provide the long-lost primary-source material related to Farrer's momentous decision to join Church of England, they do not answer the question about the location and date of his actual baptism. For that we turn to the material from the Diocese of Wakefield held in the West Yorkshire Archive Service, and there we find that another surprise awaits us: Gibbon, Farrer's col-

---

"Letter E" states that it was written on January 26, but this is an error, conflating the date of E with that of both B and C.

12. For Burge's life and career, see Matthew Grimley, "Burge, Hubert Murray (1862–1925)," in *ODNB*, 3:254–56.

13. Curtis, *A Hawk among Sparrows*, 24.

14. See J. Barry Vaughn, "Resurrection and Grace: The Sermons of Austin Farrer," *Preaching* 9 (1994): 61–63. Vaughn draws on Curtis's biography throughout this article.

lege chaplain, forgot to record the baptism! However, although this omission briefly complicated Farrer's ordination process, a creative solution was found, and all ended well. As it turned out, Farrer was baptized on May 14, 1924, and not in Christ Church but in the parish church of St. Peter-le-Bailey, which is now the Chapel of St. Peter's College, University of Oxford.

Section 1 below provides, for the first time, transcripts of Austin's missing letters as well as more fulsome and accurate transcripts of his parents' responses than those provided by Curtis.[15] More briefly, section 2 provides transcripts of the material from the Diocese of Wakefield, which explains Gibbon's gaffe and offers a statutory declaration by a witness to Farrer's baptism instead of a certificate based on an entry in the parish register. Farrer's stature as "possibly the greatest Anglican mind of the twentieth century" makes this unpublished material of considerable interest for both Anglicans and Baptists and for all those interested in charting the movement of religious conversion and allegiance in the mind of such a brilliant thinker. It is also a moving record of middle-class religious family life in 1920s England, as a father, mother, and son all negotiate an unexpected and unwelcome development that threatened the family's cohesion: namely, the beloved son's decision to leave the parents' religious tradition. Obviously much has changed for both Anglicans and Baptists (in England and around the world) in the intervening ten decades, and the rather naïve views of the nineteen-year-old Balliol undergraduate were not identical to the more mature understanding of the warden of Keble College. However, my primary interest here is in presenting this material to a wider audience, and so I shall keep commentary and analysis to a minimum.

I. Letters between Austin Farrer and His Parents

From the Farrer Papers in the Bodleian Libraries, University of Oxford, Boxes 1 and 10. Because these papers were still uncatalogued and thus unfoliated, I have designated each of the six letters transcribed here as Letters A–F, but that is only

---

15. In addition to the matters mentioned in note 8, another serious deficit of *A Hawk among Sparrows* is that comparison of the original correspondence with Curtis's citations reveals numerous inaccuracies. In addition to a new biography, a critical edition of Farrer's correspondence is greatly to be desired.

for the purpose of this article and is not part of the Bodleian reference system. I also indicate in which box each letter may be found. As much as possible I follow the original punctuation and spelling of these handwritten letters, and use underlining rather than italics for emphasis. In very rare instances some words are illegible, and there I follow my best judgment in determining the sense. I also occasionally add obviously missing words or punctuation within brackets. One purely personal and extraneous paragraph from Letter C is omitted and marked with a bold ellipsis.

Letter A, Box 10: from Austin Farrer, to his father, Augustine Farrer

Balliol College,
Oxford
January 15th [1924][16]

Dear Father

If this epistle reaches you at breakfast or any other such odd time, put it away as you do Mr. Mann's, and read it at your leisure. For it is going to be long and serious and tedious, and, I am afraid, will cost you some thought to make out.

To proceed then, or rather to begin: you remember our agreeing, last October, on the desirability of my being baptised? We have not mentioned it again this vacation. You, I expect, were waiting to see if I should speak for myself; and I promise you that I have not forgotten the matter. My desire to make this profession has increased, not deminished [sic], since our first talking of it, and to it make it in any case I am resolved. But there is one thing about which I hesitate a good deal, and have done so for some time. I waited, because I thought I could overcome my difficulty, and that, that being so, it was better nothing should be said about it. But as it is I am more perplexed than ever, and want your advice.

It is this. I told you then, as well as I can remember, that I felt no difficulty about <u>what</u> church I should join. I am afraid I imposed upon

16. Farrer is now nineteen and is in the second (Hilary) term of his first year at Oxford; note how quickly this issue arose once he left home for university studies and college life.

you, but that is scarcely to be wondered at, since I was making desperate efforts to impose upon myself; I did not want to admit even to myself that I had any doubts. I thought I had stifled them, but they have quite broken loose, and will be heard. You must know that the only other church I could think of is The Church of England.

And now I don't know how to go on. I must some how give you my reasons and thoughts about it, but they form such a formidable mass, that I don't know how to set them down. I think it will be best if I give my reasons for change first, and those against it after.

1. I like and prefer the church service. It is probably my own weakness that is to blame, but anyhow I find it much easier to concentrate my mind on prayers clearly and exactly expressed, each collect containing one idea, to which I assent one by one in the Amen. And what is more, these prayers seem much more personal, much more the act of the congregation together, than our extempore prayers, where the congregation does not pray <u>with</u> the minister, but follows <u>after</u> him; for they do not know what is coming. The Anglican priest is just the voice of his congregation. And as for the set forms—they do not trouble me; most petitions a congregation wants to make are the same every week; indeed, our own ministers repeat themselves nearly as much as the prayer-book, only not so well; and the charge, that Anglicans do not use special prayers in special times of need, is by my experience at least simply untrue.

2. I am not a fervent political democrat, and have no desire whatsoever to insist on my right to have a share in church government. Episcopacy, although it leads to some gross corruptions, seems a better working system. It is a pity the Prime Minister appoints bishops, and that patrons present to livings; but these things may yet be mended, and a churchman does not necessarily acquiesce in them any more than an Englishman necessarily acquiesces in the opium-trade with China. You know that what I have seen of Congregational government cannot increase my respect for it. To submit to ecclesiastical superiors seems to me just another act of Christian self-denial, as Thomas à Kempis says.

3. Now I come to what is hardest for me to speak about, because from the nature of my position I cannot do so with experience; I mean, the Eucharist. You say that it is a commemoration—that if it conveys any special blessing, it does so by <u>preaching</u> more vividly than anything else

can to the sacrifice of our Lord. It seems to me that this is to make it no sacrament at all. I look at the matter from the point of view of comparative religion. Other faiths have their sacraments: the Christian sacrament should be the perfect sacrament. The idea of a sacrament seems to be that by the aid of an outward symbol you visualise and realise and concentrate on one act, your faith in the grace imparted to you by the god you worship, and thus through faith obtain that grace. Imperfectly this is shewn in heathen sacrifices and more especially the mystery-feasts, and it should be perfected in Christianity. And this seems to me the plain meaning of scripture. 'This is my body': we take the outward thing, believing that our Lord does with it give us the inward. The blessing comes by the faith of the participant, not by a priestly miracle: but if it is necessary to the faith of a simple man that he should believe also in the priestly miracle, I say it is better that he believe in it. We know that millions of Christians have found grace and sustenance in this thing in the past: why should we deny it to ourselves? I am convinced that St. Paul held at least as full a doctrine as I am here setting forth; he calls it a mystery, and the mere commemoration-doctrine is no mystery at all—neither is trans-substantiation: both, I think, must be wrong. 'This is My Body': that is, I take it, Our Lord says to us 'this means for you My Body' and I myself am ready and desirous to receive it as such. Do not think that anyone has been putting this into my head; at least, I honestly believe that I have not heard these arguments from anyone else, but they seemed to me natural, from the very important place this Institution holds in the synoptic Gospels, and the mystic references to it in St. John, together with the words of St. Paul. And it seems to me that I can receive it in this spirit better in the Church of England than in our own.

Now I come to the reasons against.

1. My desire for change may only be the natural and foolish preference for what one does not know over that which one does; I may live to repent it. After all, the sect a man belongs to matters little, and it is a foolish thing to occupy in nice balancing of the claims of this sect and that faculties that might be turned to the service of God and one's own salvation which comes through no sect. (But is it not a sin to withstand the Truth?)

2. There are some things in the Apostles' Creed that one baptised into

the Church of England at an age to speak for himself must profess, about which I simply hold no belief at all. I mean these two: He descended into Hell, and the Resurrection of the Body. If the first simply means that Our Lord was dead until he rose, I believe it: if it means anything more specific, I can neither affirm nor deny. If the second means that the atoms composing this mortal frame shall be raised and reassembled, I think it probably absurd; if it means what St. Paul apparently believed, that the mortal body shall have a spiritual successor, I think it most probable but no more. (Perhaps I should say here, since I left it out in its proper place, that I cannot but feel almost a preference for infant-baptisms; scripture gives us no guidance at all, since it only tells of the baptism of converted heathens. A great deal of the machinery of it in the Church of England, the sponsors and so on, is not particularly valuable; but I cannot bring myself to condemn the thing itself.)

3. Becoming a member of the Church of England may imply a belief that a special χάρισμα[17] of the Holy Ghost is vested in Bishops, that they received it from the Apostles in the laying on of hands, and that by the same means they can give it to others, and to priests in a peculiar measure. Such a belief I will not subscribe to.[18] I have no objection to the ordering of priests or the confirmation of myself for that matter, by the laying on of Bishop's hands, if such action is merely a symbol, an outward act upon which the faith of the recipient may gather itself. But I will not and cannot subscribe to any electric current sort of doctrine, or any that gives a greater measure of the Spirit to any peculiar class of men.

4. The last reason against is the personal one. It is an immeasurably great evil to worship apart from one's family. It is not that I will not always worship with you all at least once a week when I am at home—this is a promise, you may hold me to it: I mean that if I <u>do</u> join the Church of England I will still go to church on Sunday mornings wherever you go: God forbid that I should ever be a bigot, or think uncharitably of a church in which you and Mother (for I never hope to find in any church

17. Greek: *charisma* (grace, favor, gift).
18. Here, in the margin of the page, a later reader has added an arrow pointing to this sentence with an exclamation mark before it ("! →"), no doubt expressing surprise at the young Farrer's statement, for being as yet insufficiently sacramental and Anglo-Catholic.

a better Christian than she) have lived and been brought up. If I go, I shall not go as some do, with a jaunty air, boasting to all of their liberation; I shall go grieving and unwillingly, and half ashamed, and praying that I may not be held guilty for the very real distress that I know you and Mother must feel, though you be never so liberal and open-minded, and though you say nothing of it. I suppose—it is a cruel text—that the will of God is to be set above the dearest ties of human affection, and I suppose it is His will that we follow the truth as best we know it; but it is intolerable to me to think that if I do this thing I shall be doing you a wrong, and that men may say that you who train Baptist ministers, your son left the denomination. Alas! You have done enough, all that you could to commend your own faith to me, both by example and instruction. Forgive me for what I meditate doing. And yet I speak as though my mind were made up, when it is not. I have put my thoughts before you as clearly as I can—that I desire to use the practices of the Church of England, but only if I can do so without perjury. I ask you for your advice what I should do. I do not think you can now convince me of the error of my opinions; but these last being what they are, try to imagine my state of mind, and advise me as best you can, supposing or assuming them to be true. Should I ask some Anglican divine what is entailed in the matter of belief by joining the Church? And, if so, who would be both honest, moderate and learned for the purpose? Or what shall I do? Do you consider that belief is so much more important than practise that I should make no change: or that a fuller meaning may be understood in the Sacrament even as we have it administered? Perhaps there could be no harm in consulting a churchman, provided one could be sure he were perfectly unbiased by the desire to make a convert—if such a man could be found; and if you think his opinion biased, I can always reject it. But write and tell me just what you think. You are my first advisor, anyhow.

I had rather, for the present, that no one but you and Mother should have any suspicion of this matter for the present. If you think it better to spare her the trouble of it just now, do so; just as you think proper. Do not think me so impatient as to be in a hurry for your reply. Consider as long as you like, and in any case pray for me, as I know you will, whether I ask it or no.

I have done very wrongly in hiding my doubts so long. Forgive me this also. You know it is my vice. Here, anyway, is a beginning of frankness. I am glad to be able to write before I receive any questioning from you.

Your loving son
   Austin.

Letter B, Box 1: reply from Augustine Farrer to Letter A

72 Grafton Rd
Acton, W.3.
Jan. 26. 1924

My dear Austin

I was intending to write to you tomorrow, but as Principal Robinson[19] (preaching at Church Road) is to be with us, I think I had better at least begin my letter this evening.

I have been in some doubt how, or how long I should attempt to answer your letter; and still am. You ask me for advice; but precisely at this moment I am feeling myself to be a wretchedly poor advisor. I ask myself, again and again, whether, if my instruction and example (especially the latter) had been at all what they should have been, this situation would have arisen. But then I answer myself, 'Yes, it might, quite well. He has had his Mother's example, which he acknowledges equal to that of any Christian he can ever hope to meet.' And as for instruction, well, conceivably in earlier years I might have impressed my own opinions on your mind, before it had grown firm, and was fully awake on the critical side. But, rightly or wrongly, it has not been my wish to put denominational tenets in the forefront of what I tried to teach you: and I believe

---

19. H. Wheeler Robinson, eminent Old Testament scholar, principal of Regent's Park College from 1920 until 1942, and the one who moved it from London to its current location in Oxford—which was, according to E. A. Payne, "the greatest achievement of his life." See E. A. Payne, rev., "Robinson, Henry Wheeler (1872–1945)," in *ODNB*, 47:346–47.

I have never—deliberately or consciously at least—done so. If I stand for anything, I stand for the individual's independence of thought and judgment in these matters. Moreover had I attempted such proselytism, I think it would have proved ultimately vain, in your case. From quite a small boy, you have always shown a disposition to think for yourself, and not to accept positions of which you were not personally convinced: and had I thought prematurely to mould your views, there would inevitably have come later a recoil, probably proportionate to the violence of the advantage made and taken of your childish innocence.

And now—I do not know how far your mind remains undecided. You say it is not; but then again you say that you do not think I can say anything that would convince you of the error of your opinions; and as I read your letter through, it does seem to me that your mind is more than half made up. If so, should I put you to the trouble of reading a long letter, which must repeat a good deal of what I have already said to you? Perhaps not. But 'a drowning man will catch at a straw' (that may sound exaggerated! but what I mean by it, you will know when you have read this letter to the end): and so I will go on. And that I may not seem to evade any of your points I will venture to take them seriatim, though such a method will almost certainly make a tedious letter (which yours as certainly was not).

But before doing so, I will touch here something in the close of your letter. You say you 'have done very wrongly in hiding your doubts so long.' It would not occur to me to call it wrong—only mistaken, and unfortunate. I confess that what you said to me in October about the comparative unimportance of the denominational question has had the effect of lulling me into a false security: and I cannot help regretting that when during a walk in the Christmas vacation, we got upon the subject of sacraments, episcopacy, etc, you did not take the opportunity to make the confidence contained in your letter. For we could so much better discuss the matter in conversation than by letter. But I appreciate your desire to spare me a shock which you hoped might never need to be given.

1. As for your preference of the church service, I can of course have little to say. You have a perfect right to your individual preference and it would be the merest impertinence to traverse it. I can go further, and say

that it has frequently occurred to me that, with your particular temperament and training, you might be quite likely to find the church service more congenial to you on the whole than that of the average dissenting congregation. For myself, I scarcely ever attend a service in the Church of England without things occurring that jar. Very likely you would be ready to say the same of the dissenting service. I suppose the predilection we bring with us has much to do with the way in which the service strikes us. I have occasionally been surprised at the ease with which you have excused admitted shortcomings in the clergyman, and—forgive my saying so—have wondered whether you had an equally ready charity and indulgence at the service of his free church brethren. I will only add, under this head, that the untruth 'that Anglicans do not use special prayers in special times of need' is not chargeable to me. What does seem to me true is that the provision made in the P. B. for such occasions seems insufficient in range and flexibility.

2. I am less inclined to acquiesce in what you say about church government. You 'have no desire whatever to insist on your right to a share in church government.' Are you clear that there is not a higher, and therefore more proper, standpoint? This looks to me, in part at least, like the instinctive shrinking of a naturally modest, retiring, & diffident man from possible difficulty and responsibility. Is a man, and especially a man of some gifts and educational advantages, to think exclusively or primarily of securing a form of worship congenial to himself, and not of opportunities of helping and serving others? What of the undoubtedly N. T. doctrine of the priesthood of all believers? And is not this same doctrine out of harmony with the view you express of the episcopacy? I know of course that you would not subscribe to high Anglican doctrine on the subject of episcopacy. You would not accept the apostolical succession, with its special χάρισμα [charisma] transmitted from generation to generation of bishops, making them, and the clergy ordained by them, exclusive channels of the means of grace to lay folk. I expect you would even agree with me that no form of church government has come down to us with the express direct authorisation of our Lord himself. I, on the other hand, should be ready to agree with you that the church is not to be limited to such forms of organisations, the beginnings at best of which can be traced in the N. T. We should probably concur in the view that

government should not necessarily be the same in every age & country, but can be determined on grounds of expediency. And this apparently is your defence of episcopacy. But you would not, would you, endorse a system of government out of keeping with fundamental truths of N. T. Christianity? (You know I am not for tying the church down exclusively to beliefs, practices etc which are demonstrable in the N. T.—only I say that to get nearest to the mind and will of our Lord, we must go primarily to the record made by those who had immediate contact with Him.) And does not the control[20] of the parish & the worship by the clergyman imply a distinction between him and the layman, which the N. T. not only does not recognise, but actually denies? I should still say this, on the assumption that the apparatus of appointment were such as to secure that he was a truly Christian man. But you yourself clearly acknowledge that this is not the case. You say that the abuses of patronage may be mended, and that a churchman does not necessarily acquiesce in them. That seems to me to be disposing of the matter rather easily. And moreover it is a consideration equally applicable to the weaknesses of dissenting organisation and management. That what you know of congregational government cannot increase your respect for it I am most painfully aware: your mother and I have no more poignant regret than that our family experience of church life has been so unfortunate. But are you sure that things are considerably better in the established church? You admit elsewhere in your letter that comparative ignorance of the C. of E. may have something to do with your preference. May I suggest that it may, in this point? Of course I know that the episcopal church is not liable to the same weaknesses as ours. But from what I have read and heard, it is just as liable to weaknesses of its own e.g. quarrels between clergy & wardens, clergy & choirs, scandals in the lives of unholy priests, etc. Such evils are avoidable not by any system, but only by adequate Christian character in the officers and members of the church.

Then there is all the untold mischief that has been wrought in manifold ways by the legal connection of Church & State. I cannot think that you have duly acquainted yourself with, and weighed these: but it is out of the question to enlarge on this here. I will only say further on this point, that

20. Augustine wrote "rule" and then marked through it and replaced it with "control."

I was rather startled to read that 'to submit to ecclesiastical superiors[']
seems to you 'just another act of Christian self-denial.' How far would you
be prepared to carry such submission? 'One is your Master, even Christ[,]
and all ye are brethren.'[21] Surely we should only be warranted unquestion-
ing compliance if we had reason to believe that our superior was adequately
equipped as Christ's vice-regent. And such a belief brings us again to a
distinction between cleric & lay which the N. T. does not recognise. Surely
too, your authority, Thomas à Kempis, is unfortunate. Is the monk's vow
of obedience to his superior a wholesome thing?

3. About the Eucharist I too find it a difficult thing to write, because
definition is so peculiarly difficult here I almost despair of finding words
not liable to misunderstanding: & the more so, because you are evidently
conscious of a serious cleavage between us on this point, & yet you put
down a definition which I think I could fully accept. 'The idea of a sacrament seems to be that by the aid of an outward symbol you visualise
and realise and concentrate on one act, your faith in the grace imparted
to you by the god you worship, and thus through faith obtain that grace.'
Here is faith responding to the offer of Divine Grace, and using [it] to
help its weakness, a particular symbol and act as it uses other 'means
of grace.' It is a <u>spiritual</u> transaction: the Lord vouchsafes his presence
and quickening grace to the devout soul that does this in accordance
with his word—in remembrance of Him. There is no priestly miracle,
and no mystical energy imparted to the material bread and wine. It is
the perfecting of the imperfect heathen sacrament or mystery (I agree),
in that it represents its thorough spiritualisation. If this is your view, it
is mine also. With you I protest against a mere, <u>bare</u> commemoration.
I will allow that some Dissenters—I may say, some Protestants—in their
recoil from Romanism—have carried the process of reduction too far—
have refused to recognise anything more than commemoration. And
such a jejune view may sometimes show itself in the dissenting minister's
administration of the ordinance. But surely, what the sacrament <u>means</u>
to the individual participant depends primarily on <u>him</u>—on what he
understands by it. There is the minister: there are the eloquent symbols:
there is the individual's participation. It may be a drawback if the admin-

21. Matt. 23:10.

istrant is out of sympathy with the recipient's view: but this may occur in the C. of E. as well as in the free church—the priest may mean as much more by the Eucharist, as the dissenting minister means less, than you do. Perhaps I shall make my view clearer if I add—I believe that just as our Lord promises us grace in general if we pray according to His word, i.e., believingly, in His name, so He promises us a special grace if we take the sacrament according to His word.

Now your reasons for hesitancy.

1. 'Sect matters comparatively little.' But then you query 'Is it a sin to withstand the truth?' I should answer Yes—But first comes Pilate's question (though not in Pilate's mood). You must be sure what is the Truth. And often it will be hard to be sure that matters of detail on which sects divide (as contrasted with the fundamental principles on which they unite) belong to it. And in any denomination whatsoever you will find some things that are not of the Truth. This at least we may be sure of—whatever is incongruous with the revelation that God is Love and that all His children are to love one another, is not of the Truth.

2. About the Apostles' Creed. I believe (though I cannot say for certain at the moment) that when the clause 'He descended into Hell' was added, it was understood to convey more than you say. But suppose you would be free to understand it in your own sense, just as you would be free to interpret the 'resurrection of the body' as you do, and as many clergymen (I believe) do. I think I have told you that my objection to creeds is less against their individual contents than against a creed in itself. Look at the creeds of the Established Church, including that in the Communion Service [i.e., the Nicene Creed] and the Athanasian. They include the affirmation of many beliefs which neither Christ nor His apostles ever required of the disciple, of much philosophy which inevitably becomes obsolete (some of it was never comprehensible) with lapse of time—and in any case, of propositions assent to which has nothing to do with the essence of religion. And then the profession of these is required of the loyal churchman, and in time past they have been made the means of cruel persecution—and when not that, of severe disabilities and painful divisions, to people as devout and truly Christian as the best of those who accept them. Is it not the fault of the Scribes repeated—a laying on men of a yoke which neither they nor their fathers

were able to bear?[22] Ought we to include in requirement for church-membership beliefs and practices that cannot claim the authority of the Lord of the Church?

On the subject of baptism, I agree that the argument from silence against infant baptism in the N. T. is not conclusive. There is, in the nature of the case, no instance of infant baptism recorded. But can baptism, as applied to infants, have the same significance as it had in the case of adults who thereby professed their discipleship? Can baptism in the case of infants have the significance that Paul found in it—that it symbolises the spiritual transformation of the recipient, his death to sin and resurrection to newness of life in Christ Jesus? Is not infant-baptism, indeed, contrary to the spiritual character of N. T. Christianity in general? And is it an adequate condemnation of sponsors to say that the institution 'is not particularly valuable'? Before you could speak plain, you said 'How can anyone promise in my name?' Have you yet found an answer (other than negative) to your own question?

3. You say that to the doctrine of the apostolic χάρισμα [charisma] of the bishop 'you will not subscribe.' The question for you is whether you can be confirmed in the Church of England, or baptised in it, without in effect subscribing to that doctrine, and to the doctrine of baptismal regeneration. For these doctrines are, I take it, the doctrines of the majority of churchmen, or at least church clergy, today—of that part of the C. of E. which is most living and influential today—and of those 17th century divines who are its classics.

4. I cannot tell you how thankful I am to read what you write about our worshipping united & as a family. I readily believe too, that if you left us to join the C. of E., it would be with such feelings as you describe. I eagerly welcome your promise to worship with us, in any case, once on Sundays. But forgive me if I express some misgivings. Again and again I have seen that when individuals have left us to join the Established Church they have—and usually in no long time—so fully absorbed the sympathies—and antipathies—of their new associates as to stand aloof in all religious matters from their dissenting relatives. Even if this were not so in your case, do you think we could bring ourselves to hold you to

22. Matt. 23:4.

that promise? Could we wish you to come with us if we knew that your heart was elsewhere? Nay, could we wish you to worship with us when we knew that you thought it more right to worship elsewhere, and that you would derive more benefit from so doing?

You show a beautiful and rare consideration & sympathy for my feelings (should you join another church). But may I say, you do not touch what for me would be the sorest trial. It is not what people would think and say of a Baptist professor whose son went into the C. of E. That would be humiliating, and hard to bear. But far harder to bear—the greatest loss entailed upon me by such a change—would be the loss of the consciousness of our fellowship & likemindedness in the higher things. You know I am a lonely man. I do not make or keep many friends. At my age it is most unlikely that I shall find new intimate friends to replace the loss of those of whom advancing years will increasingly rob me. Next to your mother, your sympathy and fellowship are more to me than anyone's else whatever. It is a loss the mere threat of which since I had your letter has shadowed me more & more. It is a good while now since I began to realise that part of the sacrifice involved to us in planning & contriving to give our children better education at school & University than we had had ourselves, might be some lessening of the fullness of companionship between us and them—that they would develop tastes & interests with which we could but imperfectly sympathise: that they would choose their friends in other circles than ours—that they might feel some constraint about introducing their friends at home, and so on. And eventually, behind all this rose another possibility, the possibility your letter announces. Believe me, my dear boy, I am not unresponsive to the assurances you give me: I am most grateful for them. But there remains a something that I have no power to do away, something that rather grows the more I think about the matter, a consciousness that the old happy fellowship—in <u>some</u> things—will be gone, not to return again.[23] How shall I be able to speak to you about the things that interest and concern me most, with the old assurance of your lively interest and unreserved fellow-feeling? Why, if I had been writing to

23. It looks as though Augustine began to write "is al-" (that is, "is already") and then scratched it through, replacing it with "will be."

you in the ordinary way today, one of the first or chief things I should have been telling you would have been that I had after all undertaken the task Dr. Rushbrooke asked of me.[24] But now—I know you would show interest still—but could it be the same? Indeed at the moment I feel my life all flat, stale and unprofitable. I was beginning to fret that I have not opportunities of preaching: now I feel thankful that I have not to do it. For the moment I have no longer the same interest in my College work. I know this mood will pass. Work will probably prove my most effective resource in distracting my disquietude. If this thing happens, it will be one of the reallest griefs that has yet befallen me.

But don't misunderstand me. I do not say all this as any <u>argument</u> against the course you are contemplating. You will do what you are led to believe to be right: and do you think I would ever be the man to dissuade you? I only want you not to act without an adequate realisation of the issues involved. I believe you would yourself wish to realise them. What I am pleading for today is that you will take no step for the present. No decisive step until you have given yourself time for a full consideration of the whole matter. I would venture to ask you to hold your hand until we have had a chance to meet and talk about it at length—until we can both be convinced that this course is the right one for you to take, or perhaps another.

Meanwhile, what shall you do? About consulting an Anglican divine I hardly know what to say. In proportion as he was earnest and serious, he would naturally want to proselytise. And I think he would be sure to tell you that there was fully as much latitude of interpretation of belief practised and allowed in the C of E as you desired. Also I am afraid at the moment I can think of no one I should like to suggest. Let me think about it a little longer.

I will not discuss in the abstract the relative importance of belief and practice. I will only say that practices reflect & express belief, and I have tried to show you above that adhesion to the C of E and its worship does imply some beliefs to which you are not prepared to subscribe. I have

24. James Henry Rushbrooke, English Baptist missionary, historian, and secretary of the Baptist World Alliance. See J. H. Y. Briggs, "Rushbrooke, James Henry (1870–1947)," in *ODNB*, 48:158–59.

also tried to show you that you can reconcile your view of the Sacrament with our administration of it.

I read your letter to Mother the evening of the day I received it. I felt I had no right to keep it from her any longer. She had rather a restless night but is now, I am glad to say, sleeping as usual. We know if the letter was hard for us to read, it was hard—perhaps harder—for you to write. And I say again, my thankfulness—& hers too, I know—is above our grief. Your desire to unite yourself with the Church of Christ is an answer to our constant prayer for you. And we rejoice and glory in your devotion to truth. That text you quote is a cruel one—for us all—parents & children both—but we had rather you obeyed it, though to our loss.[25] Only we want you to be sure first that that which you set above[26] family affection is indeed something demanded by the following of Christ.

> Now and ever, as always,
>   Your loving
>   Father

I will send Duff's funeral tomorrow.

Letter C, Box 1: reply from Evangeline Farrer, first to another letter from Austin to her, and then to Letter A

72 Grafton Rd
Jan 26th

My dear Austin,
    Your letter[27] did me good. I am relieved to know you are quite well again. I expect you are right about your food, but I am not quite con-

25. Augustine here echoes Austin in speaking of a "text" in the singular, but rather than a specific verse they seem to be referring generally to several passages in which Christ says that love and obedience to God must take precedence over natural family affections and commitments.

26. Augustine wrote "prefer before" and then marked it out and wrote "set above."

27. Another letter sent directly to his mother, not A.

vinced that it is good for you to be hungry for an hour before dinner every day. I have always understood that until the age of 25 the body is developing & needs as much good food as ever it can take, but I also know that you have never been able to take huge meals. But do your best in that way. We'll try the 3 meal programme at home next vac. . . .

I think I must leave your ghost stories for another time—if I begin on that subject I might write pages—& you know my thoughts all the time are on the letter you wrote to Father. You won't want a long letter from me when Father has said much in his reply that you will want to think about. I am glad & thankful that you feel the time has come for you to join a Church. When you were home at Xmas I could not bear for you to get up, & leave us to stay to the Communion service without you, & I meant after you had gone back to Oxford to write & ask you if you would not like to stay [to] that service with us, although you had not joined any Church. Our Church at least welcomes any one who 'loves Christ in sincerity and truth,' whatever are his opinions.

I feel with you in a good deal of what I think you feel about the Baptist denomination. I am very conscious of its shortcomings. I don't like the excitement of some of the services & the lack of reverence in some of the ministers & in the way the services are conducted. I find many of the people half-educated, incapable of seeing 2 sides of a question—but on the other hand, I do not know as far as I can judge another body of people who are trying to meet the needs of a sinful community as thoroughly & whole-heartedly as the Baptist Church, both in foreign missionary work & at home. If you could talk with them, you would find many of the more enlightened of its adherents fully conscious of its blemishes. Here is Mr Marsden,[28] for one, out of office in the Church where he has worshipped for nearly 30 years, because the other members cannot rise to his ideal of Church work. But he does not leave the denomination[29] for in spite of its defects, in his judgement it is the best he can find. I like some things in the Presbyterian Church, some things

28. As stated above, John Marsden, an old family friend, a solicitor from whom Austin received his middle name, and who helped support the education of the Farrer children. See Curtis, *A Hawk among Sparrows*, 2.

29. Evangeline wrote "Church," then marked it out and replaced it with "denomination."

in the Quaker worship & practices, some things in the Anglican Church (I loved those services at [illegible]) but I have to admit that none of them satisfy me & that though I see big blemishes in our own Church, it is the best I know.

But what do you know of the Baptist Church, you poor boy. It is humiliating indeed to recall the fact that from the time you were a little boy our church life has been spoiled & shadowed by split on split, at Pinner & then at Haven Green & now Horn Lane. We tried hard to avoid it at Haven Green, & made up our minds to continue there for your sakes, but when you and Joyce began to ask questions we found it no longer possible to go on taking you to hear a man whose opinions uttered from the pulpit you were criticising & combating.[30]

But I find these differences are not only in our Church. One reason for Uncle Ernest leaving Edgeware was that he had grown weary of his Vicar & couldn't agree with him. Mr and Mrs White (Kathleen's parents) have recently left a Church that they were greatly attached to because the Vicar had quarrelled with the people & half the congregation left. I heard too that the people were recovering from a split at St Matthews, Ealing. I do not repeat this as gossip but to show that other Churches have their troubles too.

I wish very much that you & Joyce & Ellie could have had the early Church life that Father & I enjoyed. It was entirely happy as far as the minister and government of the Church went. Mr Brock was over 45 years minister of Heath St & such things as stormy Church meetings or quarrels were never thought of. He was like a wise father among us, reserved and quiet in manner, but we were always sure of his sympathy in all that concerned us. I could write more about him than you would care to read, but I will say to this day when Father & I are discussing a difficult problem, we will sometimes say to each other, I wonder what Mr Brock would advise. He is our ideal of a Christian minister, & there are other happy Churches to be found. But I will admit, we are passing through a very difficult time & we need strong men. You & Joyce have had no chance of doing any Church work owing to your evenings being taken up with homework. We have always felt that was a loss in your religious

30. On this period see Curtis, *A Hawk among Sparrows*, 4–5.

life, not to learn in practice as well as in theory. I sometimes wonder that if you should join the Anglican Church under the influence of School & the University, whether when you go out into the world—& the law world will be a hard world in some respects—the Church of England will satisfy your needs.

I am conscious that I have said very little that can help you. If only I could enter into all your difficulties through love & sympathy I would, but it is true that we must each 'work out our own salvation with fear & trembling,'[31] & through lack of education & understanding I am incapable of entering into many of your thoughts. But you have your father, & better, still a thousand times, you have <u>God</u>. I am afraid I do not care so much whether you join the Baptist Church or the Church of England (God forgive me if I am disloyal to my own Church by saying it) but I <u>do</u> care that you join the Church where your own soul can best grow, & where you will best learn to use to the utmost for the benefit of others the powers that God has given you, & where you will best learn to understand the beauty of the character of our Lord, which is worth a lifetime of study. Forgive a poor letter on such an important subject. It is best my love can find words for, & it is a humiliation that it is not better but it comes with love from

Mother

Letter D, Box 10: from Austin, to his father, in response to Letters B and C

Balliol College, Oxford
Thursday[32]

Dear Father

Your letter and Mother's move me greatly. I have not made up my mind. I can tell you that if I inclined one way before, you have just about

31. Phil. 2:12–13.
32. No date, but either late January or early February 1924.

restored the balance. I am much distressed. I feel somehow that now is the time to settle the matter, before I sink back into apathy, but which way to settle it I cannot see. To be forced to perform an unpleasant duty is bad enough, but to feel the necessity of doing something without knowing what is a worse torture. Most things of importance we really settle by conscience, and in this case my conscience seems inactive, or else I cannot read it. Sometimes I think that to stay as I am would be to yield to the weakness of the flesh, and but another instance of my natural irresolution: sometimes again I think that to go into the Anglican Church would be to yield to tastes and predilections which have nothing spiritual in them, or even to a desire for ease and an easier religion, or yet again, to intellectual pride. The matter seems at present left to reason. I never yet have decided anything by reason and probably never shall; I see both sides and can convince myself of either at will.[33] I suppose I must just study the subject as much as I can, and wait for the voice of conscience, which will sometime speak, I trust. It is enough that I should be in suspense, without your being so also. What you write of yourself I see to be true, and it grieves me very much. Can you not, with an effort, set aside this sad anticipation for the present? Anticipation is always worse than the reality, and the reality is far from certain in this case. Anyhow there is not the least fear of my making any decision before we meet again. Try and put away anxiety for the present. Oh, what a fool I was, how continually do I blame myself now that I did not open the subject to you after Christmas, that we might have got used to the idea together: that I might have had your advice, and been there to convince you in a way that no letter can, that I shall never be a bigot, or ever, to anything like the extent you suppose, lose the most personal and close interest in everything you do and think. If, as far as I can see, I find one church

33. A later reader has marked this passage "NB." In my *Solved by Sacrifice: Austin Farrer, Fideism, and the Evidence of Faith* (Leuven: Peeters, 2013), 103–4, I discuss this passage as the first recorded instance of a persistent strand of fideism that was to remain present in Farrer's thought, even as he sought to develop what Rowan Williams describes as "a viable and sophisticated natural theology" (see Rowan Williams, "Theology in the Twentieth Century," in *A Century of Theological and Religious Studies in Britain*, ed. Ernest Nicholson [Oxford: Published for the British Academy by Oxford University Press, 2003], 242).

preferable to another, do you think I shall think my opinion infallible? Is this your experience of me? Have I not always told you how hard it is for me to be convinced of a thing, when I see as many good Christian men against it as for it? What can I say? The very idea of what you suggest—to give you loneliness and sorrow in your age—makes me almost feel that my own soul is not worth the causing of it. We have only to love one another truly, and surely God will find a way for our love. Love does not depend on circumstance. If it be His will that our circumstances change, if we are faithful in loving do you not believe that He will find channels, new channels, for it to flow in? Cast away such thoughts as you wrote to me, or you will not only make yourself unhappy, but put me in grievous temptation. You would not have me do wrong for your sake: no: but for all that the temptation to me to do so is none the less strong.

What more can I write? I hate thus to rake up your feelings, and to lay bare what would better be let alone. But still I cannot let you think such things. Let me know that you do as I ask you; let me see the issue clearly and on its own merits. It is not that I feel your distress an impediment to my desire to enter the Church of England, for I am just as likely to make too much allowances for the natural bias it gives, and thus be driven the other way: but I want to look at it by itself. As for realising the meaning and importance of the matter, I do that enough I think already.

I cannot now engage in controversy with you. I feel fully the weight of the points you set before me. There are some I should like to answer, but will not. For if I answer you, though I am only putting my doubts and queries, one half of my mind, yet I am forced to write as from the Anglican point of view entirely, which I have not yet come to adopt. Besides, such controversy would be endless. I do not know where to begin or end. I have two ideas on each point, and the different contradictions and objections they raise against one another are almost infinite in number. If I write them down I only misrepresent myself, as I see I have sufficiently done already. Only be sure that because I do not answer you, it is not that I do not weigh what you write.

On the Creeds and on Church-government in particular you do not convince me. For the rest I do not know what to think. In the matter of the Eucharist, it seems to me that a dissenting minister administering it as a Commemoration merely <u>would</u> prove infinitely more hindrance than an Anglican who believed in a priestly miracle. However, I will leave these points, on which, as I said, I am quite unsettled.

I am conscious of being much moved, though hardly in the region of pure reasoning, by a shadowy conception of historical continuity and the body of the Church. The Christian Church ought to be one: it is not, indeed: but I somehow feel that the Church of England is one step nearer unity, and that, with some admixture of evil, perhaps, it still preserves something of the corporate spirit that we have lost. It is an impressive thought to me to think of joining in practices and institutions which are shared to some degree at least by the other great Churches, and which have been used all down the ages. It is true that the logical form of this doctrine is Apostolical succession, which is not credible or historical. And yet, even in a mistier form the idea seems to me valuable. The Church was meant to be a visible unity. The New Testament does not seem to contemplate the possibility of belief in Christ in any other way than that of being a member of the one Body. This idea is utterly gone and lost from Nonconformity. It is true that the Church is in any case divided, but the Church of England preserves more of the great conception, more links with the past and the great churches of the present. To St. Paul the question of baptismal regeneration did not arise because belief and baptism into the one church were one thing in his mind, as it seems to me. I see that in the present day my idea is illogical, and yet—

I put this down as one of the things that draws me the other way. I have no need to put down the reverse arguments, as you know them and they are shared by all Nonconformists together.

I want very much to hear about the thing that Mr. Rushbrooke persuaded you to do. What does it involve? And has anything been settled about the future of the college? And what about the long established and exclusive firm of Greenwood Bros, those most particular of all Baptists? See that you keep Principal Robinson in order, though really I suppose nobody can. Talking of the Greenwoods and Wheeler puts me in mind of a question I have for you—do you think that there is any future among Baptists for moderate and middling opinions, whereof you seem to me at present the sole representative? Between modernists and obscurantists, bigots and critics I really do not know which I would choose, if I had to take one or the other; in fact, I could take neither. I wonder whether it is really a media via between all opinions that I am looking for?

You see that I am become for the present a terrible egoist, and cannot keep off my own thoughts and ideas. And since there is no real use in putting them down, I will stop, only repeating my request for news about the Rushbrooke business, and the College.

Your loving son
    Austin

Letter E, Box 1: reply from Augustine to Austin's Letter D

72 Grafton Rd, W.3.
Feb. 3 1924

My dear Boy

Your letter, which had been eagerly awaited, reached me last evening, and now, having read with Ellie, I sit down alone to reply, and to give you the assurance for which it asks, which I do out of a full heart, and without any reserve.

Your letter has been—is—a very great comfort to me, and after reading it, I can and do assure you that I will not allow that anxiety further place in my thoughts. My heart leaps to meet and share the confidence you utter, that if we are faithful to our love for each other, God's love will make a way for us. I can even believe that if the time should come when it is made clear that your duty calls you to join another community than mine, and you do so, not because you didn't love me but because—as you should—you love God more, I believe, I say, that our mutual affection and sympathy will be deepened and strengthened and made a fuller and realler thing. And I lift my head again in thankfulness, and look on with cheerfulness and hope to whatever the future may bring.

No, I have never known any man of your age who was less of a bigot: I have not so learned you. I have had no fear of the son I know, as I have known him hitherto: I was only fearful that under certain influences he might change, as I have known some change. But after reading what you write, I could not find it in me to retain these fears, and indeed they are banished.

And now in my turn, let me ask you not to be over-anxious about this matter. For the present you have a clear duty: it is to take advantage to the utmost of the opportunities of education and mental training which are offered to you at Oxford, and you must not let your mind brood upon this other matter in such a way as to distract your thoughts and weaken your power of application to your studies. I quite agree with the view you take of the way in which your deliverance will arise: the question will be settled by conscience rather than reason, and in due time your conscience will become clear as to the line of your duty. (Of course, indirectly reason will have played its part in determining conscience.) And when conscience declares itself, on whichever side, to that side you will go, and with your mother's and father's blessing and prayers to second you. And it shall be my faith that when that stage is reached, I too shall be entirely reconciled to the course marked out for you, though it should be what now I dread. Meanwhile, do not fear that you will fall back into apathy. You will be treading the path of God's appointment for you (that often calls for patience), as you could not be doing if you decided without a leading of conscience, and He will care for it that you do not lapse into indifference.

And now—again in agreement with you—I will abstain from controversy. Any further discussion we will postpone till we can meet again, when I am certain it will be no controversy, at least in the harder senses of that word, but a common pursuit of truth in a humble and prayerful spirit with true oneness of heart. Today I will only venture to underline two things which you yourself say of yourself.

First, I think you are right to hold in view that possibility of an unconscious influence upon your mind of 'predilections which have nothing' essentially 'spiritual in them, or even to a desire for . . . an easier religion, or yet again, to intellectual pride.' I need not explain what I mean, since it is what you mean. And second, I can quite understand the attraction to you of the idea of historic continuity and visible unity. Your training in an ancient C. of. E. school and University is calculated to impress that strongly. You will remember, will you not, that you can hardly get a central view of the matter while you are immediately under the pressure of that training. In those institutions Nonconformity necessarily appears a feeble and obscure thing, if not a nonentity. On the other hand, you probably see the C. of E. in its most favourable aspect. And your view of it is still that of an outsider. What is less favourable even there may well escape your notice. I only want now to say this further. Is it quite clear that it was a <u>visible</u> unity that Christ contemplated for the church on earth? That that is the ideal, ultimately to be attained, there can be no question. But has the church on earth, ever, even in the first generations, actually been a visible unity? And does there appear to be any prospect of such a thing? Quot homines, tot sententiae.[34] If it is to be a matter of practices and institutions, I fear I must be a pessimist. But if it is rather a question of a common spirit and life, then I am far from hopeless. Then, too, I cannot agree that the idea of unity is clean gone from Nonconformity. The Nonconformist claims to be the true Catholic, because he recognises his brotherhood in Christ with all, in every Christian community, or even outside the Churches, who share the spirit and life of Christ. At this point I can hear you strike in with your question[,] How many of such Nonconformists are there, how many among the Baptists who have that breadth of charity? Well, I do not know: but I hope there are a good many, and that the number is now on the increase.

The remainder of the letter, two-thirds of the other side of the second page, and both sides of a third page, deal with the details of Augustine's church and college life that Austin inquired about in Letter D. At this point, however, we encounter a gap and a puzzle. The three letters from Austin's parents—B, C, and E—were found uncatalogued in Box 1 of the Farrer Papers. They are all from late January or early February 1924. Curtis cites directly from them in *A Hawk among Sparrows*. Austin's two letters above—A and D—were found uncatalogued in Box 10, along with a third, Letter F below. As stated above, Curtis does not cite from either A or D, professes ignorance of their verbatim

---

34. A well-known Latin proverb, traditionally translated: "There are as many opinions as there are men."

content, and partly reconstructs what Austin wrote from Augustine's replies (see pages 20–24 of *A Hawk among Sparrows*). Despite the separate location of these six unfoliated letters, and despite the lack of clear dating on Austin's, they clearly belong together as relating to Austin's decision to join the Church of England, and their sequence thus far can be confidently determined as above. That is, Austin wrote A to Augustine; Augustine shared the letter with Evangeline; Augustine wrote B and Evangeline wrote C; Austin wrote D in response to both, although only directly to Augustine; and Augustine then replied with E.

The gap and the puzzle arrive with the following Letter F from Austin. It has no date, but simply says "Monday," and so cannot be dated accurately in relation to the others, although it clearly follows them. In it Austin addresses "a revelation of distress on [his father's] part deeper than [Austin] had supposed possible after the first surprise was past." In E (Augustine's reply to D), however, Augustine seems greatly relieved by Austin's assurances, and wonderfully composed and reconciled to whatever happens. While he admits continuing anxiety, there is no deep distress, but rather a peaceful resignation to divine providence, even promising his blessing should Austin join the Church of England, to which possibility he hopes he might be "entirely reconciled." He gives Austin everything Austin had hoped for and more. In short, it seems clear that Austin's Letter F below is *not*, as one might well wish in terms of historical tidiness, a response to E.

First of all, Letter F begins with Austin saying that he has already been to see an Anglican clergyman (the chaplain of Balliol), which he wrote to his father about in A and which Augustine asked him *not* to do in B. While it is barely conceivable that the young Farrer would impulsively go ahead with this plan before hearing back from his father, it is inconceivable that he would do so against his father's express instructions, especially since Augustine said that he wanted to discuss this situation with Austin in person. And it is clear from the end of Letter A ("Do not think me so impatient as to be in a hurry for your reply") that Austin's sense of urgency—though acute—was not so strong as to cause him to act precipitously. Second, although F is certainly a response to a letter from Augustine, it cites phrases and refers to content absent from either B or E. Third, it seems clear that an indefinite but significant period of time has elapsed since A in late January: Austin's mind is now made up to the extent that he has not only met with the chaplain but is even about to inform Mr. Marsden of his forthcoming baptism and confirmation in the Church of England, as this may affect the possibility of Austin joining Marsden's family-owned law firm, which remains "in the [Baptist] denomination."

So, despite the missing date, all the evidence points clearly toward F being a letter written sometime after Augustine's E, to yet another letter from Augustine that has been lost. Perhaps the real puzzle, however, lies in the urgent tone and pastoral content of Austin's Letter F, which indicates that even after Letters A–E (and presumably after the promised face-to-face discussion), when Austin finally made the decision to join the Church of England—perhaps in March or April 1924—Augustine found this so difficult to accept that he wrote another, now lost letter, expressing extreme anguish and desolation. If this reconstruction is correct, then Augustine found the actual decision even harder than he had thought. It is to his father's unexpected and distressing *cri de coeur* that Austin's Letter F responds:

Letter F, Box 10: Austin's reply to a letter from his father, but apparently not either B or E

Balliol College,
Oxford
Monday[35]

Dear Father,

The first thing to say is that it is done: that is, that I have applied to the Chaplain.[36] I saw him this morning. His behaviour was exemplary, but to me astonishing, for he said that he made it a rule never to encourage anyone to leave their own communion for the Church of England, and wished to be satisfied first of all that you knew what was being done and consented to it, and then that my reasons for making the change

---

35. No date, but still in early 1924, as indicated above.

36. Henry Hensman Gibbon (1861–1928)—see Curtis, *A Hawk among Sparrows*, 24, and *Crockford's Clerical Directory*. He is commemorated on the left side of the East Wall of Balliol College's Antechapel: https://tinyurl.com/4ujwuayp, number 3. The note on the website says: "Died in Baluchistan, en route to his daughter's wedding."

were sufficient. He said that of course he would be glad to help me in the matter if he was convinced that it was a serious decision on my part and a decision of my own, but that he had no wish to influence me either way. On the first head I satisfied him, but begged time for the second, and I am to see him again to-morrow morning. I have no doubt that it will be all right. I had debated with myself whether I should go to him or to the vicar of a neighbouring church. I am glad that I decided to go to him. He seems to me a better and more sensible man than I thought him before.

I do not really know how to answer your letter, and in large part shall not attempt to do so. It was to me a revelation of distress on your part deeper than I had supposed possible after the first surprise was past. I can only say again, that it takes two to make a misunderstanding, and that if we are both determined against any arising there is little fear that it should. If you begin by feeling and imagining that you lose my sympathy and then proceed to act upon your feelings and imagination, you will be putting a barrier between us; but if you resolutely refuse to entertain such thoughts and will put faith in me that all your interests will always remain mine, there is surely good hope for us. It is not I suppose possible for me to give any sort of guarantee on which you may rest: but I still maintain firmly the intention of worshipping wherever you worship on Sunday mornings when I am at home. I know and have seen from what you have said that you are prepared to come a long way to meet me: let this little determination of mine be a continual reminder and parable to you that I will go some way to meet you. Give me proof that you are taking me at my word by writing to me as much or more than ever you did of the College and its prospects—Is anything further settled yet?—and by any church or denominational affairs in which you are interested or engaged.

Do not think that I wish to minimise the many grievous disappointments and griefs that must fall to you. I can only ask you for your forgiveness for them. But what I do say is that these are in a manner accidentals which can be stripped off and laid aside, though with pain; but that the essentials can be preserved. Only let me implore you to combat with all your power of will and faith this 'feeling of a very serious loss.' The feeling is the loss: to refuse to feel is, not to sustain it. This feeling seems to me the most dangerous thing. Try to believe it a temptation. As for me I know you so well that I cannot experience such a feeling for myself. I know that your sympathy is assured to me. You have never been wont to trust blind feelings and impulses. Here indeed is one for you to distrust with all your heart and soul.

Surely 'loving the creature above the Creator' can only mean, loving in the creature accidental and not intrinsically good things, which happen to be pleasing to ourselves. Otherwise surely we are taught that to love the creature is to love the Creator. It is surely not less but more love to refuse to give up even when these accidentals turn against us.

As for your desire to be assured that I am at least clear in my own mind on the issue—I am about as clear as I am ever likely to become from looking at things from outside, which, you may say, is not saying much. Perhaps not: but hesitancy is rather my vice than precipitancy, and at the present stage of things I feel that to put it off now would be nothing but weakness. And I thought too that you would feel really easier yourself when the thing was fixed. Suspense is always worse than certainty.

As to Mr. Marsden, I shall write to him next Sunday, so that the matter come not to his ears by any side channels before he hears from me. Let me have the first word, and if you want to write, write a day or two after me. And of course you won't beg for me, will you? It is most likely that they may really wish to throw the business up, but not quite like to having once taken it on. I shall try to persuade Mr. Marsden to set all other considerations aside and act as though he had never agreed to it in the beginning. I shall tell him of course that my mind has not changed and that I do not myself foresee any positive difficulties, but that, inasmuch as he may naturally wish to keep the firm in the denomination, particularly if either of his sons are going into it, I ask him to reconsider that whole matter afresh.

After all there are various ways of life and I feel at the moment prepared to do almost anything. (This last remark is not part of my proposed letter.)

If any difficulty arises or the Chaplain tells me it is my duty to change my mind and so things are hung up, I will let you know by postcard immediately so that you do not write to Blackburn prematurely, and I may have time to consider further. Or if you wish to say anything to me about my letter to Mr. Marsden, send it to me sometime this week.

> Your loving son
> Austin

II. Documenting Farrer's Baptism

The letters transcribed in section 1 provide the missing primary source material related to Austin Farrer's momentous decision to leave the Baptist tradition of his parents and join the Church of England. However, as indicated above, determining the precise date and location of Farrer's eventual baptism was greatly complicated due to Gibbon's failure to record it. I suspect that in addition to not having Farrer's own letters to hand, Curtis made some attempt to ascertain this information, found that it was missing, and so passed over this episode in silence. However, the following three documents are included in Farrer's ordination files in the archives of the Diocese of Wakefield, now held in the West Yorkshire Archive Service, UK, Ref. WD100 Box 10. The two unfoliated letters (1) and (2) are handwritten notes from the Reverend James B. Seaton (1868–1938), then the principal of Cuddesdon Theological College (where Farrer trained for ministry), to Mr. W. H. Coles, the diocesan secretary of Wakefield. The unfoliated typewritten statutory declaration (3) is from Cyril Bailey, an eminent classics scholar and fellow of Balliol who witnessed Farrer's baptism.[37] These documents provide evidence for both the date and location of this event:

37. Cyril Bailey was, like Farrer, a graduate of both St. Paul's (1890) and Balliol (1894). He was fellow of Exeter College from 1894 to 1902, and fellow of Balliol from 1902 to 1939. A leading interpreter of both Epicurus and Lucretius, he was probably one of Farrer's classics tutors, and as a practicing Anglican may have had some influence on Farrer's decision to join the Church of England. He was certainly close enough to Farrer to attend his baptism and thus later serve as a witness, which is significant. See Jasper Griffin, "Cyril Bailey (1871–1957)," in *ODNB*, 3:254–56.

(1)

Cuddesdon College,
Oxford
15 September 1928

My dear Mr Coles,
  <u>A. M. Farrer</u>
  This letter is about a very different matter.
  Farrer is one of my students, a very brilliant Balliol man. He is to be ordained at Advent to Dewsbury Parish Church. His father is a Baptist minister: and he was brought up as a Baptist. He was baptised at Oxford in S. Peter le Bailey Church, being prepared and baptised by Mr Gibbon, the Chaplain of Balliol, either in the Spring of 1924 or 1925: and was subsequently confirmed by Dr Burge, Bishop of Oxford. I told him to get his baptismal certificate. But there is no record at S. Peter le Bailey. Mr Gibbon died this year: he was the kind of person who might easily omit to have the baptism registered at the Church (of which he was not the Vicar): Dr Burge is also dead. Farrer did not keep a note of the date. Would it be sufficient if we obtained an affidavit from one of the witnesses? Mr Cyril Bailey, Fellow of Balliol, was present and I have no doubt that he would testify. What do you advise?

  Yours sincerely,
    James B. Seaton

(2)

Cuddesdon College,
Oxford
18 September 1928

My dear Mr Coles,
  <u>A. M. Farrer</u>
  Thank you very much. We now know the actual date of the baptism. So will you kindly prepare an affidavit or Statutory Declaration for him

and let me have it. It shall be filled in with the date of which Mr Cyril Bailey, the witness, made a note at the time.

Yours sincerely,
James B. Seaton

(3)

I CYRIL BAILEY of *The King's Mound, Mansfield Rd. Oxford*, Fellow of Balliol College Oxford DO solemnly and sincerely declare

1. That *Austin Marsden* FARRER of [blank]
was baptised by the Reverend Henry Hensman Gibbon Chaplain of Balliol College Oxford at St. Peter le Bailey Church in Oxford on the *fourteenth* day of *May 1924*.

2. That I am able to make this declaration by reason of having been present at such baptism.

AND I make this solemn declaration conscientiously believing the same to be true and by virtue of the provisions of the Statutory Declaration Act 1835.

DECLARED at the City of *Oxford*	)	
this *12th* day of *October*	)	*CBailey*
One thousand nine hundred and	)	
twenty eight.	)	
Before me		

Francis Marshall [?]
Commissioner for Oaths.[38]

While the six letters in section 1 are rich in content and could be discussed in considerable detail, these three brief documents speak for themselves and

---

38. This document is in typescript, and the italicized portions have been handwritten by Bailey or the Commissioner for Oaths, whose signed surname is unclear: "Marshall" is my best guess.

require little commentary or analysis. They are, however, equally fascinating. Given that Austin and his family went through such agonies of conscience and theological travail over his decision to join the Church of England, and given that Austin went on to become "possibly the greatest Anglican mind of the twentieth century," for his baptism to have gone officially unrecorded is an irony of considerable proportions.[39] One final irony with which I shall conclude is this: very soon after writing his notes to the Wakefield diocesan secretary in regard to Farrer's baptism, in order that Farrer's ordination could proceed as planned, James Seaton left his position as principal of Cuddesdon College. On November 1, 1928, he was consecrated as third bishop of Wakefield.[40] He ordained Farrer deacon in the Cathedral Church of All Saints on Sunday, December 23, 1928, and priest on Sunday, December 22, 1929.[41]

39. The parish registers of St. Peter-le-Bailey are now held in the Oxfordshire Record Office. I have personally checked the relevant volume, and Farrer's name is indeed absent. In the Wakefield Archive, the official folder containing documents related to Farrer's ordination as a deacon has a checklist printed on the front cover with six required forms titled "Papers to Be Furnished." The first is "Certificate of Baptism," but someone has marked through "certificate" and handwritten "statutory declaration" instead.

40. Curtis discusses Seaton at various points in *A Hawk among Sparrows*, 39–57. According to *Crockford's Clerical Directory*, he was bishop of Wakefield from 1928 until his death in 1938. See also his entry in *Who Was Who, 1929–1940* (London: Black, 1941), 1213. The Diocese of Wakefield was created out of the Diocese of Ripon in 1888 and was dissolved in 2014 to create the new Diocese of Leeds.

41. Those who have assisted in the completion of this article are many. First of all, I am very grateful to the Historical Society of the Episcopal Church for a personal grant that helped fund this research. Second, I am indebted to expert assistance provided by staff at the Bodleian Libraries, Balliol College, and Christ Church College, all of the University of Oxford; the Oxfordshire Record Office; and the West Yorkshire Archive Service. For permission to publish the Farrer letters I am extremely grateful to Nick Newton of the Farrer Estate; and for permission to publish the material from the archives of the Diocese of Wakefield, I am most grateful to the West Yorkshire Archive Service. For linguistic and other assistance I must thank David Brown; for efficient help in checking citations I thank Drew Courtright; and for comments, advice, and encouragement I thank David Hein, Edward Henderson, Paul Holloway, Ben King, the late Ann Loades, Stephen Platten, James Turrell, and Michael Ward. A long-planned visit to the West Yorkshire Record Service was unexpectedly facilitated by the otherwise highly inconvenient eruption of Eyjafjallajökull in April 2010. Finally, as a philosophical theologian willfully trespassing into the realm of history, I am grateful to Ed Bond for his patience (in more ways than one).

A Fertile Friendship: C. S. Lewis and Austin Farrer

Austin Farrer (1904–1968) was an Anglican priest, philosopher, theologian, and New Testament scholar of rare brilliance, creativity, wit, and spiritual depth. Those familiar with most biographies of C. S. Lewis will know that Lewis and Farrer were good friends, and they might even know that Joy Lewis was also good friends with Farrer's wife, Katherine (Kay). But the *significance* of those mutual friendships, and the extent to which Lewis and Farrer may have *influenced* each other, has not, to my knowledge, been much explored. This is probably because Farrer himself has greatly been neglected over the years, although that is beginning to change. So this seems to be an opportune moment—and certainly an opportune forum—to begin to rectify this deficiency and to take this investigation forward. And, let me stress, this is indeed just a beginning. All I will try to do in this paper is to lay out the most obvious pieces of relevant evidence. What to make of this evidence is something we can then discuss further together.

I. Parallels and Differences

Lewis and Farrer had much in common. Consider, for example, Professor Leslie Houlden's description of Farrer as "unmistakably Anglican and Oxford Anglican at that; yet there was no better spokesman for universal, deep-rooted, mature Christian orthodoxy."[1] If you presented those words to someone without

1. Leslie Houlden, introduction to Austin Farrer, *The Essential Sermons*, ed. Leslie Houlden (London: SPCK, 1991), ix.

Originally published in *Chronicle of the Oxford University C. S. Lewis Society* [now *Journal of Inklings Studies*] 5, no. 2 (Trinity Term/May 2008): 22–45.

revealing their context, they might well be taken to refer to C. S. Lewis—and rightly so. But the similarities run even deeper than that description alone might convey. When I first encountered Farrer's work in my midtwenties after many years of reading Lewis, I had the strong sense of encountering a deeply similar mind, of entering into a similar world, of being presented with a similar vision of the Christian faith and life.

But while there are parallels, there are also differences. For example—and I mean this with no disrespect to Lewis at all—my first encounter with Farrer's work, for all of its similarity to Lewis's, also presented me with a more *professional* theological and philosophical thinker. Farrer's writings, although often exasperating for other theologians, and somewhat puzzling for other philosophers, still carry with them a sense of expertise and sophistication and technical mastery in those fields that Lewis's theological and philosophical writings—for all of their compensating virtues—sometimes lack. For those reared on and shaped by Lewis, Farrer, I would suggest, is a very good next step into the world of academic theology and philosophy.

Also, although Farrer was, like Lewis, "unmistakably Anglican and Oxford Anglican at that," Farrer's Oxford Anglicanism was decidedly more High Church than Lewis's. Although Farrer mellowed a bit in his old age, he was a card-carrying Anglo-Catholic, and indeed a leading member of the Anglo-Catholic wing of the Church of England during the 1940s, '50s, and '60s, often mentioned in the same context as such luminaries of that movement as Michael Ramsey, Kenneth Kirk, Gregory Dix, and Eric Mascall. Farrer was also a priest who frequently preached and celebrated at Pusey House, occasionally lectured at Mirfield Theological College, and ended his career as warden of the college founded in memory of one of the great saints of the Oxford Movement, John Keble.

And yet, despite his Anglo-Catholic credentials, Farrer never forgot or lost touch with his nonconformist, Baptist roots. I will get to those roots in a moment, but they perhaps explain why, rather surprisingly, the best one-sentence summary of Farrer's legacy is provided not by a fellow Anglo-Catholic but by the evangelical Anglican theologian J. I. Packer. While he was preparing for ordination at Wycliffe Hall between 1949 and 1952, Packer attended Farrer's lectures in philosophy of religion. Despite great differences in churchmanship, theological method, and conclusions on contested issues, the young neo-Puritan Packer came to revere the older Anglo-Catholic Farrer, and went on to read his works appreciatively. Naming each of the three academic fields in which

Farrer taught and wrote, Packer says that his writings on philosophy, theology, and New Testament exegesis show "an independent, lucid, agile, argumentative and articulate mind, fastidiously whimsical, witty in manner of a metaphysical poet, Newmanesque in sensitivity, incantatory in expression, and committed to a rational credal orthodoxy."[2]

Now, rather briefly, Farrer's *curriculum vita*, occasionally noting specific points parallel to and different from Lewis's.[3] Farrer was born in Hampstead, London, in 1904, just six years after Lewis. His home life, unlike Lewis's, was secure and happy, and his father was a Baptist minister, scholar, and lecturer at Regent's Park College (first in London, and then, when the college moved to Oxford, there as well). Despite his eventual defection to the Church of England, Farrer remained on very good terms with his father throughout his life. Indeed, in contrast to Lewis, commentators remark on how close Farrer and his father were. After winning a scholarship to St. Paul's School in London, which he attended as a day pupil, Farrer entered Balliol in 1923.

Farrer's religious journey was rather different from Lewis's. He never renounced the Christian faith, but even as a boy he could not reconcile himself to his parents' religion and struggled with various theological and philosophical difficulties. He was never baptized in the Baptist church, but as an undergraduate was gradually drawn to the Church of England. He was thus baptized at the age of nineteen in St. Peter-le-Bailey (now the chapel of St. Peter's College) and then confirmed by the bishop of Oxford in the Latin Chapel of Christ Church in May 1924.[4]

But, like Lewis, Farrer eventually achieved a remarkable academic distinction of earning three consecutive Firsts. Both of them initially read Greats, and so both received Firsts for Honor Moderations and Literae Humaniores. But

2. J. I. Packer, "Farrer, Austin Marsden," in *New Dictionary of Theology*, ed. Sinclair B. Ferguson and David F. Wright (Leicester, UK: Inter-Varsity Press, 1988), 253. In his biography of Packer, Alister McGrath writes that Packer "recalls attending the lectures by Austin Farrer in [philosophy of religion], and being stimulated by the ideas of this remarkable Oxford philosopher. For Packer, Farrer was a 'class A genius,' a philosopher of religion who showed a genuine concern for New Testament scholarship and systematic theology, even if Packer had misgivings concerning his exegetical methods" (*To Know and Serve God: A Biography of J. I. Packer* [London: Hodder & Stoughton, 1997], 44).

3. There are, of course, numerous biographies of Lewis, but there is only one of Farrer: Philip Curtis, *A Hawk among Sparrows: A Biography of Austin Farrer* (London: SPCK, 1985).

4. See chapter 3 of this volume for the details.

then their academic paths diverged: Lewis went on to read English, receiving his third First in 1923—the year Farrer came up—and Farrer went on to read theology, receiving his third First in 1928. Farrer trained for ordination at Cuddesdon Theological College, just outside Oxford, where he met and became good friends with Michael Ramsey, the future 100th archbishop of Canterbury.

After a curacy in Yorkshire, Farrer returned to Oxford as chaplain and tutor at St. Edmund Hall from 1931 to 1935, followed by a long and productive period as chaplain and fellow of Trinity College from 1935 to 1960. Unlike Lewis, Farrer never became a university professor. He declined the Nolloth Chair in the Philosophy of the Christian Religion and was passed over for the Regius Canon Professorship of Divinity. Farrer culminated his career not as a professor but as warden of Keble College from 1960 until his death in 1968—like Lewis, at the comparatively early age of sixty-four. Earlier that year, also like Lewis, Farrer was made a fellow of the British Academy.

In *The History of the University of Oxford*, F. M. Turner says, "More than any figure of his generation in the University, Farrer embodied the highest ideal of the college chaplain-theologian."[5] That is, he exemplified the traditional Anglican model of combining both pastoral and academic work in a university setting—a model that is now almost extinct. In addition to several posthumous collections of essays and sermons, Farrer published fifteen books of philosophy, biblical studies, doctrinal theology, and sermons. Archbishop Rowan Williams has recently said that Farrer was "possibly the greatest Anglican mind of the 20th century," and many others would agree.[6] Indeed, the American philosopher Diogenes Allen, who studied with Farrer in the 1960s, once remarked that Oxford had only produced one great theologian since John Henry Newman—and that was Austin Farrer.[7]

Farrer's book *The Glass of Vision* consists of eight chapters delivered in the University Church of St. Mary the Virgin as the Bampton Lectures in 1948, and they had an immense impact on those who listened to them. One of those present was a young philosophy tutor at Keble named Basil Mitchell. In a spiritual autobiography, Mitchell wrote:

5. F. M. Turner, "Religion," in *The History of the University of Oxford*, vol. 8, *The Twentieth Century*, ed. Brian Harrison (Oxford: Clarendon, 1994), 309.
6. Rowan Williams, "Debate on *The Gift of Authority*: Archbishop of Canterbury's Remarks," February 13, 2004, https://tinyurl.com/bdf8kzka.
7. Cited by Eric Springsted in his introduction to *Spirituality and Theology: Essays in Honor of Diogenes Allen*, ed. Eric O. Springsted (Louisville: Westminster John Knox, 1998), 3.

If there was a moment in my new life at Oxford at which I experienced a conversion, or rather realized that a conversion had occurred, it was while listening to Austin Farrer's Bampton Lectures, given in St. Mary's Church for the Michaelmas term 1948 and published under the title *The Glass of Vision*. The restrained delivery, the precision of utterance, the controlled imagination, together with the capacity, without apparent alteration of pace or emphasis, to raise the discourse to the most intense level of religious contemplation without loss of philosophical substance, were unlike anything I have ever experienced before or since.[8]

Since most of Farrer's work is out of print, without being too self-serving and self-referential, may I recommend that those wishing to explore his legacy start with the anthology I coedited with Professor Ann Loades, *The Truth-Seeking Heart: Austin Farrer and His Writings*. This is the first comprehensive anthology that tries to provide a rounded introduction to the many sides of his work, with sections on Scripture, tradition, and reason.[9]

Given that Lewis and Farrer studied and worked in different colleges, and taught in different faculties, it is unclear exactly how and when they met. Lewis became a Christian in 1931, the same year Farrer returned to Oxford as chaplain of St. Edmund Hall, but it is rather unlikely that they met immediately at that point, or even anytime soon thereafter. But they were certainly friends and colleagues ten years later, as they were both involved with Oxford's Socratic Club, founded in 1941 for what F. M. Turner called "lively interchange between committed Christians and their philosophical detractors."[10] Whenever

8. Basil Mitchell, "War and Friendship," in *Philosophers Who Believe: The Spiritual Journeys of 11 Leading Thinkers*, ed. Kelly James Clark (Downers Grove, IL: InterVarsity Press, 1993), 38–39. See Austin Farrer, *The Glass of Vision* (Westminster, UK: Dacre, 1948), now available in a critical edition: Robert MacSwain, ed., *Scripture, Metaphysics, and Poetry: Austin Farrer's The Glass of Vision with Critical Commentary* (London: Routledge, 2016). Mitchell says that the lectures were given in the Michaelmas Term 1948, but both Farrer's preface and correspondence with his father indicate that they were rather delivered earlier that calendar year during the Hilary Term.

9. Ann Loades and Robert MacSwain, eds., *The Truth-Seeking Heart: Austin Farrer and His Writings* (Norwich, UK: Canterbury, 2006).

10. Turner, "Religion," 311. Walter Hooper suggests plausibly that Lewis and Farrer became friends through the Socratic Club. See his biographical sketch of Farrer in *C. S. Lewis: Collected*

and however they met, Lewis and Farrer eventually became good friends, and J. I. Packer even describes Farrer as Lewis's "closest clerical friend."[11] Walter Hooper surmises that Farrer may have been the anonymous Anglican theologian mentioned in the introduction to *Mere Christianity*, and he gives Farrer the last word in the biographical section of his *C. S. Lewis: A Complete Guide to His Life and Works*.[12]

The Farrers were one of the very few couples in Oxford to embrace both Lewis and his new wife, Joy Davidman, as mutual friends, and so Lewis dedicated *Reflections on the Psalms* to both Austin and Kay. Austin was one of the witnesses at Lewis and Joy's first, rather unconventional civil marriage; he gave Joy the sacrament of reconciliation on her deathbed and she asked him to take her own funeral service, which he then did; he gave Lewis the last sacraments while in hospital, and read the lesson at Lewis's burial as well.[13] I have read that Farrer was Lewis's confessor, but by its very nature that relationship is private, and so I'm not sure how certain that information is.[14] After Lewis's death, Farrer preached the sermon at the memorial service for him in Oxford, in the Chapel of Magdalen College, on December 7, 1963. He also contributed an essay titled "The Christian Apologist" to the very first posthumous volume published on Lewis, *Light on C. S. Lewis*.

Letters, vol. 3, *Narnia, Cambridge, and Joy, 1950–1963*, ed. Walter Hooper (London: Harper-Collins, 2006), 1662–65, especially 1663.

11. J. I. Packer, "Still Surprised by Lewis," *Christianity Today* 47 (September 7, 1998), https://tinyurl.com/48xdeakm.

12. See Walter Hooper, *C. S. Lewis: A Complete Guide to His Life and Works* (San Francisco: HarperSanFrancisco, 1996), 119–20 and 307.

13. See Roger Lancelyn Green and Walter Hooper, *C. S. Lewis: A Biography* (London: Collins, 1974); Hooper's *C. S. Lewis: A Complete Guide to His Life and Works* (cited above); George Sayer, *Jack: A Life of C. S. Lewis* (London: Hodder & Stoughton, 2005; original 1988); and William Griffin, *Clive Staples Lewis: A Dramatic Life* (San Francisco: Harper & Row, 1986).

14. For the claim that Farrer was Lewis's confessor, see both Rowan A. Greer's foreword to *Captured by the Crucified: The Practical Theology of Austin Farrer*, ed. David Hein and Edward Hugh Henderson (New York: T&T Clark International, 2004), and the editors' introduction, 4. I must take this opportunity to correct an error for which I alone am responsible in the editors' introduction to *The Truth-Seeking Heart*. On page xiv it says that Farrer performed "the funeral services for both Joy and 'Jack.'" However, as Michael Ward pointed out in conversation, while Farrer indeed performed Joy's service, he simply read a lesson at Lewis's, which was taken by Lewis's parish priest, the vicar of Holy Trinity Headington, Ronald Head.

CHAPTER 4

II. Lewis on Farrer

Lewis wrote the preface for the American edition of the only collection of Farrer's sermons published in Farrer's lifetime. The British title is *Said or Sung: An Arrangement of Homily and Verse*.[15] The title is drawn from a familiar rubric in the Book of Common Prayer, and the subtitle refers to the eight short poems included with the sermons. The American version not only changes the main title of this collection from the nicely literary and evocative *Said or Sung* to the rather more pedestrian *A Faith of Our Own*, it also (sadly) eliminates the poems, dispenses with the subtitle, and retitles many of the sermons. However, perhaps the most important difference between these two editions was that Lewis wrote a preface for the American version. He begins by saying:

> Books like this are rather rare. We have plenty of religious literature: books
> of devotion, controversies, apologetics, Christian reflections on "the present
> situation," Drives, Recalls, Appeals, and New Approaches. But except on a
> far lower level, both literary and theological, than Dr. Farrer's, the unabash-
> edly homiletic—undisguised instruction and exhortation—is not common.
> Dr. Farrer offers it. He comes before us in this book not as a missioner, nor
> as a journalist, nor as a philosopher, but simply as a priest.[16]

As Lewis was known to be, on occasion, severely critical of the clergy of the Church of England, this is not necessarily a compliment! However, Lewis clarifies what he means when he adds that Farrer "writes everywhere as one who both has authority and is under authority. This is what constitutes his priestliness, and this dictates everything else in the book."[17]

Lewis sees Farrer's priestliness as evident first of all in his writing style, which he greatly admires, not only for its good taste, but also because of its restraint and reticence: "Because he writes with authority, he has no need to shout." But, Lewis then adds, "equally, because he speaks under authority, he must practice many

---

15. Austin Farrer, *Said or Sung: An Arrangement of Homily and Verse* (London: Faith Press, 1960).

16. C. S. Lewis, preface to Austin Farrer, *A Faith of Our Own* (Cleveland: World Publishing, 1960), 7.

17. Lewis, preface to Farrer, *A Faith of Our Own*, 8.

abstinences: no exaggerations, however effective, no half-truths, however stimulating." In other words, Farrer speaks and writes not on his own behalf, but as commissioned by his office, and that both constrains and empowers his words.

But in many ways, Lewis's highest praise and most interesting comments are reserved not for Farrer's prose but for the way Farrer explains difficulties in Christian doctrine. He says that Farrer's "severe self-discipline is nowhere more apparent than in the simplicity with which he writes." Referring to several sermons in particular, Lewis says that "they lead us through a structure of thoughts so delicately balanced that a false word, even a false tone, might land us in disaster. Opposite errors threaten from both sides, so that the author has to tread a path as narrow as a hair." He continues, "Yet I believe the simple reader will be perfectly capable of following them and will remain quite unaware of all the shoals and rocks that have been avoided. When the author was really dancing among eggs, he will seem to have been strolling across a lawn."[18] Lewis then adds the following observation, fascinating for the insight it revealed into both Farrer's intellectual character and Lewis's appreciation of it:

> It would indeed be possible—if you didn't know—to read the whole book without ever suspecting that it is written, not only by one of the most learned theologians alive but by the theologian whose critics most often accuse him of excessive subtlety. This does not mean that the simplicity of these essays is spurious. It means it is a final product. None of them began in simplicity. It is a costly distillation. The work is all done and out of sight by the time they reach us.[19]

And this leads Lewis to his final paragraph, which I will quote in full:

> Perhaps, after all, it is not so difficult to explain why books like this are rare. For one thing, the work involved is very severe; not the work on this or that essay but the life-long work without which they could not even have been begun. For another, they demand something like a total conquest of those egoisms which—however we try to mince the matter—play so large a part

18. Lewis, preface to Farrer, *A Faith of Our Own*, 8.
19. Lewis, preface to Farrer, *A Faith of Our Own*, 9–10. Although note that these pieces are technically sermons rather than essays.

in most impulses to authorship. To talk to us thus Dr. Farrer makes himself almost nothing, almost nobody. To be sure, in the event, his personality stands out from the pages as clearly as that of any author; but this is one of heaven's jokes—nothing makes a man so noticeable as vanishing.[20]

That is a remarkably interesting paragraph. Aside from telling us something about Austin Farrer, it tells us something about C. S. Lewis, and what Lewis valued most highly about the intellectual discipline required for any kind of writing, but perhaps most of all for writing philosophy and theology. The "work involved is very severe." There is an ascetic character to good writing and thinking, as they require not only a mental discipline but a moral discipline as well—in Lewis's phrase, the "conquest of those egoisms which . . . play so large a part in most impulses to authorship."

III. Farrer on Lewis

We only have one published text from Lewis on Farrer, but we have two texts from Farrer on Lewis, both written after Lewis's death. As it happens, they are two entirely different genres, the first being a sermon commemorating Lewis's life and work, the second being a more academic analysis of Lewis as a Christian apologist. I'll begin with the sermon.

A. "In His Image: In Commemoration of C. S. Lewis"

Originally published in a posthumous collection of Farrer's sermons titled *The Brink of Mystery* in 1976, this sermon was later reprinted in James Como's *C. S. Lewis at the Breakfast Table*.[21] It was delivered on the seventh of December 1963 in the Chapel of Magdalen College. Lewis's burial service at the Parish of Holy

---

20. Lewis, preface to Farrer, *A Faith of Our Own*, 10.

21. I will cite from *The Brink of Mystery*, but see also James T. Como, *C. S. Lewis at the Breakfast Table* (San Diego: Harcourt Brace Jovanovich, 1992), 242–44. In its third edition, this book has now been retitled *Remembering C. S. Lewis: Recollections of Those Who Knew Him* (San Francisco: Ignatius, 2005), and Farrer's sermon may be found on 383–86.

Trinity, Headington, on the twenty-sixth of November was only attended by a small number of people, close friends such as J. R. R. Tolkien, Owen Barfield, George Sayer, Gervase Mathew, and Lewis's stepson Douglas Gresham. Farrer, as I said earlier, read a lesson. The Magdalen service the following month was a public event for the university, and Farrer was asked to preach.

After an opening paragraph in which he reflects on the general point that "we glorify the Creator when we mark the glory in his creature," Farrer turns to Lewis himself. Remember that Farrer, although far less well known than Lewis, is still widely recognized as a genuine genius—"perhaps the greatest Anglican mind of the 20th century"—and in Lewis's own estimation was one of the most learned theologians of his day. And yet, when considering Lewis's mind, Farrer the genius was moved to write:

> Every human mind is a marvel, for is it not a focus into which the world is drawn? Yet minds differ vastly in force or range, and spirits in life or feeling: and the first thing I am moved to say about the man we commemorate is that he had more actuality of soul than the common breed of man. He took in more, he felt more, he remembered more, he invented more. The reflections on his early life right up to manhood, which he has left us in his writings, record an intense awareness, a vigorous reaction, a taking of the world into his heart, which must amaze those whose years have offered them a processional frieze in several tints of grey. His blacks and whites of good and evil, his ecstasies and miseries were the tokens of a capacity for experience beyond our scope. And yet he was far from the aesthetic type as commonly conceived—this burly man was no overstrained neurotic, whatever he was.[22]

Farrer then reports that someone wrote to him soon after Lewis's death and suggested that Lewis was a "split-personality, because the imaginative and the rationalistic held so curious a balance in his mind."[23] Admitting that Lewis himself recounts his fierce struggle to keep reason and imagination in harness, Farrer nonetheless replies: "I will not call a split personality one brave enough

---

22. Austin Farrer, "In His Image: In Commemoration of C. S. Lewis," in Austin Farrer, *The Brink of Mystery*, ed. Charles C. Conti (London: SPCK, 1976), 45.

23. Farrer, "In His Image," 45. In reading through the Farrer Papers in the Bodleian, I discovered that this correspondent was Farrer's friend the poet Martyn Skinner (1906–1993).

both to think and to feel, nor will I call it integrity that is achieved by halving human nature.... No doubt many intellectuals keep a life of feeling somewhere apart, where it will not infect the aseptic purity of their thoughts. If it is a crime to think about all you strongly feel, and feel the realities about which you think, then the crime was certainly his."[24] And this leads to the following paragraph, which I will again quote in full, for the light it sheds both on Lewis and on what Farrer valued so much in him. Farrer writes:

> It was this feeling intellect, this intellectual imagination which made the strength of his religious writings. Some of those unsympathetic to his convictions saw him as an advocate who bluffed a public eager to be deceived, by the presentation of uncertain arguments as cogent demonstrations. Certainly he was a debater, and thought it fair to make the most of the case: and there were those who were reassured by seeing that the case could be made. But his real power was not proof, it was depiction. There lived in his writings a Christian universe which could be both thought and felt, in which he was at home, and in which he made his reader at home. Moral issues were presented with sharp lucidity, and related to the divine will; and once so seen, could never again be seen otherwise. We who believe will ask no more. Belief is natural, for the world is so. It is enough to let it be seen so.[25]

Farrer continues the sermon with some appreciative comments about Lewis's great generosity, with both his time and his money—"I will not say," says Farrer, "what I know about his charities," which comes pretty close to saying what he knows about his charities—and concludes with some thoughts about Lewis as a friend, Lewis as a scholar, Lewis's grief at the loss of his wife but his peace regarding his own approaching death. But rather than survey those passages, I want to move on now to what is probably Farrer's best-known commentary on Lewis's legacy, his chapter "The Christian Apologist" in the very first collection of posthumous essays on Lewis. And in this chapter Farrer picks up the same thread of thought he developed in the paragraph I just read, namely, the way in which Lewis's religious writings draw their power not from a purely philo-

24. Farrer, "In His Image," 45–46.
25. Farrer, "In His Image," 46.

sophical or rationalistic or argumentative skill, but from joining intellect and imagination into a "feeling intellect," an "intellectual imagination."

B. "The Christian Apologist"

Farrer begins by defining an apologist as a "writer who answers an attack," as one engaged in the battle of "book answering book."[26] Apologetics is thus to be distinguished from both systematic theology and pure philosophy. In some ways it may indeed be a lesser discipline than those two, but it is still a necessary enterprise. In words that should be inscribed upon the heart of every priest, preacher, Christian teacher, theologian, and philosopher, Farrer writes:

> It is commonly said that if rational argument is so seldom the cause of con-
> viction, philosophical apologists must largely be wasting their shot. The
> premise is true, but the conclusion does not follow. For though argument
> does not create conviction, the lack of it destroys belief. What seems to be
> proved may not be embraced; but what no one shows the ability to defend
> is quickly abandoned. Rational argument does not create belief, but it main-
> tains a climate in which belief may flourish.[27]

Those five sentences are a perfect example of what Lewis said regarding Farrer's priestly authority: "Because he writes with authority, he has no need to shout." But in those five concise, even terse sentences, Farrer has actually thrown a hand grenade into the contemporary Christian neglect or fear of reason, a fear that has crippled us in so many ways, particularly in contemporary theology. Argument, he grants, may not *create* conviction—but the *lack* of it destroys belief.

Lewis, however, did not shrink from the necessary apologetic challenge of seeking to provide the arguments that allow faith to flourish, and Farrer tells us that Lewis "was an apologist from temper, from conviction, and from modesty. From temper, for he loved an argument. From conviction, being traditionally orthodox. From modesty, because he laid no claim either to the learning which

---

26. Austin Farrer, "The Christian Apologist," in *Light on C. S. Lewis*, ed. Jocelyn Gibb (London: Geoffrey Bles, 1965), 23.
27. Farrer, "The Christian Apologist," 26.

would have made him a theologian or to the grace which would have made him a spiritual guide." Note that Farrer does not deny that Lewis was in fact a spiritual guide for many, and a gifted lay theologian as well, but simply that Lewis did not claim such titles for himself. Farrer went on to say that Lewis's apologetic gifts were not limited to the purely—or merely—rational, for he also had the capacity to evoke imaginatively the realities he was seeking to defend. Lewis's apologetics were "many-sided." That is, he had both a "feeling intellect" and an "intellectual imagination."

Thus, in a well-known account of Lewis's performance in the Socratic Club, Farrer wrote:

> So far as the argumentative business went, he was a bonny fighter. His writing gave the same impression as his appearances in public debate. I was occasionally called upon to stop a gap in the earlier programmes of Lewis's Socratic Club. Lewis was president, but he was not bound to show up. I went in fear and trembling, certain to be caught out in debate and to let down the side. But there Lewis would be, snuffing the imminent battle and saying "Aha!" at the sound of the trumpet.[28] My anxieties rolled away. Whatever ineptitudes I might commit, he would maintain the cause; and nobody could put Lewis down.[29]

But Lewis's apologetic effectiveness, according to Farrer, was due at least as much—if not more—to his powers of description than to his powers of persuasion. Or rather, Lewis described *to* persuade, depicting a Christian world that his readers or listeners were invited to step in and explore for themselves. And, having once stepped in, they often found they could not so easily step out and return to the world as they once knew it. As Farrer said in his commemoration sermon, Lewis's "real power was not proof, it was depiction," and the world "once so seen, could never again be seen otherwise." Similarly, in his chapter on Lewis as an apologist, Farrer writes: "You cannot read Lewis and tell yourself that Christianity has no important moral bearings, that it gives no coherence to the whole picture of existence, that it offers no criteria for the decision of

28. A humorous allusion to Job 39:19–25, with Farrer comparing Lewis to a (literal!) warhorse.
29. Farrer, "The Christian Apologist," 25–26.

human choices, that it is no source of strength or delight, no effective object of loyalty."[30] And, at its best, Farrer believes that Lewis's writing can open up the possibility of a genuine religious experience. In such transcendent passages, Farrer says, "We think we are listening to an argument, in fact we are presented with a vision; and it is the vision that carries conviction."[31]

That sentence has been quoted to suggest that Farrer was gently criticizing Lewis's rational arguments as being insufficient to carry the weight of their conclusions, and thus claiming that imagination was being smuggled in to shore up a tottering foundation.[32] But in context it is clear that this is not Farrer's intent at all. He is saying that in such passages Lewis rises *above* the purely rational, not that he falls beneath it. It is not a criticism but a compliment. Note also that nowhere in this essay on Lewis's apologetics does Farrer refer to the famous Lewis-Anscombe debate and suggest that somehow as a result of this encounter Lewis himself lost confidence in his apologetic work and withdrew from the arena.

But Farrer does have some criticisms of Lewis's apologetics, and it would be misleading not to mention them. Farrer points out that the academic discipline of philosophy is "an ever-shifting, never-ending public discussion, and that a man who drops out of the game drops out of philosophy."[33] And this is precisely what happened to Lewis once he began to focus professionally on literature. As Farrer says, "Philosophy was not Lewis's trade and he had many other irons in the fire." Consequently, according to Farrer writing in 1965, Lewis "was never quite at home in what we may call our post-positivist era: his philosophical commendations of theism cannot usefully be recommended to puzzled undergraduate philosophers of the present day. His literary, his moral, and his spiritual development was continuous; his philosophical experience belonged to the time of his conversion."[34] And so, if Farrer thought Lewis's apologetic works were not useful among philosophical undergraduates in 1965, what would he think about their use to philosophical undergraduates today? We can discuss the justice of Farrer's claims in a moment if you wish—I think his

---

30. Farrer, "The Christian Apologist," 27.

31. Farrer, "The Christian Apologist," 37.

32. See, for example, Humphrey Carpenter, *The Inklings: C. S. Lewis, J. R. R. Tolkien, Charles Williams, and Their Friends* (London: HarperCollins, 1978), 221.

33. Farrer, "The Christian Apologist," 31.

34. Farrer, "The Christian Apologist," 30–31.

inferences here are rather debatable. The important thing to say immediately, however, is that in fact Farrer does *not* think that Lewis's alleged lack of contemporary philosophical *nous* necessarily counts against his effectiveness as an apologist—*except as* an apologist to philosophers. So, Farrer says, "It does not follow that a Christian apologist who drops out of professional philosophy is left with nothing to say."[35]

No, Farrer's real criticism of Lewis's apologetics is twofold. One is that he believes Lewis is overly moralistic in his understanding of the ways of divine providence with human nature. According to Farrer, Lewis's background in idealist philosophy led him to think of humans too narrowly as "moral wills" detached from what Farrer calls "the full involvement of the reasonable soul in a random and perishable system"—that is, the physical universe.[36] So when it comes to explaining the problem of pain, for example, Farrer is more willing than Lewis to say that some pains at least—even life- and self-destroying ones—have no *specific* purpose in God's plan other than being the necessary concomitants of our existing as rational animals in a physical universe. God may indeed draw good out of our sufferings, but on an individual basis our particular sufferings are not necessarily part of some detailed divine pedagogy. And that is what Farrer took Lewis to be claiming.[37]

Second, despite all of what I said above regarding Farrer's deep appreciation for Lewis's "feeling intellect" and "intellectual imagination," despite Farrer's defense of Lewis against those who thought he had a split personality with reason at war with fantasy, even Farrer felt that sometimes the two components of Lewis's mind came into conflict with each other. And this is precisely what has occurred, Farrer fears, in Lewis's determination to retain a realistic understanding of a prehuman Fall of the cosmos in the face of evolutionary theory, and in particular his speculations about possible animal immortality. Here, Farrer says, "Imagination has slipped the leash of reason—even if it is a traditionalist imagination."[38] Farrer, by contrast, despite his own basic Christian orthodoxy, was

35. Farrer, "The Christian Apologist," 31.

36. Farrer, "The Christian Apologist," 41.

37. For more on this, see Ann Loades, "C. S. Lewis: Grief Observed, Rationality Abandoned, Faith Regained," *Literature and Theology* 3 (1989): 107–21. This essay was recently reprinted in Ann Loades, *Explorations in Twentieth-Century Theology and Philosophy: People Preoccupied with God*, ed. Stephen Burns (Melbourne: Anthem, 2023), 75–87.

38. Farrer, "The Christian Apologist," 42.

far more willing than Lewis to rethink some features of Christian doctrine in light of what science and philosophy seem to be telling us about the universe.

For example, unlike Lewis, Farrer was inclined not to think of our world as somehow deeply twisted and fallen away from God's plan for it. Rather, the world as it now is—death and disease and carnivorous creatures included—is the world God intended. Likewise, Farrer was inclined not to accept the existence of a literal devil, a fallen angel responsible for much of the evil and suffering in the world, because he believed it was an unnecessary hypothesis. In regard to creation, Farrer thought that God started with atoms and worked upward, rather than starting with archangels and working downward. In regard to such aspects of Lewis's apologetic, where he felt Lewis was trying to use either reason or imagination to defend the impossible, Farrer wrote: "What a pity it is that by such superfluous unrealities he should furnish the public with excuses to evade the overwhelming realism of his moral theology!"[39]

IV. Conclusion

Much more could be said about C. S. Lewis's and Austin Farrer's respective strategies in apologetics, their views of reason, their theodicies, their doctrinal beliefs, their churchmanship, and so on. For example, in 1944, Lewis published a short essay titled "Myth Became Fact," and the very next year Farrer delivered a paper to the Socratic Club titled "Can Myth Be Fact?"[40] Aside from the perhaps telling transition from indicative to interrogative, comparing and contrasting these two essays would be an interesting exercise. And there are perhaps other points of interaction and influence as well.[41]

39. Farrer, "The Christian Apologist," 42. For Farrer's own theodicy, which picks up many of these themes at greater length, see *Love Almighty and Ills Unlimited* (New York: Doubleday, 1961; London: Collins, 1962).

40. Lewis's essay was republished in C. S. Lewis, *God in the Dock: Essays on Theology and Ethics*, ed. Walter Hooper (Grand Rapids: Eerdmans, 1971), 39–43, and Farrer's in Austin Farrer, *Interpretation and Belief*, ed. Charles Conti (London: SPCK, 1976), 165–75.

41. Since this essay was published, two other comparative studies of Lewis and Farrer have appeared: Judith Wolfe, "Austin Farrer and C. S. Lewis," in *Austin Farrer: Oxford Warden, Scholar, Preacher*, ed. Markus Bockmuehl, Stephen Platten, and Nevsky Everett (London: SCM, 2020), 70–85, and Philip Irving Mitchell, *The Shared Witness of C. S. Lewis and Austin*

I want to conclude this essay, however, by suggesting that the importance of Lewis and Farrer's friendship with one another was probably less about "influence" in some sort of direct and quantifiable and documentable way—that is, Lewis got idea X from Farrer and Farrer got idea Y from Lewis—although such exchange of intellectual DNA probably occurred. Rather, I think, the mutual importance of this friendship had more to do with *encouragement*. By being faithful to the immense gifts and responsibilities they had both been given, Lewis and Farrer each encouraged the other to best fulfill their respective callings as the Imaginative Debater and the Philosophical Priest. I have titled this paper "a fertile friendship," but friendship does not need to be utilitarian and instrumental to be "fertile." Rather, it can be so by more fully bringing out—and so helping to create and form—the character of the friend. It's not that either Lewis or Farrer somehow dominated the other, and made over the other in his image. No, Lewis was more Lewisian and Farrer was more Farrerian as a result of their friendship, and so more fully the person that God created them to be. The image they brought out in the other was the image of Christ.

I would like to close with a passage from one of Austin Farrer's sermons, titled "Responsibility for Our Friends," preached in Keble College Chapel in 1967. The date explains his noninclusive language, which I will not revise in quotation. At one point in this sermon, Farrer tells us that paying attention to the needs of our friends should get our focus off of ourselves and should remind us that "our concern is not with our own holiness, but with other men's happiness, health, or well-being." He then returns to this theme at the very end, connecting such simple acts of thoughtful, other-regarding friendship with the very being of God. Farrer says:

> These are very plain lessons. But they are the foundation of great virtues. What is the greatest height we Christians think to climb? Can we climb higher than the blessed Trinity, to find our place in that movement of mutual devotion which is the pulse of being, and the life of God? And the school of divine love is common charity. He that loves not the brother he has seen, how shall he love the God whom he has not seen?

Farrer: Friendship, Influence, and an Anglican Worldview (Kent, OH: Kent State University Press, 2021). Both of them consider the topic of myth in more detail.

But now I am sorry I said that we have to climb, for love has come down to us, the heart of heaven is here: and it is with the impulse of the Holy Ghost, and by the leading of the Eternal Son, that we give the Father of our lives our hearts.[42]

---

42. Farrer, *The Brink of Mystery*, 60. As noted in the introduction, I was invited to address the C. S. Lewis Society of Oxford University in 2008 due to my involvement in a volume subsequently published as Robert MacSwain and Michael Ward, eds., *The Cambridge Companion to C. S. Lewis*, Cambridge Companions to Religion (Cambridge: Cambridge University Press, 2010). I am grateful to Michael for collaborating with me on this volume and to Judith Wolfe for the invitation.

CHAPTER 5

Imperfect Lives and Perfect Love: Austin Farrer, Stanley Hauerwas, and the Reach of Divine Redemption

As Brian Hebblethwaite observes in his contribution to her Festschrift, over several decades Ann Loades established herself as one of the leading scholars associated with the legacy of Austin Farrer (1904–1968).[1] In a number of books and articles, Ann expresses her deep appreciation for Farrer's creative fusion of philosophy, theology, biblical interpretation, and sacramental spirituality as held within the matrix of a firm commitment to Anglican Christianity. Typically, however, appreciation does not blunt her critical edge.

This became abundantly clear to me in 2004 at the Farrer centenary conference in Baton Rouge, Louisiana. During this conference, Ann summarized Farrer's life and work for an audience of respectful Americans. In the midst of a primarily positive assessment, she paused to consider the

1. See Brian Hebblethwaite, "Ann Loades and Austin Farrer," in *Exchanges of Grace: Essays in Honour of Ann Loades*, ed. Natalie K. Watson and Stephen Burns (London: SCM, 2008), 130–41. Hebblethwaite begins by listing Ann's participation in a series of international Farrer conferences and various related publications, including coediting *For God and Clarity: New Essays in Honor of Austin Farrer* with Jeffrey C. Eaton (Allison Park, PA: Pickwick, 1983), authoring "Austin Farrer on *Love Almighty*" in that volume, 93–109, and also "The Vitality of Tradition: Austin Farrer and Friends," in *Captured by the Crucified: The Practical Theology of Austin Farrer*, ed. David Hein and Edward Hugh Henderson (London: T&T Clark International, 2004), 15–46. These two essays were recently reprinted in Ann Loades, *Explorations in Twentieth-Century Theology and Philosophy: People Preoccupied with God*, ed. Stephen Burns (Melbourne: Anthem, 2023). And one could also add Ann's entry on Farrer in *The SPCK Handbook of Anglican Theologians*, ed. Alister McGrath (London: SPCK, 1998), 120–23.

Originally published in *Exchanges of Grace: Essays in Honour of Ann Loades*, ed. Natalie K. Watson and Stephen Burns (London: SCM, 2008), 142–54.

brief appendix—"Imperfect Lives"—to his book on the problem of evil, *Love Almighty and Ills Unlimited.*[2] Here, Farrer engages in some pessimistic speculation regarding God's capacity to "immortalise" those whose mental faculties are below what some might consider "human": namely, infants and the mentally handicapped. Speaking of an infant who dies soon after birth, Farrer writes, "The baby smiled before it died. Will God bestow immortality on a smile?" Ann quoted this passage, then suddenly looked up from her notes, glared at us defiantly, and asked, "Well, why the hell not?"

I take this anecdote as my point of departure for two reasons. First, it's "pure Ann" and nicely captures her distinctive combination of intellectual energy, vigorous engagement, keen compassion, and moral sensitivity. Ann may deeply appreciate Austin Farrer, but she does not defer to him—or anyone—uncritically. Second, and more significantly, Farrer does indeed seem to have thought himself into a corner in this appendix, and in the remainder of this essay I'd like to see if he can be helped out of it. I thus offer this essay to celebrate Ann's own engagement with Farrer, express some of what I have learned from her, and acknowledge her concern about "Imperfect Lives." To this end, I will also look to another theologian mentioned by Hebblethwaite in connection with Ann's work, who also contributed a chapter to her Festschrift, namely, Stanley Hauerwas.[3] In short, Hauerwas's arguments about the place of the mentally handicapped in the life of the church challenge the intellectualism expressed in "Imperfect Lives," and in so doing point us back to another, more helpful element in Farrer's own theology: that is, his belief that our salvation is "bodily." Accentuating this aspect of Farrer's thought allows us to include the deaths of infants and the mentally handicapped within the reach of divine grace. Imperfect lives, including our own, may still be redeemed by perfect love.

---

2. Austin Farrer, *Love Almighty and Ills Unlimited* (London: Collins, 1962). "Imperfect Lives" covers pages 189–91.

3. See Stanley Hauerwas and Samuel Wells, "An Apostle with Reservations: On Judas and the Vocation of Christian Ethics," in Watson and Burns, *Exchanges of Grace*, 35–45.

I. "Imperfect Lives"

Ann is not the only Farrer scholar worried by this appendix. Brian Hebblethwaite says that "one could imagine Farrer's arguments being called upon to justify not only abortion but also infanticide," although he adds (rightly) that "Farrer himself certainly would not have approved of that."[4] And Robert Boak Slocum complains that Farrer's conclusions here are "strikingly disappointing and inconsistent with his other positions."[5] But what exactly does Farrer say?

He begins the appendix with the observation that one of the "commonly reckoned evils of human life is the death of speechless infants, before they reach the stature of humanity; another is the survival of imbeciles, who are incapable of ever reaching it."[6] These are obviously controversial and disturbing claims about such individuals, and they will be considered extensively below.[7] But,

4. Brian Hebblethwaite, "God and the World as Known to Science," in *The Human Person in God's World: Studies to Commemorate the Austin Farrer Centenary*, ed. Douglas Hedley and Brian Hebblethwaite (London: SCM, 2006), 72–73. Here Hebblethwaite cites Peter Singer's influential book *Practical Ethics*, 2nd ed. (Cambridge: Cambridge University Press, 1993) as an example of a text that draws precisely the conclusions that Farrer denies.

5. Robert Boak Slocum, *Light in a Burning-Glass: A Systematic Presentation of Austin Farrer's Theology* (Columbia: University of South Carolina Press, 2007), 48. As will be seen further below, I think Slocum is only partially right here: Farrer's position in "Imperfect Lives" is consistent with some aspects of his thought and inconsistent with other aspects of it. In short, his anthropology was not fully integrated with his eschatology.

6. Farrer, *Love Almighty and Ills Unlimited*, 189.

7. Farrer wrote this book in 1961 when the term "imbecile" was still in common usage. The *American Heritage Dictionary* provides the following definition: "A person of moderate to severe mental retardation having a mental age of from three to seven years and generally being capable of some degree of communication and performance of simple tasks under supervision. The term belongs to a classification system no longer in use and is now considered offensive." Even so, it is thus unclear if "imbecile" fits the criteria of "speechlessness" and consequent total lack of reasoning ability Farrer seems to have in mind. Throughout this chapter, I follow Hauerwas in using the still-controversial term "mental handicap" to cover perhaps a wider range of ability and disability than Farrer may intend in this appendix. In addition, as will be discussed further in the course of the chapter, one may question the three assumptions (expressed if not explicitly defended by Farrer) (i) that infants have not yet reached "the stature of humanity," (ii) that even the severely mentally handicapped are incapable of ever attaining such status, and (iii) that the birth and survival of such handicapped individuals are an "evil" (i.e., a misfortune) to be regretted.

having made this observation, Farrer continues that the *theological* problem "specially posed by these disorders is not that they should be permitted to befall our kind, but that we do not know how we should relate to the mercy of God beings who never enjoy a glimmer of reason. Are they capable of eternal salvation, or are they not?"[8]

One can already see the danger lurking in Farrer's restriction of "human" status to those of us capable of speech and reason, but his justification for this is complex and will be considered in a moment. Meanwhile, he immediately moves to block the threat of infanticide or euthanasia: "Out of natural piety, and a respect for the divine image in man, we treat [such individuals] as human. We do not kill our imbeciles; we baptise dying infants and give them Christian burial."[9] So, as Hebblethwaite argues, while Farrer's theory may be disturbing, his practice is sound. Natural piety and respect provide moral guidance where speculative reason is confounded. But this agnosticism, we may feel, is neither a safe nor a satisfactory state of affairs. Thus, we want to determine why Farrer's theory seems to have gotten out of sync with his practice, and to bring the two back into harmony.

Farrer proceeds to make an uncomfortable but defensible point. In regard to such individuals, he says, "We are inclined to think of a rational person walled up, as it were, in their bodies, and bricked in with stupid flesh; he is cruelly treated in being denied light, air, and utterance. This, at least, is a fallacy of sentiment; the rational person is not there."[10] In taking this uncomfortable position, however, Farrer is in complete agreement with much contemporary thinking—even much contemporary Christian thinking—about human nature. If we abandon a Platonic or Cartesian substance dualism that identifies our rational selves with an essentially immaterial, immortal soul, then in what does our rationality, humanity, or personhood subsist? More specifically, how do we think—and with what?[11]

8. Farrer, *Love Almighty and Ills Unlimited*, 189.
9. Farrer, *Love Almighty and Ills Unlimited*, 189.
10. Farrer, *Love Almighty and Ills Unlimited*, 189.
11. These questions are of course hugely controversial and complicated, and cannot be settled here. While currently on the defensive, substance dualism is still a viable position in both philosophy and theology, and it would be a mistake to simply assume its falsity or defeat. For a brief discussion within the context of a larger argument, see pages 123–27 of David Brown's *Discipleship and Imagination: Christian Tradition and Truth* (Oxford: Oxford University Press,

Farrer's description of the supposedly rational person "denied utterance" by being "walled up" in "stupid flesh" recalls Wittgenstein probing Augustine's account of his speechless yet supposedly thoughtful infancy, struggling to find the words to express his already developed concepts.[12] Like Wittgenstein, Farrer turns this common story upside down and identifies reason with speech. We do not first think and then learn to talk; rather, we first talk and then learn to think. And we learn to talk by being talked to by others. Thinking is internalized talking. Mentality is not individual and internal but social and cultural. For those with Wittgensteinian sympathies, in making these various claims Farrer is on good, solid ground.[13]

But he then goes on to associate the achievement of speech-reason-mentality with personhood. Earlier in *Love Almighty and Ills Unlimited*, in the chapter "Man Redeemed," he spells this out very clearly: "Man, in being man, is both a body and a beast. . . . But if he is a beast, he is a talking beast, and in his speech lies his reason. Through reason he shares, however faintly, that truth which is the mind of God, and becomes a copy or reflection of the divine likeness: in short, a person."[14] This linkage of reason and personhood is, of course, a very common move in contemporary ethical thought, and I will come back to it in a moment. For now, however, note Farrer's *theological* application of this move: "the rational person offers an opening to God's mercy which humbler creatures do not. . . . Man is not first an immortal soul; he is an animal on whom

---

2000). And, indeed, Farrer's own precise position on the nature of soul and its relation to body cannot be determined simply from *Love Almighty and Ills Unlimited*; rather, a full account would need to take in his major philosophical volumes *Finite and Infinite* (Westminster, UK: Dacre, 1943) and *The Freedom of the Will* (London: A&C Black, 1958), as well as other writings. For the sake of argument and brevity, however, I will in the remainder of this chapter adopt a "Wittgensteinian" reading of Farrer.

12. See Augustine's *Confessions* 1.6–8, and Ludwig Wittgenstein's *Philosophical Investigations*, part 1, paragraphs 1–3, 32, and 206. For a good discussion of Wittgenstein's understanding of Augustine in these passages, see Fergus Kerr, *Theology after Wittgenstein*, 2nd ed. (London: SPCK, 1997), 38–42.

13. Among several other passages expressing this Wittgensteinian view, see Farrer's sermon "Thinking the Trinity," reprinted in *The Truth-Seeking Heart: Austin Farrer and His Writings*, ed. Ann Loades and Robert MacSwain (Norwich, UK: Canterbury, 2006), 157, and *Love Almighty and Ills Unlimited*, 114.

14. Farrer, *Love Almighty and Ills Unlimited*, 106–7. Hereafter, page references from this work will be given in parentheses in the text.

the capacity for everlasting life has been conferred. For he has been enabled to talk, and in acquiring speech has acquired the rudiments of reason" (107). Thus, Farrer identifies reason with speech, links the achievement of speech and reason with the status of personhood and humanity, and further argues that—unlike "humbler creatures"—such rational beings provide a unique "opening to God's mercy." That is, only such speaking, reasoning, human persons have the "capacity for everlasting life."

Returning to "Imperfect Lives," this general argument is then further developed and specifically applied to "speechless infants [and] imbeciles." Farrer asserts that if "there ever was a speaking and loving person, there is a creature for God to immortalize" (190). He then sets up the rhetorical question Ann finds so vexing: "But if the reasoning person never developed, what are we to think? The baby smiled before it died. Will God bestow immortality on a smile?" After this question, Farrer raises the further complication of both natural and medical abortions, the many millions of embryos—indeed, the majority—that fail to survive the womb or even the earliest stages of gestation. Are they bound for an immortal existence? And he makes things even more difficult for himself by stating that, even if we grant "the origin of an immortal soul with the attainment of speech and reason," we may still be driven to ask, "What degree of reason?" Mental handicap comes in various stages. Is there a cutoff point beneath which God does not have sufficient material with which to build an immortal soul? What IQ level is required for heaven? Farrer's conclusion is both bleak and hopeful, granting his assumptions: "We do not know where to draw the line; that is to say, we do not know where God draws it. But we may be sure that he loves and saves whatever there is to be saved or loved; if his love or power does not act, it is because there is nothing for it to act upon. He makes no arbitrary discrimination" (190).

In short, within the broader context of *Love Almighty and Ills Unlimited*, Farrer's argument in "Imperfect Lives" may be expressed as follows:

1. "Man is not first an immortal soul; he is an animal on whom the capacity for everlasting life has been conferred. For he has been enabled to talk, and in acquiring speech has acquired the rudiments of reason" (107).
2. Thus, in failing to acquire both speech and reason, "speechless infants" and "imbeciles" do not "reach the stature of [either] humanity" or personhood (189).
3. We "do not know how we should relate to the mercy of God beings who never

enjoy a glimmer of reason" (189), but if "there ever was a speaking and loving person, there is a creature for God to immortalize" (190).

4. Indeed, God "loves and saves whatever there is to be saved or loved" (190).

5. Therefore, although we "do not know where to draw the line," we know that God "makes no arbitrary discrimination" (190).

The conclusion of the argument—(5)—is thus an expression of agnosticism regarding the eternal fate of those described in (2), rather than a confident dismissal of such individuals from the halls of heaven. Still, given their apparent lack of an immortal soul, the vexing question lingers: "Will God bestow immortality on a smile?"

It is important not to dismiss Farrer's line of reasoning too quickly, but rather to identify where it seems to go wrong. While I cannot speak for Ann, I am happy to consider (1), (4), and (5). But (2) is ethically repugnant in its limitation of the set of "humans" or "persons" to those with speech and reason, and the theological problem is most obvious in (3). Rather than immediately address these various difficulties, however, I now wish to bring "Imperfect Lives" into conversation with the very different thought of Stanley Hauerwas on the place of the mentally handicapped in human society generally and in the church in particular.

II. Stanley Hauerwas, the Mentally Handicapped, and the Church

What makes Hauerwas such an interesting contrast with Farrer here is that they both agree on (1) above. Like Farrer—and at least partly under his influence—Hauerwas accepts a basically post-Wittgensteinian, nondualistic understanding of human nature. Like Farrer, Hauerwas does not assume that infants, the mentally handicapped, or indeed any of us are born with an immortal soul "in addition to" our bodies that essentially qualifies us for "personhood" and automatically destines us for eternal life with God. In fact, Hauerwas's position on the relation between body and soul, on the unity and stability of the "self," is arguably more radical and further removed from conventional dualistic conceptions than Farrer's. But where Hauerwas decisively parts company with Farrer is in the conclusions he draws from their mutual starting point.[15]

15. See "The Sanctified Body: Why Perfection Does Not Require a 'Self,'" in Stanley Hau-

In short, Hauerwas consistently inverts our standard assumptions—assumptions prevalent in both philosophical *and* theological anthropology—that privilege "normal" adult reasoning capacities as the criteria for either humanity or personhood. Indeed, he regards the latter term as a dangerously ambiguous and elusive concept best to be avoided. By contrast, inspired by the work of Jean Vanier and his L'Arche communities, Hauerwas lifts up those described by our contemporary culture as "mentally handicapped" (Farrer's "imbeciles") and argues that both they and those who care for them in fact provide for us an icon of *true humanity*—and, indeed, even an icon of true divinity. While not necessarily to be desired, the birth of a mentally handicapped child is also not an evil to be deplored, but rather a gift to his or her family and to the wider community—a gift to be welcomed, cherished, and benefited from. In other words, Hauerwas offers a radical transposition of values regarding what constitutes both human nature and society and divine nature and society. By dispensing with our normative assumptions about such matters, he clears a space for the mentally handicapped to survive and even flourish, and further invites us to consider the challenging possibility that such a space is actually more "human" and thus more conducive to our own flourishing as well—that is, those of us who are not mentally handicapped.[16]

Professor John Swinton of the University of Aberdeen has collected ten of Hauerwas's most important and influential essays on the mentally handicapped and invited various other scholars and practitioners to critically interact with

---

erwas, *Sanctify Them in the Truth: Holiness Exemplified* (Edinburgh: T&T Clark, 1998), 77–91, especially 78, 86, and 90n15. For the record, Farrer was an important influence on Hauerwas's early thinking on the topics of character, selfhood, and agency: see Stanley Hauerwas, *Character and the Christian Life: A Study in Theological Ethics* (San Antonio, TX: Trinity University Press, 1975), 27n41 and 87n6. Although I will not develop the contrast further in this chapter, it should also be noted that Hauerwas's general approach to the problem of evil is very different from Farrer's in *Love Almighty and Ills Unlimited*, being less abstractly theoretic and more thickly narrative. See Stanley Hauerwas, *Naming the Silences: God, Medicine, and the Problem of Suffering* (Grand Rapids: Eerdmans, 1990).

16. Since this essay was originally published, posthumous revelations of emotional manipulation and sexual abuse by Jean Vanier (1928–2019) have led to intense study and reevaluation of his personal legacy. For example, Hauerwas has coedited with Hans Reinders an essay collection dealing with these difficult and painful questions: *The Betrayal of Witness: Reflections on the Downfall of Jean Vanier* (Eugene, OR: Cascade, 2024).

this body of work. In response to these critics, friendly and otherwise, Hauerwas writes:

> One of the most frustrating aspects of my work, for friend and foe alike, is I have always tried to do theology by indirection. By indirection I mean I have tried to resist the temptation to make theology another set of ideas that can be considered in and of themselves. For example, anyone concerned to discover what "my" doctrine of God might be or what my "theological anthropology" entails will look in vain for any essay or book on those theological topics. But that does not mean I do not think about questions classically associated with the doctrine of God or theological anthropology; I try to write about such issues in relation to material practices that exemplify what is at stake.[17]

Having revealed his method, Hauerwas then says, with admirable if disarming candor:

> My reflections on the challenge the mentally handicapped present to some of our most cherished conceits about ourselves is best understood as my attempt to develop a theological anthropology. In brief, I "use" the mentally handicapped to try to help us understand what it means for us to be creatures of a gracious God. For I think it a profound mistake to assume that a strong distinction can be drawn between those who are mentally handicapped and those who are not mentally handicapped once it is acknowledged that we are equally creatures of a God, who as Augustine observed, created us without us, but who refuses to save us without us.[18]

And Hauerwas rounds out his position by making an additional crucial, liturgical, ecclesial move:

17. Stanley Hauerwas, "Reflection on Dependency: A Response to Responses to My Essays on Disability," in *Critical Reflections on Stanley Hauerwas' Theology of Disability: Disabling Society, Enabling Theology*, ed. John Swinton (Binghamton, NY: Haworth, 2004), 192–93. Subsequent references to Hauerwas's essays will be from this volume, which was also published as *Journal of Religion, Disability, and Health* 8, nos. 3/4 (2004).

18. Hauerwas, "Reflection on Dependency," 193.

The mentally handicapped remind us that the "us" that is saved is the body constituted through Christian baptism that is anything but an individual. If we take seriously practices of the church such as baptism, we are all, mentally handicapped and the non-mentally handicapped, creatures drawn into a kingdom of patience making possible our friendship with God and one another.[19]

Near the end of the response, Hauerwas offers some striking reflections on the human capacity for communication through gesture and body that bears directly on Farrer's emphasis on speech and reason as outlined in section 1 above. He argues that "the language of gesture" can be as cognitive as speech, indeed may even be "the most determinative cognitive claims we can make," given that they "cannot be abstracted from the ones making the claim." Even those who cannot speak may still communicate with their bodies. Such gestures remind us of "the significance of the body whose silence often tells us what we most need to know to be with one another."[20]

Finally, he concludes the essay with a vision of the church that he has articulated and defended over the decades, namely, as a community that includes, values, celebrates, cares for, and lives with the mentally handicapped: "here we see a people who believe that there is nothing more significant to be done in a world of such deep injustice than to take the time to be friends with the handicapped. I know of no better vision of peace."[21] Earlier in the essay, Hauerwas goes so far as to describe the church as "a community that is constituted by our sharing our lives with the mentally handicapped."[22] If this is what truly *constitutes* the church, then one may say that Hauerwas has made such mutual sharing the *bene esse*—or even the *esse*—of the church, rather than other, more familiar candidates (such as bishops!).

---

19. Hauerwas, "Reflection on Dependency," 193. I have presented Hauerwas's position here from a single piece of writing because in this essay he condenses thirty years of groundbreaking thought on the relation between Christian doctrine, the mentally handicapped, and the church. Much could be drawn from these compact statements, but I will instead point interested readers toward the volume as a whole. Despite its regrettably many minor typographical errors, I highly recommend this book for those who wish to further explore Hauerwas's theology on this topic.

20. Hauerwas, "Reflection on Dependency," 197.

21. Hauerwas, "Reflection on Dependency," 197.

22. Hauerwas, "Reflection on Dependency," 195.

III. The Body of Christ

As stated at the conclusion of section 1, rather than deal directly with the problematic elements of Farrer's "Imperfect Lives," I first wished to contrast Farrer's position on the mentally handicapped with that of Stanley Hauerwas. While I must resist the temptation to develop these points in detail, it is clear that they agree on (1) above, and perhaps also (4) and (5), but that they radically disagree on (2) and (3). As for (2), Hauerwas rejects Farrer's linkage of speech and reason with humanity and personhood.[23] Characteristically, Hauerwas reverses the onus of proof and requires the non–mentally handicapped to prove *their* humanity by their treatment of those with such handicaps.[24]

But, readers may object, how can I maintain that Hauerwas rejects (3)—that is, that we "do not know how we should relate to the mercy of God beings who never enjoy a glimmer of reason," but if "there ever was a speaking and loving person, there is a creature for God to immortalize"—when Hauerwas is and has been and remains conspicuously silent on the topic of *eschatology*, whether individual, corporate, or cosmic? That is, does Hauerwas really even address Farrer's *theological* concern in (3), or does he simply deal with the *ethical* issue of (2)? And, while Hauerwas has certainly written extensively about the mentally handicapped, what about Farrer's other problem in "Imperfect Lives," the death of infants?

It is true that Hauerwas has rarely discussed the traditional topics of Christian eschatology—but remember his comments above regarding his method of theological indirection.[25] Through this method, he has spent his career trying

23. See especially Hauerwas's critique of Joseph Fletcher in "The Retarded and the Criteria for the Human," reprinted in Swinton, *Critical Reflections on Stanley Hauerwas' Theology of Disability*, 127–34. Fletcher holds that "any individual who falls below the I. Q. 40 mark in a Stanford-Binet test is 'questionably a person,' and if you score 20 or below you are not a person" (131). Transposed into theology, this exactly parallels Farrer's concern about intellectual capacity and eternal redemption: If such individuals are not persons, then how can they be saved?

24. Hauerwas, "The Retarded and the Criteria," 132.

25. A possible exception to his avoidance of eschatology would be his brief, passing comment in *Naming the Silences* that, in contrast to the heroine of E. B. White's *Charlotte's Web* (1952), a child's fate is not that of a spider (148). Since the original publication of this chapter, Hauerwas has published a volume titled *Approaching the End: Eschatological Reflections on Church, Politics, and Life* (Grand Rapids: Eerdmans, 2013), but even here he is not writing primarily about the traditional topics of eternal salvation or damnation, etc., but rather about

to demolish the distinction between theology and ethics. Thus, I would argue that if his writing on the mentally handicapped is his way of developing a theological anthropology "in relation to material practices that exemplify what is at stake,"[26] then such anthropological conclusions have eschatological implications. Likewise, his ecclesial conclusions have eschatological implications. Hauerwas does not need to tell us explicitly that the mentally handicapped are "going to heaven," because once you see *and practice* his understanding of their central place in the church, the body of Christ, the question answers itself. "The way to solve the problem you see in life is to live in a way that will make what is problematic disappear."[27] If the church, the body of Christ, is *constituted* by the mentally handicapped and those who share life with them in mutual friendship, then to ask whether God is able to "immortalize" the mentally handicapped is nonsense. If the mentally handicapped are, as Hauerwas argues, "a prophetic sign of our true nature as creatures destined to need God and, thus, one another,"[28] then our salvation is inextricably linked with—and perhaps more precarious than—theirs. And if, as Hauerwas says, "we take seriously practices of the church such as baptism, [then] we are all, mentally handicapped and the non–mentally handicapped" (thus including, let us add, mentally handicapped and non–mentally handicapped infants) "creatures drawn into a kingdom of patience making possible our friendship with God and one another."[29]

---

how the corporate and individual Christian life is lived within the transformed "apocalyptic" context created by Christ's life, death, and resurrection. For a brief but lovely contemporary articulation of a Christian eschatology, which pays proper attention to our bodily nature, see the chapter "Love Actually" in Rowan Williams, *Tokens of Trust: An Introduction to Christian Belief* (Norwich, UK: Canterbury, 2007), especially 139–41.

26. Hauerwas, "Reflection on Dependency," 193.

27. Ludwig Wittgenstein, *Culture and Value* (Chicago: University of Chicago Press, 1980), 27e.

28. Stanley Hauerwas, "Suffering the Retarded: Should We Prevent Retardation?" reprinted in Swinton, *Critical Reflections on Stanley Hauerwas' Theology of Disability*, 105.

29. Hauerwas, "Reflection on Dependency," 197. Since the original version of this chapter was published, the question of whether those who are mentally or physically disabled will retain these conditions in the afterlife has become a topic of intense debate. While others have written on this question, the current primary disputants are Amos Yong (who says yes, at least in some cases) and R. T. Mullins (who is far more dubious). For summaries in the midst of further discussion, see Kevin Timpe, "Defiant Afterlife—Disability and Uniting Ourselves to God," in *Voices from the Edge: Centering Marginalized Perspectives in Analytic Theology,*

This mention of baptism reminds us of Hauerwas's strong emphasis on the body and its significance—but it also sends us back to Farrer, albeit to a different text than "Imperfect Lives." Nine years before *Love Almighty and Ills Unlimited*, Farrer published a remarkable essay titled "The Body of Christ."[30] Beginning with a consideration of Christ's presence in the Eucharist, he then discusses

---

ed. Michelle Panchuk and Michael Rea (Oxford: Oxford University Press, 2020), 206–31, esp. 218–20, and John Swinton, "Disability Theology," in *The New Cambridge Companion to Christian Doctrine*, ed. Michael Allen (Cambridge: Cambridge University Press, 2022), 249–66, esp. 261–65. A major point of dispute between Yong and Mullins relates to what is now called "Hauerwas's dictum" in this literature: "To eliminate the disability means to eliminate the subject." This claim may indeed be found in Stanley Hauerwas, "Marginalizing the 'Retarded,'" in *The Deprived, the Disabled, and Fullness of Life*, ed. Flavian Dougherty (Wilmington, DE: Michael Glazier, 1984), 69, which is the reference cited by Yong, Mullins, and others. However, if one looks at the passage, it is important to clarify that in context Hauerwas is speaking specifically of the human medical treatment of those with congenital cognitive disabilities, such as Down syndrome, "rather than cancer, polio, or heart diseases, as these diseases exist independently of the subject. The disease can be eliminated without eliminating the subject of the disease. The same is not true of the person mentally impaired. To eliminate the disability means to eliminate the subject." He is thus not making an absolute necessary claim about all disabilities, nor speaking of divine eschatological redemption. Indeed, God is not even mentioned in this passage. Even more substantially, when Hauerwas republished this essay two years later in his collection *Suffering Presence: Theological Reflections on Medicine, the Mentally Handicapped, and the Church* (Notre Dame: University of Notre Dame Press, 1986), under the new title, "Suffering the Retarded: Should We Prevent Retardation?" 159–81, he revised this passage to make it even more specific, cautious, and contingent. It now reads: "The [physical] disease can be eliminated without eliminating the subject of the disease. But the same is not always true of the retarded. To eliminate retardation may sometimes mean to eliminate the subject" (160). This is also the version of the essay reprinted in Swinton, *Critical Reflections on Stanley Hauerwas' Theology of Disability*, 87–106, and in a slightly abridged form with a slightly different title in *The Hauerwas Reader*, ed. John Berkman and Michael Cartwright (Durham, NC: Duke University Press, 2001), 556–76, but in both of these cases the passage in question still follows the revision in *Suffering Presence* (see 89 and 557, respectively). It thus seems that this later version best represents Hauerwas's position here, rather than "Hauerwas's dictum." And, obviously, "To eliminate retardation may sometimes mean to eliminate the subject" is a very different claim than "To eliminate the disability means to eliminate the subject."

30. Austin Farrer, "The Body of Christ," originally published in *The Crown of the Year: Weekly Paragraphs for the Holy Sacrament* (Westminster, UK: Dacre, 1952), reprinted in Loades and MacSwain, *The Truth-Seeking Heart*, 117–24.

the incorporation of Christians into the body of Christ through baptism. In a deeply lyrical and suggestive passage, he writes:

> Our bodies are to extend the body of Christ, his body is to annexe our bodies to itself—our bodies, not our bare souls. Body is the foundation, we start from body. My thoughts and actions lift themselves out of my body, play around it, alter and pass; my body remains. By virtue of my body I am founded in time and place, through it I am inserted in my environment. Jesus, conceived by the Holy Ghost in the womb of Mary, established in the world a body joined uniquely to the life of God, and our bodies are to be united with his body in one extended body, the mystical Church. Our state of redemption, like our existence, like his incarnate existence, is to begin with the body.[31]

The method by which we become part of this body is also bodily: the links between its members "are not merely mental, Christ will not have them to be so. He will have us all grafted into his body by baptism. Here is a physical fact: each of us has either been baptised, or he has not; the baptismal water has either flowed upon us, or it has not." The Eucharist is likewise physical: "actual bread, actually blessed and consecrated by the one apostolic priesthood. Here is bodily fact once more, a fact constantly repeated, through which Christ renews, actualizes and reveals his mystical body on earth." In short, through baptism and Eucharist, Christ has instituted "a web of bodily relations binding our bodies together."[32]

And this web of bodily relations is not purposeless, but rather exists for our salvation:

> It is the mercy of Christ to begin my salvation with my body. This me, the mere opaque bodily fact, the me which is there before my will, and whether I will or no, and which I can only remove by self-destruction, by the insane pretence to dispose of what is not mine either to create or to destroy . . . ; Christ takes this me, and annexes it to himself by bodily bonds, without

---

31. Farrer, "The Body of Christ," 119.
32. Farrer, "The Body of Christ," 119.

waiting for the sanctification of its acts and uses. He takes it, and presents it as a part of himself that it may be sanctified.[33]

In reading these passages, particularly in the context of Hauerwas's work, one realizes the radically physicalist nature of Farrer's soteriology. True, he immediately follows the preceding quote by adding, "Meanwhile [Christ] acknowledges [my body] for his, his body and blood, *so long as I have faith*, and repent my deadly sins" (emphasis added). But this is the only subjective, mentalistic note in what is an overwhelmingly objective, physicalistic score. Clearly, Christ's choice and action precedes—or "prevents"—ours both onto-logically and chrono-logically. Thus, even our faith is a mere—though literal—afterthought.

In other words, nine years before he wrote "Imperfect Lives," Farrer already had all the pieces in place to solve his own problem. Our redemption is not mental, but bodily. "Speechless infants" and "imbeciles" are as "capable of eternal salvation" as any of us, and for precisely the same reason: not that we have speech and rationality and so are persons, but because we have bodies and so are creatures. Farrer got into a muddle in "Imperfect Lives" because he did not follow through with the full implications of his insights in "The Body of Christ." Or, put differently, in "Imperfect Lives" he reverted to a *structural* dualism, albeit a linguistic dualism rather than a substance dualism, with a linguistic soul rather than a substantial one. Instead of the bodily nature of salvation so beautifully described in "The Body of Christ," it again becomes a matter of rational ability. Even in "Imperfect Lives," however, Farrer remembers Catholic practice: "We do not kill our imbeciles; we baptise dying infants and give them Christian burial."[34] But rather than bring his theory back in line with his practices, he wonders why the practices don't seem to make sense—and so inadvertently opens the door for the practices to be abandoned.[35]

33. Farrer, "The Body of Christ," 122.

34. Farrer, *Love Almighty and Ills Unlimited*, 189.

35. Of course, one may ask whether Farrer's view in "The Body of Christ" entails the traditional position that only the baptized can be saved. I cannot argue this point here, but I would contend that even in this text the primary category is the body that is baptized rather than baptism itself. Human bodies, including infants and the mentally handicapped, may be saved, not because they have or have not been baptized, but because they are *baptizable*.

By contrast, Hauerwas's theology may be seen as a relentlessly consistent attempt to bring Christian theory in line with Christian practices, rather than vice versa. Thus, instead of wondering how God could possibly redeem the mentally handicapped, Hauerwas concludes that such individuals are "reminders that before God none of us are whole; but God makes possible the joining of our bodies through which we become whole."[36] Thus, we cannot contrast "imperfect" lives with "perfect" ones, because we are all imperfect. But we are also all redeemable, as the bodily, created objects of a perfect love.[37]

36. Hauerwas, "Reflection on Dependency," 197.

37. I am grateful to David Brown, Joe Cassidy, Ed Henderson, and Stanley Hauerwas for comments on an earlier version of this chapter, and I am especially grateful to Ann Loades for inspiring it.

"The Evidence of Faith":
Austin Farrer, Diogenes Allen, and Reformed Epistemology

One of the most important and controversial movements in twentieth-century Anglo-American philosophy of religion developed in the early 1980s with Alvin Plantinga, Nicholas Wolterstorff, and their associates under the title "Reformed epistemology." While not all those gathered under this banner were Calvinists, they shared a common set of convictions on the rationality of religious belief. Reformed epistemologists rejected what they called "classical foundationalism" and the concomitant need for religious belief to depend upon propositional *arguments* and *evidence* for the existence of God in order to be considered rational. Rather, they insisted, belief in God was "properly basic"—that is, based upon noninferential modes of perception or an inbuilt sense of the divine—or rightly held on the basis of communal testimony and formation. If so, then religious belief may be rational without depending upon the traditional arguments of natural theology. To be more precise, religious belief was "innocent until proven guilty," in that it still needed to defend itself when called upon by answering objections such as the problem of evil or other standard criticisms. But religious belief did not need to justify its basic content in some foundationalist, rationalist, or evidentialist manner.[1]

---

1. Although other publications followed as their arguments became more sophisticated, the *locus classicus* is Alvin Plantinga and Nicholas Wolterstorff, eds., *Faith and Rationality: Reason and Belief in God* (Notre Dame: University of Notre Dame Press, 1983). In his introduction to the volume (1–15), Wolterstorff already noted that the term "Reformed epistemology" was not entirely felicitous (7), and Plantinga later expressed regret that some readers interpreted it in a triumphalist manner: see his "A Christian Life Partly Lived," in *Philosophers Who Believe: The Spiritual Journeys of 11 Leading Thinkers*, ed. Kelly James Clark (Downers Grove, IL: InterVarsity, 1993), 45–82, citing 67.

Originally published in *Austin Farrer for Today: A Prophetic Agenda*, ed. Richard Harries and Stephen Platten (London: SCM, 2020), 84–97.

With that background information in place, this essay will proceed as follows. I first summarize a recent survey of contemporary Anglo-American epistemology, both general and religious, that links four important trends with philosophers associated with Reformed epistemology, and in particular Alvin Plantinga and William P. Alston (d. 2009). I then show how Austin Farrer anticipated all four of these current trends in his philosophical work beginning with *Finite and Infinite* in 1943 and concluding with *Faith and Speculation* in 1967. The next section argues that Farrer's American student Diogenes Allen (d. 2013) developed proposals in the early 1960s that not only influenced Farrer's *Faith and Speculation* but bore a striking resemblance to the project Reformed epistemologists developed independently two decades later. The implications of all this will then be considered in a brief conclusion.

I. Four Trends in Contemporary Epistemology, General and Religious

In a recent survey of general epistemology relevant to religious epistemology, John Greco identifies four trends dating from the 1980s that continue to shape contemporary discussions: (1) rejecting narrow foundationalism, (2) rejecting internalism, (3) knowledge versus understanding, and (4) explanation versus vindication.[2] He begins by noting the broad rejection of narrow foundationalism, which he describes as "a theory that tries to explain all knowledge in terms of a narrow range of sources."[3] More specifically, narrow foundationalism is

2. John Greco, "Knowledge of God," in *The Oxford Handbook of the Epistemology of Theology*, ed. William J. Abraham and Frederick D. Aquino (Oxford: Oxford University Press, 2017), 9–29. For my purposes here, I will take Greco's survey at face value and not engage critically with either his choice of trends or his interpretation of them. However, in comments on an earlier version of this essay, David Brown observed that, despite being presented as a general account, Greco's survey is in fact more focused on the American than the British context, a thought to which I return in note 15 below.

3. Greco, "Knowledge of God," 10. "Foundationalism" refers to a family of epistemic theories that all conceive of belief along the architectural analogy of a building with a foundation on which higher levels are then built. "Narrow" and "classical" foundationalism, while not identical, are both restrictive about what belongs in the foundational level, whereas other versions are more generous: Reformed epistemology is a form of generous or broad foundationalism (see n. 6 below). Foundationalism is often contrasted with "coherentism," a family of theories that construes belief along the organic analogy of a web.

preoccupied with "a narrow range of evidence, or kinds of evidence"—that is, with what counts as legitimate evidence for a rational belief and what does not. Rationalists and empiricists answer this question differently, with rationalists focusing on "certainty" and empiricists focusing on "experience," but narrow foundationalists go on to insist that only their preferred form of evidence is acceptable. Such narrow foundationalism is traditionally manifest in religious epistemology by insisting that knowledge of God requires "proofs" or "demonstrations." By contrast, Greco says, "contemporary religious epistemology takes seriously the idea that our knowledge of God is a kind of knowledge of persons. But in general our knowledge of persons is by means of our interpersonal interactions with them as well as by what they reveal about themselves with their own words and actions. Religious epistemology is nowadays interested in pursuing analogous models of our knowledge of a personal God."[4]

The second trend, "rejecting internalism," could also be described positively as "accepting externalism." Both of these theories come in various forms. The primary claim of internalism is that for a belief to be rational, its basis must somehow "be 'immediately' accessible to one; that is, it must be immediately knowable, or knowable 'by reflection alone.'"[5] That is, everyone is personally responsible to ensure that their beliefs are rational by the exercise of appropriate reasons or arguments. There is thus a close connection between such internalism and what the Reformed epistemologists call classical foundationalism, "which restricts the sources of knowledge to such things as a priori reason, conscious introspection, and what is 'given' in experience."[6] But such internalist theories are now widely (although by no means universally) rejected in favor of externalism. By contrast with internalism, externalist theories insist that "knowledge requires appropriate causal contact with the object of knowledge. It also requires . . .

4. Greco, "Knowledge of God," 10–11.

5. Greco, "Knowledge of God," 11.

6. Greco, "Knowledge of God," 11. For Plantinga, classical foundationalism restricts the foundational or "basic" beliefs to what is self-evident, evident to the senses, or incorrigible (cannot be doubted), but it also allows for additional rational beliefs validly derived by argument from these foundations. By contrast, Reformed epistemology allows for belief in God to be included among the foundations, even if it is not self-evident, evident to the senses, or incorrigible: see Plantinga's "Reason and Belief in God," in Plantinga and Wolterstorff, *Faith and Rationality*, 16–93. An abridged version of this essay was reprinted in *The Analytic Theist: An Alvin Plantinga Reader*, ed. James F. Sennett (Grand Rapids: Eerdmans, 1998), 102–61.

healthy cognitive functioning and an enabling cognitive environment."[7] That is, externalism says that what makes a belief rational is "external" to the direct individual consciousness and more dependent on reliable mental functions in appropriate contexts. Like the first trend, when applied to religious epistemology, externalism also discourages emphasis on theistic arguments: while they may play some role, "there is a general consensus that they are not the basis for ordinary beliefs about God." Greco writes: "there is now increased interest in how religious believers might come to know God through experience or revelation. Just as general epistemology has turned its attention to the actual grounds of 'ordinary' knowledge, and away from the rational reconstructions of philosophers, religious epistemology is now concerned with ordinary persons in the pew (or in prayer, or in distress, or in joy, or in service to others)."[8]

The third trend, "knowledge versus understanding," both distinguishes between these two concepts and prioritizes the former over the latter, at least in regard to ordinary beliefs. As Greco puts it, "there is an important difference between *knowing that* such-and-such is the case and *understanding why* or *how* such-and-such is the case."[9] For example, one might *know* that food is good for one's health without *understanding* the biology of nutrition, digestion, and so forth.[10] Understanding is thus important and valuable in its own right, but it is not necessary for knowledge. Therefore, Greco says, "there is now logical space for ordinary knowledge of God without philosophical or theological understanding. For example, one might know that God loves His people and wants His creation to flourish, but not understand how suffering is compatible with this."[11] This distinction also provides a legitimate role for natural theology, after all: not to justify basic religious knowledge but to enable deeper understanding.[12]

7. Greco, "Knowledge of God," 12.

8. Greco, "Knowledge of God," 12.

9. Greco, "Knowledge of God," 12.

10. I take this example from C. S. Lewis, *Mere Christianity* (London: Macmillan, 1953), 43–44.

11. Greco, "Knowledge of God," 13.

12. Greco, "Knowledge of God," 13. For this claim, Greco cites Nicholas Wolterstorff, "The Migration of the Theistic Arguments: From Natural Theology to Evidentialist Apologetics," in *Rationality, Religious Belief, and Moral Commitment: New Essays in the Philosophy of Religion*, ed. Robert Audi and William J. Wainwright (Ithaca, NY: Cornell University Press, 1986),

The fourth and final trend is "explanation versus vindication." If the epistemic project is vindication, then we must engage skeptics on their own ground and try to establish by *their* criteria that we know anything at all: a game impossible to win and thus pointless to play. But if the epistemic project is explanation, then "the aim is not to establish (against the skeptic) that we have knowledge, but to explain (to ourselves) the difference between knowing and not knowing. It is also to consider how beings like us, in the circumstances we find ourselves, might achieve the sort of knowledge in question." Greco thus concludes:

> What this means for religious epistemology and the epistemology of theology is a retreat from apologetics. In older days, the task was to develop arguments in favor of God's existence, to answer objections against these, and to critique arguments against God's existence. The entire process was framed as a debate, with each side trying to prove its case against the other, using only premises that all could accept. This makes perfect sense if the project is vindication, but no sense at all if the project is explanation. Accordingly, present-day religious epistemology deals more in explanations than in proofs; that is, theories are put forward regarding what knowledge of God would require for beings like us, and models are put forward regarding how we might fulfil those requirements.[13]

Having presented these four recent trends, Greco goes on to associate them in both general and religious epistemology with the groundbreaking work of Plantinga and Alston, both of whom are still historically identified with "Reformed" epistemology despite Alston's avowed Anglicanism and Plantinga's later preference for what he more ecumenically calls an "Aquinas/Calvin model." Greco then considers various objections to their views such as counterevidence, the lack of universal religious belief, and religious diversity.[14] In the

---

38–81. This essay was later reprinted in Nicholas Wolterstorff, *Practices of Belief: Selected Essays*, ed. Terence Cuneo, vol. 2 (Cambridge: Cambridge University Press, 2010), 173–216.

13. Greco, "Knowledge of God," 13.

14. Greco, "Knowledge of God," 14–23, 25–26. In this section Greco focuses on Plantinga's "Reason and Belief in God"; Alvin Plantinga, *Warranted Christian Belief* (New York: Oxford University Press, 2000); and William P. Alston, *Perceiving God: The Epistemology of Religious Experience* (Ithaca, NY: Cornell University Press, 1991). For my previous engagements with

final section of his essay, Greco offers an interesting take on what he calls the "social turn" in contemporary epistemology—that is, "how the knowledge of individuals depends in various ways on the knowledge, activities, and properties of groups"—and in particular on the epistemology of testimony.[15]

II. Austin Farrer: From Rational Theology to the Evidence of Faith

Greco's four trends are all associated with Reformed epistemology and thus contrasted sharply from previous views, and that may well be the case in regard to mainstream Anglo-American discussions of natural theology, apologetics, and religious epistemology. However, I will now show that all four of these trends were anticipated by Farrer between 1943 and 1967, sometimes explicitly, sometimes incipiently.[16] As I have argued at greater length elsewhere, Farrer's mature thinking on faith and reason passed through various stages, so my presentation

---

these figures and texts, see Robert MacSwain, "An Analytic Anglican: The Philosophical Theology of William P. Alston," *Anglican Theological Review* 88 (2006): 421–32 (republished in this volume as chapter 1) and *"Sensus Divinitatis* or Divine Hiddenness? Alvin Plantinga and J. L. Schellenberg on Knowledge of God," *Anglican Theological Review* 99 (2017): 353–62.

15. See Greco, "Knowledge of God," 23–27, and here citing 23. As noted above, David Brown points out that Greco's survey is arguably more focused on the contemporary American context than the British one. Without denying the influence of Plantinga, Wolterstorff, and Alston in British philosophy of religion, Brown observes that Richard Swinburne's inductive and probabilistic approach remains the standard point of reference on the rationality of theism (in either agreement or disagreement), and also that the so-called New Atheists still accept the foundational and evidentialist frameworks rejected by Reformed epistemology. For Swinburne's position see *The Existence of God* (Oxford: Clarendon, 1979), republished in a substantially revised second edition in 2004. A more accessible version may be found in Richard Swinburne, *Is There a God?* (Oxford: Oxford University Press, 1996; rev. ed. 2010). Exploring the comparison between Farrer and Swinburne would thus be a worthwhile project for another essay. For an interesting comparison between Swinburne and Wolterstorff in conversation with Farrer, see Basil Mitchell, "Two Approaches to the Philosophy of Religion," in *For God and Clarity: New Essays in Honor of Austin Farrer*, ed. Jeffrey C. Eaton and Ann Loades (Allison Park, PA: Pickwick, 1983), 117–90.

16. Although I will not cite them below, for helpful and relevant analyses, see two essays by Edward Henderson, "Knowing Persons and Knowing God," *Thomist* 46 (1982): 394–422, and "Valuing in Knowing God: An Interpretation of Austin Farrer's Religious Epistemology," *Modern Theology* 1 (1985): 165–82.

here will be chronological rather than topical, but along the way I will note how Farrer's developing thought intersects with Greco's contemporary trends.[17]

In his first major work, *Finite and Infinite*, Farrer took his basic cosmological and analogical inspiration from Thomas Aquinas in the twin task of arguing against (i) logical positivism's rejection of metaphysics as well as (ii) Karl Barth's insistence on revelation alone as the source of human knowledge of God. And to that extent, Farrer seemed more sympathetic to the project of traditional natural theology. Yet in this book Farrer also rejected textbook Thomism's conviction that human knowledge of divine reality depended on valid deductive arguments. Farrer thus asserted that *Finite and Infinite* was an exercise in what he called "rational theology," even though he was not committed to "the perfect demonstration of even one basic theological proposition. We may find that we can only show its possibility or probability."[18] Here we already see a rejection of narrow foundationalism and the emergence of what has been called soft rationalism.[19] Farrer goes on to clarify that by "rational theology" as opposed to "natural theology" he means a focus on *analysis* rather than *dialectic*, which precisely mirrors Greco's contrast between explanation and vindication.[20]

In regard to the contested question of the existence of God, Farrer argues that while it cannot be formally *demonstrated*, it can still be rationally *apprehended*.[21] By "apprehension" Farrer means a noninferential, intuitive grasp of divine reality on the basis of what he calls the "cosmological idea": that is, through directly experiencing our own existence, as well as through recogniz-

17. For more detail on the material covered in this section, see Robert MacSwain, *Solved by Sacrifice: Austin Farrer, Fideism, and the Evidence of Faith* (Leuven: Peeters, 2013), chapters 3 and 4. For a brief introduction to Farrer's thought, including his work in biblical studies and theology as well as philosophy, see Robert MacSwain, "Austin Farrer," in *Twentieth Century Anglican Theologians*, ed. Stephen Burns, Bryan Cones, and James Tengatenga (Chichester, UK: Wiley-Blackwell, 2021), 54–64.

18. Austin Farrer, *Finite and Infinite: A Philosophical Essay* (Westminster: Dacre, 1943; 2nd ed. 1959), v.

19. The term seems to have been coined by Rod Sykes in "Soft Rationalism," *International Journal for Philosophy of Religion* 8 (1977): 51–66, and it is often used to refer to the position developed by Basil Mitchell in *The Justification of Religious Belief* (London: Macmillan, 1973).

20. See Farrer, *Finite and Infinite*, 5–6. Farrer thus also anticipates the later focus of analytic philosophical theology in engaging directly with Christian doctrines such as Trinity and incarnation without initially seeking to demonstrate their truth.

21. Farrer, *Finite and Infinite*, 8.

ing the existence of other finite realities, including other persons, we come to understand our source in the unique creative activity of an infinite Agent. In light of Greco's emphasis on explanation rather than vindication—that is, putting forward theories and models rather than demonstrations and proofs—note Farrer's interesting claim that "the theist's first argument is a statement; he exhibits his account of God active in the world and the world existing in God, that others may recognise it to be the account of what they themselves apprehend—or, if you like, that others may find it to be an instrument through which they apprehend, for perhaps apprehension is here not separable from interpretation."[22] The noninferential, interpretative character of apprehending God is at least analogous to Reformed epistemology's emphasis on proper basicality, and I will return to the crucial connection between knowing persons and knowing God below.

In regard to Greco's trend of "knowledge versus understanding," even in 1943 Farrer explicitly endorsed Greco's view that (religious) epistemology is more about ordinary (religious) belief and less about formal philosophical reconstructions of it, and this conviction became even more pronounced as Farrer's thought developed further, as we will see in the following section. Thus, in *Finite and Infinite* Farrer says that he is simply seeking to understand "the Jacob's-ladder of living religion," and in his correspondence with Diogenes Allen in the 1960s, he summarized Allen's thesis by saying: "Justification ought not to construct bypasses to God, but to test the roads by which he comes to us."[23]

So far we have seen Farrer's early articulation of ideas expressed in Greco's trends of "rejecting narrow foundationalism," "explanation versus vindication," and "knowledge versus understanding." Since there is an admittedly strong internalist element to Farrer's argument in *Finite and Infinite*, and since contemporary externalist theories of epistemology did not develop until the 1970s, to claim that in Farrer we also find Greco's "rejecting internalism" may seem implausible. But in an intriguing passage, Farrer suggests that even revelation must be intelligible to the human mind before it can be accepted, and so we must be properly designed to receive it: "unless I had some mental machinery for thinking the bare notion of God, could I recognise His revelatory action as

22. Farrer, *Finite and Infinite*, 9–10.

23. Farrer, *Finite and Infinite*, 4, and Farrer's 1963 letter to Allen on 241–42 of MacSwain, *Solved by Sacrifice*.

that of God?"[24] The term "mental machinery" has a strongly externalist ring. And in a later passage in *Finite and Infinite*, we find even more explicitly externalist ideas. To understand human cognition it is necessary to "abandon the path of logical rectitude, and to consider evolutionary theory and biological probability."[25] That is, we must recognize that we are not immaterial "thinking substances" but evolved organic beings who can only understand things in similarly embodied ways within environments conducive to such knowledge. This is how what Greco calls "beings like us" come to know things.

Recall that in articulating the religious significance of the move away from narrow foundationalism, Greco says that "contemporary religious epistemology takes seriously the idea that our knowledge of God is a kind of knowledge of persons. But in general our knowledge of persons is by means of our interpersonal interactions with them as well as by what they reveal about themselves with their own words and actions. Religious epistemology is nowadays interested in pursuing analogous models of our knowledge of a personal God."[26] Recall also his statement that externalism requires "appropriate causal contact with the object of knowledge."[27] Given these comments, it is thus fascinating to see how Farrer's thought moved increasingly in both of these directions in the 1950s and '60s.

For example, his 1957 Gifford Lectures at the University of Edinburgh marked an epistemic shift from his earlier focus on what we might call "contemplative apprehension" to "causal interaction." Even in *Finite and Infinite* Farrer had argued that "we cannot think about anything about which we can do nothing but think,"[28] and that "we know things as they condition or effect our vital operation."[29] This minor theme in *Finite and Infinite* assumed more prominence in Farrer's later philosophical work where it was eventually applied not just to our knowledge of the physical world but—perhaps surprisingly—to God as well. Thus, in *The Freedom of the Will* Farrer wrote that "the physical is known to us by the way it conditions our physical motion; and the divine will, which is God himself, is known to us in limiting or evoking our dutiful action,

24. Farrer, *Finite and Infinite*, 2.
25. Farrer, *Finite and Infinite*, 232.
26. Greco, "Knowledge of God," 10–11.
27. Greco, "Knowledge of God," 12.
28. Farrer, *Finite and Infinite*, 294.
29. Farrer, *Finite and Infinite*, 231.

through all the persons with whom we have to do."[30] That is, it is precisely through recognizing our moral obligations to others *and acting accordingly* that we come to recognize and respond to the divine reality as well. Likewise, in *Faith and Speculation*, Farrer maintained that

> to know real beings we must exercise our actual relation with them. No physical science without physical interference, no personal knowledge without personal intercourse; no thought about any reality about which we can do nothing but think. Is not this the highest possible generalisation of the empirical principle? Theology must be at least as empirical as this, if it is to mediate any knowledge whatsoever. We can know nothing of God, unless we can do something about him. So what, we must ask, can we do?[31]

Farrer's answer regarding what we can "do" about God is that we can "devote ourselves to [God's] will; that is, we can place ourselves in [God's] action as we suppose it to be disclosed." And in such obedient devotion we find a confirming response of "life" and "blessing."[32]

In these various statements we hear a significant development in Farrer's thought that arguably finds its clearest (although not final) expression in the opening chapter of *Saving Belief*, titled "Faith and Evidence." The crucial question is how what Farrer here calls "the evidence of faith" is perceived and evaluated.[33] The question is crucial because Reformed epistemology self-consciously defines itself as a form of noninferential "anti-evidentialism," and yet Farrer

---

30. Austin Farrer, *The Freedom of the Will: The Gifford Lectures Delivered in the University of Edinburgh, 1957* (London: Black, 1958; 2nd ed. 1963), 309.

31. Austin Farrer, *Faith and Speculation: An Essay in Philosophical Theology* (London: Black, 1967), 22. Note the self-quotation from *Finite and Infinite*, 294.

32. Farrer, *Faith and Speculation*, 57. In making these claims Farrer was influenced by Diogenes Allen: what Farrer calls "blessings" Allen calls "nourishment." In context it is clear that both Farrer and Allen are speaking of spiritual rather than material benefits, and so such talk should not be confused with what is sometimes called the "prosperity gospel." I am grateful to Ben Cowgill for pointing out the need for clarification here.

33. Austin Farrer, *Saving Belief: A Discussion of Essentials* (London: Hodder & Stoughton, 1964), 11–34. "Faith and Evidence" has been reprinted in *The Truth-Seeking Heart: Austin Farrer and His Writings*, ed. Ann Loades and Robert MacSwain (Norwich, UK: Canterbury, 2006), 168–84; the phrase "evidence of faith" is found on 26 of the original and 179 of the reprint.

insists that evidence for God is still necessary for rational belief. However, Farrer also insists that we must be properly positioned to perceive the evidence correctly, and what positions us is "faith" understood as a form of openness and receptivity to God—or at least to reality. The attitude of faith is required to interpret the objectively-compelling evidence. Thus, he says that without

> the readiness of faith, the evidence of God will not be accepted, or will not convince. This is not to say that faith is put in place of evidence. What convinces us is not our faith, but the evidence; faith is a subjective condition favourable to the reception of the evidence. . . . The evidence is intrinsically and of itself convincing, but only under conditions which allow it to be appreciated. Faith supplies the conditions.[34]

III. Diogenes Allen and Reformed Epistemology

The previous section argued that Farrer exemplified in proleptic fashion all four of Greco's contemporary trends in both general and religious epistemology. Assuming that Greco's account is correct, Farrer anticipated these trends about forty years before they became widely influential in Anglo-American philosophy. Precisely why Farrer was so far ahead of his time, on these and many other issues (such as his literary approach to biblical interpretation), is an interesting question that cannot detain us further here, other than to note that it might help explain his relative obscurity both then and now.

However, although Greco associates all four trends with Reformed epistemology, I have not argued that Farrer himself was a proto-Reformed epistemologist. Things are rather different with Diogenes Allen, who, as an American PhD student at Yale, spent a year in Oxford working with Farrer on his doctoral thesis in 1963/1964.[35] The son of Greek Orthodox immigrants from Turkey

---

34. Farrer, "Faith and Evidence," 22; in reprint, 176. For more detail, see MacSwain, *Solved by Sacrifice*, 160–72. In my view, this development amounts to a shift from soft rationalism to a subtle form of moderate fideism, although this claim has been contested: see, for example, Brian Hebblethwaite's review of *Solved by Sacrifice*, *Faith and Philosophy* 31 (2014): 490–92. For a more sympathetic response to this aspect of my argument, see Sergio Sorrentino's review, *European Journal for Philosophy of Religion* 9 (2017): 209–12.

35. For the basic details of Allen's life and career, see MacSwain, *Solved by Sacrifice*, 40–41

who became a Presbyterian as an undergraduate at the University of Kentucky, after one year of graduate studies in philosophy at Princeton University, Allen was then a Rhodes Scholar at St. John's College, Oxford, before returning to the USA for further theological and philosophical studies at Yale. Allen, Plantinga, and Wolterstorff were all born in 1932, and Allen's undergraduate mentor was Jesse DeBoer (1912–1990), who studied and taught at Calvin College, the Dutch Reformed *alma mater* of Plantinga and Wolterstorff. Although two decades older than they, DeBoer shared the experience of being taught by their mentor, William Harry Jellema (1893–1982).[36] Especially given Allen's early embrace of Presbyterianism (albeit moderated by his Orthodox upbringing and modified yet further by his later membership and ordination in the Episcopal Church), it is plausible to suggest that his studies with DeBoer provided some shared intellectual DNA with Plantinga and Wolterstorff.

Such biographical speculations notwithstanding, Allen's doctoral thesis and subsequent publications advanced a proposal remarkably similar to early Reformed epistemology, although twenty years beforehand. As Farrer engaged with Allen on these topics in 1963/1964, Farrer was himself challenged and stimulated by Allen's argument, as his correspondence with Allen and published citations bear witness.[37] In a series of letters Farrer summarized and raised various objections to Allen's position. The penultimate letter, written on June 29, 1966, after Allen sent Farrer an *American Philosophical Quarterly* article containing the core of the thesis, reads as follows:

---

and 174–75. He eventually succeeded John Hick as the Stuart Professor of Philosophy at Princeton Theological Seminary.

36. For DeBoer, see https://tinyurl.com/zxvhmusc; for Jellema, see https://tinyurl.com/ymah286y. Allen dedicated his book *Philosophy for Understanding Theology* (Atlanta: John Knox, 1985) to DeBoer, and discusses his relationship with him in *Steps along the Way: A Spiritual Autobiography* (New York: Church Publishing, 2002), 104–6.

37. The version of Allen's doctoral thesis read by Farrer was *Motives, Evidence, and Religious Commitment* (1964), the revision accepted by Yale for the PhD was *Faith as a Ground for Religious Beliefs* (1965), and the final version was published as *The Reasonableness of Faith: A Philosophical Essay on the Grounds for Religious Belief* (Washington, DC: Corpus Books, 1968). Allen presented the central argument in "Motives, Rationales, and Religious Beliefs," *American Philosophical Quarterly* 3 (1966): 111–27. For Farrer's letters to Allen, see *Solved by Sacrifice*, appendix (B), 240–49. Farrer acknowledged Allen's influence in the preface to *Faith and Speculation*, vi, and cited Allen's "Motives, Rationales, and Religious Beliefs" in the first chapter on 10.

Dear Diogenes,

Thank you for the offprint of your very substantial paper, which I have read with high appreciation. By the time I received it I had completed the MS of a book containing the Deems Lectures of 1964 [*Faith and Speculation*], in which your ideas (not unacknowledged) furnish the substance of the first chapter ["The Believer's Reasons"]. I do not altogether agree with you but I think what you say is very important. I think it comes to this: The believer, qua believer, rightly says "I believe because the grace of God" (or the like) "persuades me." But the philosopher's business is not (mainly) to say: "Quite right, my boy, that's how believing goes" but to examine the assumptions upon which the facts through which "the grace of God persuades" come to be taken as instruments, effects or evidences as the Grace of God.[38]

Readers are directed toward the first chapter of *Faith and Speculation* to see Farrer's public engagement with and partial endorsement of Allen's ideas, but in the remainder of this section I turn directly to Allen's article. Allen first proposes a distinction between what he calls "motives" and "rationales." A motive is the *actual reason* why someone holds a certain belief. It is specific to her as an individual, and Allen sometimes refers to it as "biographical." A rationale, by contrast, is a *possible reason* that one *could* provide, not to justify the belief itself as *actually* held by the person but as a general reason why the belief *might* be true or even *ought* to be held. So whereas motives are actual and personal reasons, rationales are possible and impersonal.[39]

In regard to religious beliefs, Allen holds that most people's motive for belief is faith, aroused biographically. In some rare instances, the *actual reason* someone believes might indeed be the cosmological or some other theistic argument, but this is neither normal nor necessary. Crucial to Allen's position is the claim that not only is it *actually* the case that most people's religious beliefs are based on faith (which is fairly uncontroversial), but also that this situation is perfectly *rationally acceptable*. As he puts it, such faith-based "biographical" reasons are "a proper basis for the affirmation of Christian beliefs. The motives one has for one's adherence to religious beliefs are not grounds which warrant other kinds of assertions, but they are a basis for the assertion of religious beliefs. To

38. MacSwain, *Solved by Sacrifice*, appendix (B), Letter 6, 248.
39. Allen, "Motives, Rationales, and Religious Beliefs," 111–12.

believe on the basis of one's motives is not to act arbitrarily, blindly, or without any reason."[40]

Furthermore, Allen makes the stronger claim that to insist that religious beliefs must be based on arguments is to distort their true character: "To seek to give religious beliefs an evidential basis results in turning them into something else. In particular, it makes religious beliefs appear to be like other kinds of metaphysical assertions."[41] Metaphysical beliefs are based on reasoning that makes inferences about realities beyond empirical investigation. Religious beliefs, on the other hand, while they may well imply or even entail certain metaphysical commitments, are not based on such reasoning. Rather, they arise in response to personal confrontation with a message about God—the "gospel"—which one encounters either through growing up in a religious community, or reading the Bible, or hearing a street preacher, etc.[42]

Although Allen maintains that to grow up within the Christian community is itself a valid motive to hold Christian beliefs (assuming, as we shall see in a moment, that one has not encountered insurmountable objections to them), in fact there is more to faith on his account than biographical considerations, namely, appropriate *grounds*. According to Allen: "The grounds are that a man has come to have faith in response to the witness of the Christian community and in the condition of faith he finds his soul nourished. By praying, by reading the Scriptures, by fellowship with other Christians, he finds his life is beginning to conform to what Paul described as the new life. This nourishment is his assurance and ground for the condition of faith in which he finds himself; and the very response of faith itself (which includes receiving nourishment) is a ground for faith."[43] Thus, having faith is not merely assenting to a particular set of groundless beliefs just because one was taught them as a child, but rather to actively receive what Allen calls "nourishment" from them—nourishment that itself provides the necessary grounds on which they are rationally held.

What then of "rationales," or possible reasons? Do they play any role at all in this scheme? Yes, for religious believers often encounter *objections* to their belief,

---

40. Allen, "Motives, Rationales, and Religious Beliefs," 111.

41. Allen, "Motives, Rationales, and Religious Beliefs," 111.

42. Allen, "Motives, Rationales, and Religious Beliefs," 112–13. The first two examples are Allen's, but he clearly does not limit himself to them.

43. Allen, "Motives, Rationales, and Religious Beliefs," 113.

objections that arise either internally or externally, that cause them to doubt or perhaps even to abandon their faith. Although Allen holds that religious beliefs are "innocent until proven guilty," he fully acknowledges that sometimes they do need to be defended. Rationales may thus be a necessary component of the life of faith, answering accusations and dealing with doubt. However, as with metaphysical beliefs, Allen insists that rationales still need not—and perhaps even should not—become the believer's *actual* motive or ground: she should still believe because of the *nourishment* she has actually received from the gospel, not because of an impersonal, objective argument.[44]

I do not have space to make a close comparison between Allen's position here and the original version of Reformed epistemology articulated by Plantinga, Wolterstorff, Alston, and others in the 1980s, but the parallels are remarkable. In both cases we see an emphasis on the *prima facie* rationality of ordinary religious belief, a pervasive anti-evidentialism, the idea of "grounds" rather than "arguments" as the basis of belief, and the need for "negative apologetics" to answer objections. It is also striking to recall Greco's claim that "religious epistemology is now concerned with ordinary persons in the pew (or in prayer, or in distress, or in joy, or in service to others)."[45] Such common and communal practices of faith are precisely what Allen presented in the mid-1960s as the primary justification for religious belief as well. And if Farrer did not follow Allen all the way in this regard, his final book, *Faith and Speculation*, still wrestled with this then-radical and still-controversial epistemic proposal, namely, that "it is the actual motives or grounds for religious believing which demand the philosopher's attention."[46]

IV. Conclusion

I thus conclude with a question and an observation. The question is, "Why are Farrer and Allen not better recognized for their trailblazing accomplishments

---

44. The preceding five paragraphs were adapted from MacSwain, *Solved by Sacrifice*, 177–82.

45. Greco, "Knowledge of God," 12.

46. Farrer, *Faith and Speculation*, 1, and note how he explicitly used Allen's terms of "motives" and "grounds."

in religious epistemology?" More specifically, why is Farrer not included in contemporary epistemological discussions, and why has Allen's anticipation of Reformed epistemology been so neglected? My brief answer is that they were both so far ahead of their time that their work fell on the proverbial rocky soil. More empirical and formalist forms of philosophy were so deeply entrenched in the United Kingdom and the United States during the 1940s, '50s, and '60s that it took several decades for an atmosphere more congenial to alternative approaches to develop. It may also be the case that Farrer and Allen simply were not as effective as others in getting a hearing for their ideas, either because of their style of presentation or because of their chosen publishers. So I am certainly not accusing Greco of negligence or Reformed epistemologists of conspiracy: the absence of Farrer and Allen here is pervasive and systemic rather than accidental or intentional. But that situation should be remedied and their work engaged with more deeply.

My observation is that both Farrer and Allen continued to develop as thinkers in commendable ways, and they continue to be relevant to the current conversation. Consider, for example, the crucial question of "the evidence of faith": that is, should religious belief be based on evidence or not, and if so, then what kind and how much? Despite being challenged by his proposals, Farrer thought that Allen had gone too far in his youthful anti-evidentialism—and Allen later agreed. That is, Allen eventually came around to Farrer's position in "Faith and Evidence" that the evidence "is intrinsically and of itself convincing, but only under conditions which allow it to be appreciated."[47] Accepting this claim then opens important connections between epistemology and both moral and spiritual development (that is to say, matters of the *heart*), for what does it take for those necessary faith conditions to obtain? Thus, against Reformed epistemology, William J. Wainwright defends the thesis that "mature religious belief can, and perhaps should, be based on evidence but that the evidence can be accurately assessed only by men and women who possess the proper moral and spiritual qualifications." He adds, "This view was once a Christian commonplace; reason is capable of knowing God on the basis of evidence—but only

---

47. See Diogenes Allen, "Faith and the Recognition of God's Activity," in *Divine Action: Studies Inspired by the Philosophical Theology of Austin Farrer*, ed. Brian Hebblethwaite and Edward Henderson (Edinburgh: T&T Clark, 1990), 197–210, and *Christian Belief in a Postmodern World: The Full Wealth of Conviction* (Louisville: Westminster John Knox, 1992).

when one's cognitive faculties are rightly disposed."[48] Likewise, Sarah Coakley argues for the essential but neglected role of spiritual practices and increased attention to both body and gender in the *transformation* of our epistemic capacities to become more astute in recognizing the reality of God.[49] And while Harriet Harris is less convinced than Wainwright and Coakley about the need for evidence in establishing the rationality of religious belief, she claims that a major problem with Reformed epistemology is precisely that it "wastes the opportunity" to turn its commendable epistemology into a more robust spirituality.[50] Whether fair in this specific instance or not, her general challenge for philosophers to better integrate their intellect and affect, head and heart, mind and spirit is worth heeding. And in this respect, both Farrer and Allen offer valuable models to emulate.[51]

48. William J. Wainwright, *Reason and the Heart: A Prolegomenon to a Critique of Passional Reason* (Ithaca, NY: Cornell University Press, 1995), 3. See also his *Reason, Revelation, and Devotion: Inference and Argument in Religion* (New York: Cambridge University Press, 2015), 60.

49. See, for example, Sarah Coakley, "Response" to William P. Alston, "Biblical Criticism and the Resurrection," in *The Resurrection: An Interdisciplinary Symposium on the Resurrection of Christ*, ed. Stephen Davis, Daniel Kendall, SJ, and Gerald O'Collins, SJ (Oxford: Oxford University Press, 1997), 184–90; "The Resurrection and the 'Spiritual Senses': On Wittgenstein, Epistemology and the Risen Christ," in Sarah Coakley, *Powers and Submissions: Spirituality, Philosophy, and Gender* (Oxford: Blackwell, 2002), 130–52; and "Dark Contemplation and Epistemic Transformation: The Analytic Theologian Re-meets Teresa of Ávila," in *Analytic Theology: New Essays in the Philosophy of Theology*, ed. Oliver D. Crisp and Michael C. Rea (Oxford: Oxford University Press, 2009), 280–312.

50. See Harriet A. Harris, "Does Analytical Philosophy Clip Our Wings?" in *Faith and Philosophical Analysis: The Impact of Analytical Philosophy on the Philosophy of Religion*, ed. Harriet A. Harris and Christopher J. Insole (Aldershot, UK: Ashgate, 2005), 100–118.

51. I am grateful to David Brown, Ben Cowgill, Richard Harries, Stanley Hauerwas, the late Ann Loades, and Stephen Platten for helpful comments on earlier versions of this essay.

Human Holiness as Divine Evidence:
The Hagiological Argument for the Existence of God

In an autobiographical essay titled "My Priests," the author and activist Paul Monette wrote: "There is no God, I'm sure of that. But the more they've sought me out, the more convinced I am that there *are* holy men and women. . . . And if they like, they're welcome to include me in their prayers. Can't hurt. None of us will free the world of intolerance alone. We need the people of God, especially if He isn't there."[1] Monette, who left the Episcopal Church for atheism as an adolescent, and who won the National Book Award for Nonfiction in 1992, clearly found human holiness a more vivid and palpable reality than the existence of God—and he is hardly alone in this regard.[2] A surprising number of philosophers and theologians, however, have argued that human holiness is evidence *for* God, and perhaps even the *best* evidence. I say "surprising" because, despite the various defenders of this claim that I discuss in this essay, it has not yet been formally identified and classified among the standard theistic arguments such as the cosmological argument, the teleological argument, ontological argument, the moral argument, or the argument from religious experience.[3] Nevertheless, the claim exists, and I propose calling it the "hagiological argument for the

1. Paul Monette, *Last Watch of the Night: Essays Too Personal and Otherwise* (New York: Harvest Books, 1995), 88.

2. See Paul Monette, *Becoming a Man: Half a Life Story* (New York: Harcourt Brace Jovanovich, 1992).

3. Stephen T. Davis, *God, Reason, and Theistic Proofs* (Edinburgh: Edinburgh University Press, 1997), remains a useful book-length introduction to the standard arguments. For a more recent study, compare C. Stephen Evans, *Natural Signs and Knowledge of God: A New Look at Theistic Arguments* (Oxford: Oxford University Press, 2010). Neither volume considers the argument from saints or human holiness.

Originally published in *Sewanee Theological Review* 62, no. 4 (Michaelmas 2019): 647–73.

existence of God": that is, the argument from (human) holiness or sanctity. In this brief essay I will not go so far as to *defend* this argument. Here I simply wish to document its existence from several sources, consider a neglected earlier engagement with it, suggest three distinct versions of the argument, and finally pose some questions that these versions must answer if they have any chance of holding their own against obvious criticisms.[4]

I. Three Examples

Antecedents of the hagiological argument may be found in earlier writers, but I first clearly encountered it through the twentieth-century Oxford philosopher, theologian, New Testament scholar, and Anglican priest Austin Farrer (1904–1968). For example, in his sermon "Narrow and Broad"—a discussion of the nature and sources of theistic evidence—Farrer describes a close personal friend, the Reverend Hugh Evelyn Jackson Lister (1901–1944). After considering Lister's remarkable but short life as an Anglican priest, labor union organizer, and British army officer—a life that he both lived and sacrificed for others—Farrer concludes: "Such a life, then, is evidence, and what other evidence could you hope to find? . . . Humanity knows God only by yielding to God; we do not know the fountain of our being, so long as we are occupied in stopping it with mud. So the saint is our evidence, and other persons, of course, for the glimpses of sanctity we see in them."[5] Note that although Farrer uses the term "saint" here, he is clearly not limiting it to official canonized figures, but includes exemplary human lives that we personally encounter, even people that we might actually know well or intimately.

---

4. I initially explored some of these claims in Robert MacSwain, *Solved by Sacrifice: Austin Farrer, Fideism, and the Evidence of Faith* (Leuven: Peeters, 2013), 221–35, and I am currently writing a monograph on the evidential value of saints and holiness. This current chapter therefore presents a summary status report of work-in-progress rather than a final statement.

5. "Narrow and Broad" (1960) is here cited from *The Truth-Seeking Heart: Austin Farrer and His Writings*, ed. Ann Loades and Robert MacSwain (Norwich, UK: Canterbury, 2006), 187—I have adapted the language to be gender-inclusive. For more on Lister and his importance for Farrer, see David Hein, "Farrer on Friendship, Sainthood, and the Will of God," in *Captured by the Crucified: The Practical Theology of Austin Farrer*, ed. David Hein and Edward Hugh Henderson (London: T&T Clark International, 2004), 119–48.

For a rather different example of the claim that human sanctity provides evidence for God, consider the American Episcopal philosopher Peter van Inwagen's report that such lives were a primary factor in his conversion from atheism to Christianity. In a spiritual autobiography he writes that although he cannot convey the evidence he is in possession of, nevertheless he knows five or six Christians who, "for all the rich individuality of their lives and personalities, are like lamps, each shining with the same dearly familiar, uncreated light that shines in the pages of the New Testament. . . . When one is in the presence of this light—when one so much as listens to one of these people speak—it is very difficult indeed to believe that one is not in the presence of a living reality that transcends their individual lives."[6] Like Farrer, van Inwagen uses the term "evidence" to describe the epistemic value of these holy lives, but here he seems to construe such theistic evidence in a directly perceptual manner. Somehow, simply being in their presence helps make belief in God possible for him. Somehow, in their "light" he sees God.

My third and final example is the former archbishop of Canterbury Rowan Williams, writing in dialogue with Etty Hillesum, a Dutch Jew who died in Auschwitz at the age of twenty-nine in 1943. In an All Saints' Day sermon preached in 2009, Williams said: "Witnesses establish the truth by giving evidence. It really is as simple as that. When we celebrate the saints, we celebrate those who have given evidence, who have made God believable by how they have lived and how they have died. The saints are the people who recognise that arguments will finally not win the day. God does not make himself credible by argument [but] by lives and deaths that make him credible, that make Jesus tangible here and now."[7] And in his book *Tokens of Trust: An Introduction to Christian Belief,* Williams makes the same point and connects it to a claim made by Hillesum about how some people are called to "take responsibility for God's believability," not through rational argument but through their lives. Williams writes:

6. Peter van Inwagen, "Quam Dilecta," in *God and the Philosophers: The Reconciliation of Faith and Reason,* ed. Thomas V. Morris (New York: Oxford University Press, 1994), 57–58. In correspondence about this interesting passage, Jeffrey Stout astutely noted that van Inwagen's language shifts from the direct first-person "I" to the more ambiguous "one" and how that elides the fact that others might not respond to this group of Christians in the same way that he did.

7. Rowan Williams, All Saints' Day sermon at All Saints' Margaret Street, London (November 1, 2009), https://tinyurl.com/4at3x95j. In the quotation above I have joined two sentences together from the same paragraph of Williams's sermon.

The Bible has no arguments for the existence of God. . . . But Abraham, Moses and St. Paul don't sit down to work out whether God exists; they are already caught up in something the imperative reality of which they can't deny or ignore. At one level, you have to see that the very angst and struggle they bring to their relation with God is a kind of argument for God. . . . Faith has a lot to do with the simple fact that there are trustworthy lives to be seen, that we can see in some believing people a world we'd like to live in. It puts quite a responsibility on believing people, of course. It would be much nicer for all of us if we could just rely on arguments, not on the uncertainties of human lives. But nevertheless, the remarkable fact remains. Some do take responsibility for making God credible in the world.[8]

II. An Early If Ambiguous Engagement: Sherry on Price

Having provided three examples of what I have in mind, I will in the next section go on to identify three different versions of the hagiological argument, loosely paired to each of these three examples. First, however, I want to give credit to the contemporary English philosopher Patrick Sherry, who presented something along these lines several decades ago in conversation with the work of H. H. Price (1899–1984). Given the surprising general neglect of the "hagiological argument," Sherry's engagement with and development of Price's proposal is thus groundbreaking and yet has not itself received the attention it deserves. In his 1977 essay "Philosophy and the Saints," Sherry says that his broad purpose is "to discuss the philosophical issues raised by the existence of saints" (not only epistemological ones) and then defines saints as "those who have achieved an extraordinary degree of goodness, without necessarily gaining any official recognition, e.g. through canonization."[9] While Sherry initially provides a *moral* rather than a religious or ecclesial definition of sainthood, as the discussion continues it becomes clear that for him such "extraordinary

8. Rowan Williams, *Tokens of Trust: An Introduction to Christian Belief* (Norwich, UK: Canterbury, 2007), 21–23. See also David Brown, "Why 'Saints' Matter," in David Brown, *God in a Single Vision: Integrating Philosophy and Theology*, ed. Christopher R. Brewer and Robert MacSwain (London: Routledge, 2016), 157–70.

9. Patrick J. Sherry, "Philosophy and the Saints," *Heythrop Journal* 18 (1977): 23–37, quoting from 23.

goodness" is not entirely natural or solely due to human striving, but is regarded as the transformative, sanctifying work of God in the saintly person: not just virtue, but sanctification.[10] Sherry thus goes on to explore the relationship between religious experience and human sanctification, noting that the former is often understood to be private and momentary, while the latter is more public and typically occurs slowly over a long period within a given person's life. Furthermore, "whereas those who appeal to religious experience tend to speak of God's presence, those who are more concerned with [human] sanctification often prefer to speak of [God's] *activity*."[11]

Sherry then states that such holiness can also be used as a natural theological argument. In the published version of his 1960 Gifford Lectures at the University of Aberdeen, H. H. Price claimed that what he reluctantly (and thus rather vaguely) called "spiritual people" have religious experiences that most human beings do not, experiences that apparently provide evidence for and thus justify their own beliefs about God. Crucially, however, Price then continued that "the existence of such persons [and not just their experiences] is in practice the most persuasive argument in favour of a religious world-outlook, and probably always has been. When we meet such a person, we can hardly help wishing that we ourselves could be like him, and we cannot help wondering whether there may not be something to be said for the world-outlook which he accepts, however strange or even absurd that outlook may seem to us to be."[12]

Sherry thinks that Price's claims here are novel, interesting, and problematic, and thus subjects them to sustained scrutiny. They involve the topics of human transformation for the better (its causes and the epistemological significance of them), the moral and conceptual criteria of sanctity, and the power of religious experience to create individuals of such attractive charisma. As Sherry puts it, "Price seems to be arguing that the radiating love and serenity of saintly or 'spiritual people' are important because they attract others and so make them disposed to investigate the claims of theism, and because they are visible fruits of genuine religious experience."[13] Note that Sherry himself is responsible for

---

10. See also the parallel discussion in Patrick Sherry, *Religion, Truth, and Language-Games* (London: Macmillan, 1977), 109–16, esp. 115.

11. Sherry, "Philosophy and the Saints," 25.

12. H. H. Price, *Belief* (London: Allen & Unwin, 1969), 475.

13. See Sherry, "Philosophy and the Saints," 27–31, with this quotation on 31.

importing the loaded term "saintly" to describe Price's admittedly vague "spiritual people."

So what should we think of Price's argument, thus construed? Sherry is intrigued but not convinced. As he wrote in a parallel discussion published the same year:

> Certainly it is tempting to appeal to spiritual transformation as evidence for the existence of a transformative power, i.e. God. But clearly such a line of argument would be fraught with great difficulties. It is not perhaps to the point to object that different religions with mutually incompatible dogmas produce a similar sanctity in their adherents, for [here] we are simply concerned with *theism*. But it is unclear whether [someone] who acknowledges the sanctity of some religious believers and yet refuses to admit God's existence is making a *mistake* and, if so, of what kind. Surely it could be argued that the existence of saintly people merely shows that all [people] have certain latent capacities which can be developed, but not necessarily that there is some external power which fosters this development?[14]

Note the interesting resonance with Monette's claim at the very beginning of this essay, namely, his affirmation that holy people exist but that God does not: although Sherry himself believes in God, here he admits that it would be difficult to accuse someone such as Monette of making a logical mistake or an error in reasoning. Note also the explicit acknowledgment that "sanctity" is found both in and beyond the boundaries of Christianity and so therefore "saints" in the relevant sense may be found in all religions: the "hagiological argument" is indeed an argument for God or the divine, not any one religious tradition in particular.[15]

14. Sherry, *Religion, Truth, and Language-Games*, 111. The parallel passage in "Philosophy and the Saints" is on 31–32, but I think it is less clearly expressed.

15. And to this extent the versions of the hagiological argument that I am interested in contrast with the otherwise very similar view of Hans Urs von Balthasar, for whom holiness in the relevant sense is restricted to Christianity and thus saints are evidence for this religion only, and in particular for Roman Catholicism: see Victoria S. Harrison's helpful article "Human Holiness as Religious *Apologia*," *International Journal for Philosophy of Religion* 46 (1999): 63–82, and her monograph *The Apologetic Value of Human Holiness: Von Balthasar's Christocentric Philosophical Anthropology* (Dordrecht: Kluwer Academic Publishers, 2000).

And yet, the focus on transformative holiness certainly has special relevance to the Christian claim that God both saves and sanctifies. Returning to "Philosophy and the Saints," Sherry goes on to argue that while he is not entirely convinced by Price's argument,

> it has pointed to an important fact, namely that the Christian belief in God has certain truth-conditions, and at least some of these refer to the present. If Christians were never changed by the practice of their religion, this would count against, if not decisively refute, certain important Christian doctrines: in particular, I would be prepared to argue that it would tell against the doctrines of grace and of the Holy Spirit, and that it would involve some modification of the doctrine of God. But this suggests that we should be considering *falsification* rather than, as Price does, *verification*. And if this is so, we must look for a looser logical relationship between the process of sanctification and the existence of God than that sought by Price.[16]

Sherry therefore concludes: "(i) The existence of a causal link between sanctification and God's action does not necessarily mean that we can construct a direct argument from one to the other, as Price does," but "(ii) Nevertheless Price is right in regarding the existence of saintly people as a truth-condition of Christianity and many other theistic religions."[17] In short, even if they are not *proofs* of God's existence, perhaps "saints are *signs* of God's continuing activity."[18]

Seven years later, in 1984, Sherry returned to these themes in a short book titled *Spirit, Saints, and Immortality*. In the preface he acknowledges the continuing (and, to him, surprising) paucity of attention to this topic, stating, "Over the past few years I have come to think that the existence of saintly people is of much greater import for theologians than is usually realised, for it raises questions about grace, redemption, the Holy Spirit, the nature of God, the

16. Sherry, "Philosophy and the Saints," 32. Both for his own position and in regard to Price's argument, Sherry considers both (a) the external perception of "saints" and (b) the internal experience of those undergoing some degree of personal transformation understood as sanctification. I have focused on (a), but for a very similar recent argument focusing on (b), see Steven L. Porter, "The Evidential Force of Spiritual Maturity and the Christian Doctrine of Sanctification," *Religious Studies* 55 (2019): 111–29.

17. Sherry, "Philosophy and the Saints," 36.

18. Sherry, "Philosophy and the Saints," 33.

possibility of attaining a likeness to [God] and immortality. . . . Moreover, the existence of saints should be considered by philosophers, too, for it is a rare and precious occurrence and one which requires evaluation and explanation."[19] In this volume Sherry thus explores in more detail than the earlier article a range of philosophical and theological issues illuminated by sainthood. Most important for our purposes, however, is that under the influence of Richard Swinburne's distinctive understanding of evidence, Sherry is now more willing to grant that "the phenomenon of sanctity has an evidential value."[20] That is, while he freely admits that a "non-believer [like Monette] may well recognise and admire the phenomenon of sanctity [and yet] reject its religious interpretation," and while he still insists that "it would be a mistake to use the occurrence of saintliness as the premise of an argument to prove God's existence," nevertheless Sherry now accepts that it is "possible that the occurrence of sanctification *is evidence for* the existence of God: for if the occurrence requires explanation, the activity of God is one possible explanation; moreover, looking at it another way, the occurrence is something to be expected, given belief in the Judaeo-Christian God, and therefore it confirms this belief (assuming that we have other grounds for it)."[21] In short, Sherry importantly modifies his previous conclusion from "Philosophy and the Saints" as follows: "The existence of saintly people is a truth-condition of Christianity and many other theistic religions, in that the absence of saints would tend to falsify some doctrines. I do not think that the existence of saints verifies theism in the strong sense of conclusively establishing its truth; but *it is evidence for* its truth—a weaker relationship—for the existence of saintliness is something which requires an explanation, and theism provides one such explanation, in terms of the presence of God's spirit."[22] Thus,

19. Patrick Sherry, *Spirit, Saints, and Immortality* (Albany: State University Press of New York; London: Macmillan, 1984), ix.

20. Sherry, *Spirit, Saints, and Immortality*, 31.

21. Sherry, *Spirit, Saints, and Immortality*, 45, 46, and 47. The last quotation from page 47 ends with footnote 34, the text of which is on page 92: "My argument at this point owes much to Richard Swinburne, *The Existence of God* (Oxford, 1979)." That is, the publication of Swinburne's book between "Philosophy and the Saints" and *Spirit, Saints, and Immortality* gave Sherry a different way to think about evidence than his previous one, a way that enabled him to see how saintly lives could provide evidence for God, after all. Swinburne's *The Existence of God* was republished in a second edition in 2004.

22. Sherry, *Spirit, Saints, and Immortality*, 48.

Price (as interpreted by Sherry) says, "If saints, therefore God," whereas Sherry (influenced by Swinburne) says, "If God, therefore saints"—and thus, "If no saints, then no God."

III. Three Versions

There is much to reflect on in Sherry's claims above, particularly his provocative assertion that saints are a "truth-condition" of Christianity and other theistic religions. But having first provided three examples of the idea that some exemplary human lives provide evidence for God, and having then considered Sherry's evolving engagement with Price's similar proposal, I now want to suggest that instead of just one generic version of the hagiological argument shared by all of these various figures, there are in fact three distinct versions of the hagiological argument to consider, what I propose we call the *propositional*, the *perceptual*, and the *performative* versions. And while they correspond more or less to the examples from Farrer, van Inwagen, and Williams presented above, each of these thinkers may well represent more than one version, as indeed does Sherry's development of Price. In short, the versions are *conceptually* distinct even if the figures espousing them defend more than one at a time or do not clearly distinguish them in quite the way that I suggest here.

Farrer's view of the evidential value of human holiness actually cuts across more than one version, but his straightforward claim that "the saint is our evidence" parallels in an inchoate form what Sarah Coakley has recently dubbed the "moral-teleological" argument. In her inaugural lecture as Norris-Hulse Professor of Divinity at Cambridge, Coakley asks: "Are there indeed evidences of supreme manifestations of cultural altruism that far exceed what could be accounted for in terms of well-calculated projections of genetic and cultural fitness? If so, would they perhaps best be accounted for, as part of another argument to the 'best explanation,' in terms of a hypothesised participation in the life of a loving and sacrificial God? Can the lives of the saints, in other words, manifestators of Christian altruism well beyond the calculations of 'fitness,' provide, at the end of the day, the best argument for God's existence?"[23] Here

23. Sarah Coakley, *Sacrifice Regained: Reconsidering the Rationality of Religious Belief* (Cambridge: Cambridge University Press, 2012), 26–27.

is what I call the *propositional* version of the argument. Coakley does not break down this argument into its component propositions, the precise steps of the "inference to the best explanation," but in its most basic form she presumably has in mind something like this:

1. There are human individuals manifesting supreme altruism.
2. These lives point beyond themselves to a transcendent personal (e.g., loving, generative, sacrificial, etc.) reality.
3. The best explanation for these exemplary lives is that transcendent personal reality.
4. Therefore, that transcendent personal reality probably exists.

The moral-teleological argument is distinctive inasmuch as it identifies "supreme altruism" (rather than morality as such, or design, or consciousness . . .) as the otherwise inexplicable trait or property or feature in our world requiring divine explanation by inference to the best explanation. This propositional argument thus must be evaluated by the standard tests of logic and empirical evidence. It is a formal argument about the alleged implications of human holiness construed in a primarily moral form as "supreme altruism." Such altruism either exists or it does not, and God is either the best explanation for it or not. This is thus a rather public, objective argument. As we saw earlier, Paul Monette (and many others) would be willing to accept (1) but not the subsequent steps of this argument. Likewise, Sherry would still prefer to argue that the absence of saints falsifies theism rather than the presence of saints verifies it, but even he is now more willing to grant that such saints do indeed provide evidence for God.

The *perceptual* version of the hagiological argument corresponds to standard arguments from religious experience but is distinctive inasmuch as it makes the locus of such experience our encounter with specific human lives. Rather than a process of inferential propositional reasoning, it emphasizes vivid awareness of divine reality mediated though holy individuals. In addition to van Inwagen's testimony, a similar view may be found in William James's famous *Varieties of Religious Experience*. For just one example, although it is more about saints themselves than the God they manifest, James says: "The greatest saints . . . show themselves, and there is no question; everyone perceives their strength and stature. Their sense of mystery in things, their passion, their goodness, irradiate about them and enlarge their outlines while they soften them. They are like pictures with an atmosphere and background; and placed alongside of them, the strong men of this world and no other seem as dry as sticks, as hard and crude as blocks of stone or brickbats."[24] Note how both van Inwagen and James appeal to metaphors of *light* as they seek to describe their perception of saintly lives: they "irradiate" goodness. Unlike the first version, divine reality is thus not an inference or the conclusion of a reasoning process ("If *a*, then *b*; *a*; therefore *b*") but a direct perception, even if "perception" is construed broadly, along the lines of William Alston's *Perceiving God: The Epistemology of Religious Experience*.[25] It also thus has more of a private character than the first argument: it's more difficult to say to someone, "You are wrong about what you claim to have seen," but of course we can and do say this when it seems necessary.

As distinctive subspecies of other theistic arguments, the propositional and perceptual versions of the hagiological argument presumably have the same strengths and weaknesses of—and are thus subject to the same familiar objections to—the moral and teleological arguments and appeals to religious experience, respectively. Nevertheless, further analysis and critique of these first two versions may yet help us better understand the phenomenon of sainthood as well as the patterns of reasoning associated with those standard theistic arguments.

But the performative version of the hagiological argument takes us into less familiar territory. In *The Evidence for God: Religious Knowledge Reexamined*, Paul Moser puts forward a similar claim to what we heard earlier from Williams and Hillesum, but in more formal terms. He says:

> This book approaches the question of whether God exists from a new perspective, in which humans themselves are put under moral question, before God's authority, in raising the question of whether God exists. . . . The resulting evidence for God is not speculative, abstract, or casual but is, instead, morally and existentially challenging for inquirers as they themselves

24. William James, *Varieties of Religious Experience* (1902; reprint, London: Fontana, 1960), 364. Cited in John Cottingham's helpful chapter "Saints and Saintliness," in *The Oxford Handbook of the Epistemology of Theology*, ed. William J. Abraham and Frederick D. Aquino (Oxford: Oxford University Press, 2017), 79–80. James has several chapters on saintliness in *Varieties*, but Cottingham's use of this particular passage suggested its appropriateness in this context.

25. William Alston, *Perceiving God: The Epistemology of Religious Experience* (Ithaca, NY: Cornell University Press, 1991).

responsively and willingly become evidence of God's reality in receiving and reflecting God's moral character for others. The book calls this personifying evidence of God, because it requires the evidence to be personified in an intentional agent, such as a purposive human, and thereby to be evidence inherently of an intentional agent.[26]

Here the evidence for God is not expressed propositionally but is *personified*—that is, in my terms, *performed* across a specific life-narrative and not abstracted from it. *Analogically*, then, the person and the "argument" are the same thing. And, unlike the first two versions that evaluate the phenomenon of human holiness *externally*, this version turns the focus and burden of proof *within*. Moser thus asks, "are we ourselves willing to become, in volitional interaction with God, evidence of God's reality, thereby reflecting God's reality for others?"[27] According to Moser, people of faith are called to generate personified evidence for God. In other words, *ask not what theistic evidence can do for you, ask what you can do for theistic evidence*!

Moser contrasts his position with the conventional teleological and cosmological arguments of natural theology—what he dismissively calls "spectator evidence that makes no demand or call on the direction of a human will or life, such as either observational evidence from design or order or theoretical evidence concerning the need for a first cause of experienced contingent events."[28] Instead, he argues for what he calls a "volitional theism" that acknowledges that "a perfectly loving God would seek noncoercively to transform the wills of wayward humans, and thereby to have humans themselves become personifying evidence of God's reality, in willingly receiving and reflecting God's powerful moral character for others and thus bringing God's presence near to others."[29] Like Hillesum and Williams, Moser wants religious believers to "take responsibility for making God credible in the world" by themselves becoming or personifying evidence that makes such belief rational for both others and themselves.

26. Paul K. Moser, *The Evidence for God: Religious Knowledge Reexamined* (Cambridge: Cambridge University Press, 2010), ix.

27. Moser, *The Evidence for God*, 15. See also Porter's article cited in note 16 above.

28. Moser, *The Evidence for God*, 37.

29. Moser, *The Evidence for God*, 16.

In the terms of my typology, this third version of the hagiological argument does not present a propositional inference (from saints to God), nor does it claim a numinous perception (in seeing the saint we also "see" God), but it rather invites a performative response of personal transformation (to somehow act out and thereby generate evidence for God), and thus to become a personified "argument," analogically speaking. It thus does not seem to correspond easily to some other standard theistic argument, which adds to its interest and value. On the other hand, Moser's claim to novelty is somewhat diluted by the similar views of Williams and Hillesum, and Farrer in other writings. Likewise, historian John Boswell states: "A life can be an argument; being can be a reason."[30] Boswell appeals to the Gospel of John's identification of Jesus as the Logos, which in Greek means not just "word" but also "reason" and "argument."[31] Thus, he says, God "sent an argument in the form of a human being, a life, a person. The argument became flesh and blood: so real that no one could refute or ignore it."[32] Boswell further claims that such identification between person and argument is not a uniquely Christological phenomenon, but that all Christians are also called to be "*logoi* in this sense, arguments incarnated in persons."[33] Moser does not seem to be aware of these parallels to his epistemic proposals, and so one of my goals here is to make these connections and suggest that Moser's *The Evidence for God* might be construed as contributing a rare defense of the performative version of the hagiological argument.[34]

30. John Boswell, "[Logos and Biography]," in *Theology and Sexuality: Classic and Contemporary Readings*, ed. Eugene F. Rogers Jr. (Oxford: Blackwell, 2002), 359.

31. Boswell, "[Logos and Biography]," 359.

32. Boswell, "[Logos and Biography]," 360.

33. Boswell, "[Logos and Biography]," 360–61. He makes this claim explicitly in regard to gay and lesbian Christians who, "like all the outsiders who have remained loyal to the church in the face of its hostility . . . thereby made their commitments, their lives, their beings an unanswerable, living statement of faithfulness and love" (360). But his specific claim about "incarnating arguments" in persons is clearly intended to be more broadly applicable.

34. In addition to my book *Solved by Sacrifice* cited in note 4, some of these thoughts were also previously worked out in my contributions to the symposium on the book in *Syndicate Theology* 3, no. 5 (September/October 2016): 2–37; see also the online version, which contains some material from me and some of the other symposiasts not included in the print edition: https://tinyurl.com/4w8ye9s7.

IV. Questions and Objections

Having begun with Paul Monette's atheistic affirmation of human holiness but not of God, let me now circle back to pick up some questions for and objections to the hagiological argument in all three of these versions. It is of course possible to end the conversation before it begins by refusing to acknowledge the existence of human holiness at all. But I think it is both more interesting and more plausible to agree with Monette that "there *are* holy men and women." The question then becomes, can we acknowledge human holiness *without* also acknowledging God? Clearly, many do, and as we have seen, even Sherry is dubious about whether this is a problematic position to hold, but the hagiological argument in all three versions seeks to move us, legitimately or not, *from* human holiness *to* God.

But there are other essential questions that must be asked as well. So far in this essay I have implicitly identified human holiness with altruism, mostly for the ease of expositing Farrer and Coakley and her aptly named *moral*-teleological argument. But I believe it is a mistake to *reduce* holiness to exemplary moral goodness, or to construe it in entirely moral terms. Jacqueline Mariña observes that such a reduction is a distinctively Kantian move, but it is one that I think should be resisted.[35] Holiness is indeed entangled inevitably in issues of altruism and supererogation, but a well-known exchange between Susan Wolf and Robert Merrihew Adams on sainthood should remind us that real saints are not clenched-teeth do-gooders driven by a purely utilitarian calculus. Adams acknowledges that saints are often "devoted to improving the lives and circumstances of other people" and that there is indeed "unusual moral goodness in the saints," but he denies that ethical or political concerns are their primary motivation, for "sainthood is essentially a religious phenomenon, and even so political a saint as Gandhi saw his powerful humanitarian concern in the context of a more comprehensive devotion to God." What Adams calls the "substance of sainthood" is not "sheer willpower striving . . . to accomplish a

---

35. See Jacqueline Mariña, "Holiness," in *A Companion to the Philosophy of Religion*, ed. Charles Taliaferro, Paul Draper, and Philip Quinn (Oxford: Wiley-Blackwell, 2010), 235–42. I have contributed the entry on this topic to *The Wiley-Blackwell Encyclopedia of Philosophy of Religion*, ed. Stewart Goetz and Charles Taliaferro, vol. 2 (Hoboken, NJ: Wiley-Blackwell, 2022), 1087–91, and online at https://tinyurl.com/ycy657zb.

boundless task" but "goodness overflowing from a boundless source. Or so, at least, the saints perceive it."[36] Adequate definitions of the categories or properties of "holiness" and "sainthood" require substantial philosophical, theological, and interreligious homework, but obviously the hagiological argument needs such definitions to get off the ground.

So the first two questions that the argument must answer are "Is there holiness?" and "If so, what is it?" If those questions are given acceptable answers, all versions of the argument must then show how some human lives exemplify holiness to such a remarkable extent that the existence of God is thereby made more plausible than not. In other words, they must show why human holiness provides evidence for God. But to display this rational advantage the argument must face strong and obvious objections. As noted above, the propositional and perceptual versions face the familiar objections to the moral and teleological arguments and appeals to religious experience, respectively: That is, *is* the best explanation of human holiness really the existence of God or are there more plausible naturalistic explanations? And *do* alleged perceptions of divine reality in saints really make it more likely than not that God actually exists, or again are naturalistic explanations of such alleged perceptions more convincing? More specifically, does the specific appeal to *saints* in each version of the argument help overcome these familiar objections, or does it succumb to them?

Given its more distinctive character, the performative version of the argument faces distinctively different challenges. First, it must be asked whether some human lives actually do "personify" evidence for God, whatever that "personification" is ultimately construed to mean. Second, at least some expressions of the performative version (such as those offered by Williams and

---

36. For the original exchange see Susan Wolf, "Moral Saints," *Journal of Philosophy* 79 (1982): 419–39, and Robert Merrihew Adams, "Saints," *Journal of Philosophy* 81 (1984): 392–401. Wolf's essay was reprinted in her *The Variety of Values: Essays on Morality, Meaning, and Love* (New York: Oxford University Press, 2015), 11–29, and Adams's was reprinted in his *The Virtue of Faith and Other Essays in Philosophical Theology* (New York: Oxford University Press, 1987), 164–73: the quotations above are from page 168 of this version. I have explored this debate in more detail in "Are Effective Altruists Saints? Effective Altruism, Moral Sainthood, and Human Holiness," in *Effective Altruism and Religion: Synergies, Tensions, Dialogue*, ed. Dominic Roser, Stefan Riedener, and Markus Huppenbauer (Baden-Baden: Nomos, 2022), 211–33. This volume is also available in an online open access format, and my chapter may be accessed at https://tinyurl.com/mrmvfjp5.

Moser) denigrate the propositional arguments of conventional natural theology and privilege saintly human lives over them: Is this denigration necessary or helpful? But, third, and more generally, even if such personified evidence is acknowledged and agreed to be significant, the greatest objection to the argument from saints is the sadly less controversial existence of *antisaints*—or, perhaps better, the suggestive anagram *stains*. And by "antisaints" or "stains" I mean adherents of a given religious tradition whose moral and spiritual character has not been *enhanced* but instead *corrupted* by their religious belief and practice. Examples are legion and much in the news. If saints provide evidence *for* God's existence, then does it not unfortunately follow that antisaints or stains provide evidence *against* it?[37]

I think the most promising reply to this third objection is to insist that the hagiological argument offers not quantitative but *qualitative* evidence. Saints, if they exist, are by definition rare and wonderful. The hagiological argument in all three versions can remain open to the empirical (if unanswerable) question of whether, in regard to sheer numbers of practitioners and their collective behavior, religious belief even might do more harm than good. It is not an argument on behalf of religion as such or its positive and negative effects, but on behalf of God or the divine. Accepting that there are saintly lives, it then asks what holiness is and where it comes from. It argues in each version that a specific aspect of human life identified, or perceived, or experienced in such holy lives, perhaps even including the believer's own life, somehow helps to support belief in the transcendent reality of God or the divine. And yet, at the same time, it must remain open to the worry about falsification raised by Sherry, and thus the problem of antisaints or stains cannot be evaded so quickly. Thus, Craig Hovey poignantly writes that "if Christians cannot point to Christianity's goodness, they should refrain from claiming that, despite all appearances to the contrary, it really is quite true."[38]

37. An earlier version of this paper was presented at the Society of Christian Philosophers, Eastern Regional Conference: "Acquiring Faith," held at Rutgers University and New Brunswick Theological Seminary, New Brunswick, NJ, on October 21, 2016. In response to this question, Daniel Rubio interestingly argued that antisaints or stains would not provide evidence *against* the existence of God but rather *for* the devil! The question therefore entails thinking more deeply about the kinds of explanation we are inclined to offer to account for extreme human goodness and extreme human evil.

38. Craig Hovey, "Christian Ethics as Good News," in *Imaginative Apologetics: Theology,*

V. Conclusion

In this essay my primary goals have been to identify and classify what I call the hagiological argument for the existence of God, not to defend it and not to analyze the three versions in any substantial detail. In brief, the hagiological argument questions whether one can agree with Paul Monette that human holiness exists while affirming that God does not. Patrick Sherry's concerns about falsification versus verification notwithstanding, he now acknowledges that saints *can* be construed as evidence for God: as he puts it, "the phenomenon of sanctity has an evidential value." The three identified versions approach this question in different ways, some of which may well be better than others. And there are certainly other philosophically, theologically, and spiritually interesting questions one could ask about saints and holiness.[39] But at the very least, on the basis of the testimony gathered here, the hagiological argument in its various forms seems to be an important but neglected way to understand how some people do in fact acquire and maintain their belief in God or the divine.

For example, in his essay on saints cited earlier, Robert Merrihew Adams defined them as "people in whom the holy or divine can be seen."[40] Then in a later discussion he wrote: "The Holy is fascinating, the Holy is beautiful, the Holy is bliss, the Holy is just, . . . the Holy is love. . . . But 'nice' is definitely not the word for it. From a human point of view, the Holy has rough edges. It screams with the hawk and laughs with the hyenas. We cannot comprehend it. It is fearful to us, and in some ways dangerous." And yet, Adams says, "The strangeness of the Holy can be reflected in ideals of human life, or of sainthood. . . . Indeed . . . it is

---

Philosophy, and the Catholic Tradition, ed. Andrew Davison (London: SCM, 2011), 110. As just one example of this problem, Hovey goes on to say: "Because it seriously affects Christian claims about goodness, the sex-abuse scandal currently plaguing the Roman Catholic Church really does threaten the truth of the gospel" (110–11). Obviously, however, this scandal is far more pervasive and thus even more problematic for Christian truth claims.

39. For example, John Hick's *An Interpretation of Religion: Human Responses to the Transcendent*, 2nd ed. (New Haven: Yale University Press, 2004) contains a significant discussion of sanctification and saintliness that is highly relevant here, although for him these realities have more of a soteriological than an epistemological significance. See also David Brown's essay cited in note 8 above, in which he considers three roles that saints can play in the life of faith: exemplarity, evidence (following my argument in *Solved by Sacrifice*, 221–35), and emphasizing our social interdependence.

40. Adams, "Saints," in *The Virtue of Faith*, 170.

often precisely in the unnaturalness, or better the supernaturalness of the saints' goodness that their wonderfulness is found. In them it seems we can glimpse or touch a goodness that is more than theirs, a superhuman, a transcendent goodness that we too long for."[41] It is this complex and ambiguous phenomenon with which the hagiological argument in each of its forms must engage.[42]

41. Robert Merrihew Adams, *Finite and Infinite Goods: A Framework for Ethics* (Oxford: Oxford University Press, 1999), 52–53.

42. Earlier versions of this essay were presented at the Society of Christian Philosophers conference on October 21, 2016, as cited in note 37; the "World Religions Café" at the Center for the Study of World Religions, Harvard Divinity School, on February 1, 2017; the Appalachian College Association Summit in Kingsport, TN, on September 29, 2017; and the Logos Institute for Analytic and Exegetical Theology Seminar at St. Mary's College, University of St. Andrews (May 7, 2021, via Zoom). I am grateful to all those who attended each presentation and especially for those who engaged in conversation afterward. I am also grateful to the late Robert Merrihew Adams, David Brown, Chris Bryan, and Ben Cowgill for comments on earlier versions of the text, and to Jeffrey Stout for some very helpful correspondence on the themes of the paper. Some of this research occurred during my 2016–2017 sabbatical as a visiting scholar at Harvard Divinity School, funded in part by a Post-Doctoral Faculty Fellowship from the Appalachian College Association, and some was made possible through the support of a 2019–2020 grant from the Templeton Religion Trust. The opinions expressed in this publication are those of the author and do not necessarily reflect the views of the Templeton Religion Trust.

Contemporary Anglican Systematic Theology: Three Examples in David Brown, Sarah Coakley, and David F. Ford

JASON A. FOUT, BENJAMIN J. KING, AND ROBERT MACSWAIN

In our own time, we are well aware of the imperialism of earlier claims of the Church of England to speak for the whole Communion. Gone are the days when a book written only by members of the Church of England and (at most) two representatives of the Scottish Episcopal Church would dare to use the subtitle *By Members of the Anglican Communion*. But the poor choice of subtitle does not invalidate the important contribution that *Essays Catholic and Critical* made to Anglican theology in 1926.[1]

The present writers do not claim that the three theologians whose works are reviewed in this essay, and who taught in England and Scotland, speak for Anglicanism worldwide. But we do claim that each has made an important contribution to Anglican theology. By keeping Scripture as well as ecclesial practices (and disagreements) in mind, they exhibit a characteristically Anglican approach to their academic work. Although all three were Oxbridge educated, we are also not saying that an English education is required in order to be an Anglican theologian, nor that these are the only contemporary Anglican theo-

---

1. See Edward Gordon Selwyn, ed., *Essays Catholic and Critical: By Members of the Anglican Communion*, 3rd ed. (London: SPCK, 1929). The only "member of the Communion" not resident in England was in fact still English, the philosopher A. E. Taylor, who attended a congregation of the Scottish Episcopal Church while a professor at Edinburgh. Contributor Will Spens was born in Scotland.

Originally published in *Anglican Theological Review* 94, no. 2 (Spring 2012): 319–34.

logians we could have selected—far from it. Rather, these three happen to be our teachers, and putting them together enables the more general conversation of which Timothy Sedgwick writes: "Without this conversation . . . distinctive claims are lost from view, . . . claims which provide insight into what is central to Anglican understandings of Christian faith and life and what within Anglicanism remains captive to its Englishness."[2]

The accounts of what is *distinctive* in the work of David F. Ford, David Brown, and Sarah Coakley *at the same time* show what these theologians have in common. That commonality we take to be central to Anglicanism, and we hope to show that there are reasons why a tradition with its roots in Great Britain still offers virtues to be practiced across the Communion, and provides answers to knotty epistemological problems inside and outside the academy. Put briefly, all three begin their theology with (more or less critical) readings of Scripture and with ecclesial practice. But each demonstrates that, from there, contemporary Anglican theology makes many border crossings: into the theology of other denominations and faith traditions, into analytic and Continental philosophy, into the arts and natural sciences, even into divine life. It should be noted that Donald MacKinnon (1913–1994), who taught all three of these theologians the importance of "border crossing" into other disciplines, himself crossed the border from Scotland to England and back; and geographical border crossings are important to these three as well, as will be seen from their biographies. In fact, only one of the three is English—and she spent a large part of her teaching career in the United States. Moreover, Coakley and Ford both received American master's degrees and wrote doctorates on German theology, providing the Harvard/ Troeltschian and Yale/Barthian tenor of their respective early work.

Perhaps these transatlantic crossings explain why Coakley and Ford have lower levels of engagement with earlier Anglican theologians than does Brown, who self-consciously upholds the empirical tradition of Bishop Butler and John Henry Newman. Coakley is more likely to engage with Judith Butler than Joseph Butler, but she puts her into conversation with the early church fathers— typical Anglican dialogue partners. Ford might not be an obvious choice as an Anglican theologian—as opposed to a theologian who is a committed Anglican—because he interacts so little with historic Anglican theologians or the

2. Timothy F. Sedgwick, "The Anglican Exemplary Tradition," *Anglican Theological Review* 92 (2012): 229-30.

church fathers. Yet while Ford may not engage with earlier Anglicans nor with typical Anglican dialogue partners, the form of his theology is unmistakably Anglican, involved with border-crossing conversations, immersed in Scripture and worship, and alert to the possibility of the contingent character of things bearing witness to God. The contexts and themes of each person's theology will now be examined.

I. David F. Ford: A Review by Jason A. Fout

Born in 1948, David F. Ford grew up in a "not particularly practicing" Church of Ireland family.[3] His interest in God and theology grew out of life's upheavals, including the death of his father when Ford was twelve, and later—while studying classics at Trinity College, Dublin—wrestling with the social issues raised by student riots, the civil rights movement, and "the troubles" in Northern Ireland. He sensed that deep responses were required, and he wondered how Christian faith might approach these matters. He accepted a scholarship from St. John's College, Cambridge, to study whatever he wanted; he chose theology. While there, he met and worked with a number of varied and influential Anglican theologians who combined deep intelligence with a sincere faith, not least Stephen Sykes (1939–2014) and Donald MacKinnon. Following on from this, he moved to Yale, where he took a master's degree, working with Hans Frei, among others. He then returned to Cambridge for his doctorate, taking a term away in Tübingen; he wrote his dissertation under Sykes and MacKinnon on the use of biblical narrative in Karl Barth's *Church Dogmatics*.[4]

Ford's first teaching post was in the University of Birmingham, where he taught for fifteen years. The dynamic diversity of Birmingham affected him greatly, particularly its multifaith character. Alongside this engagement with other religions, Ford also began longer-term collaborations with two colleagues, Frances Young and Daniel Hardy. Young taught New Testament and patristics; together, she and Ford authored *Meaning and Truth in 2 Corinthians*, an effort

3. David S. Cunningham, "The Way of Wisdom: The Practical Theology of David Ford," *Christian Century* 120, no. 9 (May 3, 2003): 31.

4. Published as *Barth and God's Story: Biblical Narrative and the Theological Method of Karl Barth in the* Church Dogmatics (Frankfurt: Lang, 1981).

to bring hermeneutical, theological, and biblical-studies perspectives together in the task of scriptural interpretation.[5] The result is a creative, text-focused, multidisciplinary account that takes seriously the questions raised by each discipline yet seeks to do full justice to the text of the ancient letter. Above all, Young and Ford intended the work to go beyond textual concerns to an apprehension of the truth communicated, and in that, to be transformed.[6]

Ford's second long-term collaboration begun at Birmingham, with Daniel Hardy, who also taught theology,[7] led to the coauthored work entitled *Jubilate: Theology in Praise*, renamed *Living in Praise: Worshipping and Knowing God* in its second edition.[8] In it, they seek to relate knowing and praising God, exploring praise as the way by which human knowing and living are integrally related "to God and God's purposes."[9] This book, above all, is a constructive work of theology, attempting to show something of God, the human "in" God, and the myriad implications of this understanding for life. Ford and Hardy engage in a distinctive "voice" for doing theology, experimenting with various discourses: this is not a work of traditional systematic or dogmatic theology, but something much more exploratory.[10]

Ford returned to Cambridge in 1991 to become Regius Professor of Divinity, the first Anglican not in holy orders to hold the post, which he held until his retirement in 2015. Professionally, his period as Regius Professor began a new phase of building and guiding institutions, including founding the Centre for Advanced Religious and Theological Studies, and the Cambridge Inter-Faith Program. Theologically, three major works mark this period. The first, *Self and Salvation: Being Transformed*, constructs a theological anthropology of the self before God.[11] In this work Ford continued the pattern that he developed

5. Frances Young and David F. Ford, *Meaning and Truth in 2 Corinthians* (London: SPCK, 1987).

6. Young and Ford, *Meaning and Truth*, 7.

7. David F. Ford, "Faith Seeking Wisdom: How My Mind Has Changed," *Christian Century* 127, no. 24 (November 18, 2010): 30–34.

8. David F. Ford and Daniel W. Hardy, *Living in Praise: Worshipping and Knowing God* (Grand Rapids: Baker Academic, 2005).

9. Ford and Hardy, *Living in Praise*, 194.

10. Ford and Hardy, *Living in Praise*, 3.

11. David F. Ford, *Self and Salvation: Being Transformed* (Cambridge: Cambridge University Press, 1999).

earlier, of creatively expounding the church's faith through the lenses of theological engagement with Scripture, emphasizing the centrality of worship and conversational engagements with a wide range of thinkers. As before, he does not rest content within the boundaries of dogmatic theology, but draws into consideration a variety of thinkers who have influenced him, including Emmanuel Levinas, Paul Ricoeur, Eberhard Jüngel, Thérèse of Lisieux, and Dietrich Bonhoeffer. While he intends to make a contribution to systematic theology, he does so in part by detouring around typical perennial disputes within the discipline, drawing instead on resources such as phenomenology in order to make a constructive statement. Further, the tone of this work is much more of synthesis than analysis: Ford is convinced that the truth of doctrine cannot be considered apart from ethical, philosophical, liturgical, or biographical considerations, and these run throughout the book. The result is a theology that is not dryly conceptual, but self-involving.[12]

The second major work of theology written during this time, *Christian Wisdom: Desiring God and Learning in Love*, explores "key elements of Christian wisdom and its relevance to contemporary living."[13] Ford engages this topic particularly through the interpretation of Scripture, not only its historical composition and context but also with its historical and contemporary reception and interpretation in view: Scripture is not just read, it is reread, and this ongoing, expansive, communal engagement is extraordinarily generative for all aspects of life. The result is an account of wisdom that embraces love and desire as well as knowledge and practice.

Unlike *Self and Salvation,* in which wide-ranging conversations with others are initially to the fore and exploration of the specifically Christian self is left until later, *Christian Wisdom* features a close reading of scriptural texts in the first part and then proceeds to set out three case studies that draw Christian wisdom into "cross-border" engagements: with Jews and Muslims in the "Scriptural

---

12. For an overview of Ford's project, see Luther Zeigler, "The Many Faces of the Worshipping Self: David Ford's Anglican Vision of Christian Transformation," *Anglican Theological Review* 89 (2007): 267–85. Although Zeigler shows well how Ford may be understood as an Anglican theologian, he overstates the degree to which Ford is philosophically committed to phenomenology (as opposed to finding phenomenology heuristically useful).

13. David F. Ford, *Christian Wisdom: Desiring God and Learning in Love* (Cambridge: Cambridge University Press, 2007), 2. "Wisdom" in this case goes beyond the biblical genre of wisdom literature.

Reasoning" movement, with the contemporary university, and with the developmentally disabled in the L'Arche communities. Each of these engagements grows out of long-standing commitments in Ford's own life.

One of these engagements, the practice of Scriptural Reasoning, has figured prominently in Ford's recent work. Scriptural Reasoning features Muslims, Christians, and Jews gathering to read and study their scriptures together in mutual hospitality. Space forbids deeper consideration of this important movement, except to note the centrality of friendship to the practice.[14]

A third publication marks Ford's final years of teaching and the first years of his retirement, *The Gospel of John: A Theological Commentary*.[15] The project took twenty years, over which Ford maintained an ongoing fascination with John, exploring it through many shorter publications and presentations,[16] reading it with friends and scholars Richard Bauckham and Richard Hays, and his own deep, prayerful rumination on the text itself. Originally intended for the Westminster John Knox Belief series of commentaries, it overflowed the strictures of that series (in accord with the abundance that Ford finds in John!) and later found a home as a stand-alone work with Baker Academic.

The commentary itself is theological in orientation, written with rigor and engaging all the relevant scholarly literature. Yet it is much more than a run-of-the-mill biblical commentary, even as a theological commentary. Ford attends with great care to John's writing, and to Jesus as found in the gospel: one could say that he is listening *with John* for Jesus. Ford notes the abundance present in the gospel, not least in John's vocabulary, which simultaneously refers to the

14. Space also forbids consideration of a number of Ford's other works, among which are included *The Shape of Living: Spiritual Directions for Everyday Life*, 2nd ed. (Grand Rapids: Baker Books, 2004); *The Modern Theologians*, ed. David Ford with Rachel Muers, 3rd ed. (Oxford: Blackwell, 2005); *Shaping Theology: Engagements in a Religious and Secular World* (Oxford: Wiley-Blackwell, 2008); (with Daniel W. Hardy, Deborah Hardy Ford, and Peter Ochs) *Wording a Radiance: Parting Conversations on God and the Church* (London: SCM, 2010); *The Future of Christian Theology* (Oxford: Wiley-Blackwell, 2011); *Theology: A Very Short Introduction*, 2nd ed. (Oxford: Oxford University Press, 2013); *The Drama of Living: Becoming Wise in the Spirit* (Norwich, UK: Canterbury, 2014); and (with Ash Cocksworth) *Glorification and the Life of Faith* (Grand Rapids: Baker Academic, 2023).

15. David F. Ford, *The Gospel of John: A Theological Commentary* (Grand Rapids: Baker Academic, 2021).

16. Including the unpublished Bampton Lectures delivered at Oxford in 2015, entitled "Daring Spirit: John's Gospel Now."

mundane but also to "deeper meanings" that "stretch the thought and imagination of the reader."[17] And perhaps above all, Ford undertakes this work in the spirit of the evangelist himself, inviting the reader along with him into the love of Jesus, enticing the reader to go deeper into the abundance that John bears witness to and is found in Jesus.[18]

I have deliberately set forth Ford's career in more of a biographical than a systematic fashion, as this fits the sort of theologian Ford is. The conversations, relationships, and friendships that constitute Ford's life are intrinsic to his identity (as are the border crossings that these entail). He draws all of these into the task of theologizing, of speaking adequately of the encompassing reality of God, and of relating all things to God.

There are four aspects of this work that bear highlighting as distinctly Anglican. First, there is a care to attend to the contingent and particular as themselves theologically significant. Friendships, the experience of the Eucharist, encounters with the developmentally disabled, readings of Scripture, conversations with colleagues: all of these are significant for theologizing, rather than being accidents to be forgotten when thinking of God. There is in this a view of the world that sees creation, in its present reality, as capable of mediating knowledge of God, a sacramental view of reality, a view that some Anglicans in particular would call "incarnational."

Second, and closely related to this, Ford's theology does not dwell in the abstract and universal, nor does it tend to speak finally and authoritatively. While Ford does not deny the value of dogmatic theology, his work is much more exploratory, interrogative, and heuristic, sensitive to particular contexts, and carried out as much in the subjunctive mood—asking "what if?"—as in the indicative and imperative. This frees him to explore ideas and engagements, alert to their potential for illuminating Christian faith, without being committed to them as more final or more basic than Christian faith. This is fully consistent with the tendency of Anglicans to do theology through essays, pamphlets, sermons, and poetry, rather than single- or multivolume works of systematic theology. It is also consistent with the Anglican willingness to "borrow" outside of their tradition, without feeling thereby committed to the whole of the tradition from which they are borrowing.

17. Ford, *The Gospel of John*, 1.
18. Ford, *The Gospel of John*, 24.

Third, Ford's theology is deeply scriptural. It arises from close readings of the Bible, without being precommitted to a single hermeneutical strategy, stubbornly resisting any kind of reductivism, whether historical-critical or dogmatic. Whether writing theology or theological commentary, Ford is always concerned to do justice to the generativity of a text, particularly when it comes to Jesus. In a sense, Ford's is less a theology done on the basis of reading Scripture, and more on the basis of *rereading* Scripture: of praying it in worship, dwelling on it in love, and struggling with it to do full justice to the One who is revealed therein. This echoes broader Anglican theological tendencies that are not exclusively exegetical, nor so wedded to historical-critical methods so as to be left with a hypothetical historical reconstruction and nothing more. While certainly more complex than this, it reflects in some measure the Anglican use of the Bible more broadly, being found most regularly and prominently in the public prayer of the church: in Morning Prayer and Evening Prayer, and in the service of Holy Communion, in the Psalter and the lectionaries. The Bible is to be studied, yes, but it is also to be read and listened to in prayer and worship of God. Theologically this rereading is never completed, never exhausted: the depths of Scripture are never fully plumbed.

Finally, Ford's theology is deeply formed and informed by the practices of Christian life and specifically worship of God. For Ford, knowledge of God cannot come apart from the praise, love, and desire of God. And so to speak truly of God, and of all in relation to God, will necessarily involve one in the life of worship. In this regard, Ford is a paradigmatic Anglican theologian, seeing worship not as a response to a conceptual account of God, but seeing both worship and theology as themselves responding to the One in whom we "live, move and have our being."[19]

II. David Brown: A Review by Robert MacSwain

David Brown was born in Scotland in 1948.[20] He studied classics at the University of Edinburgh; studied philosophy and theology at Oxford; and received

19. Ford's work has been celebrated in Tom Greggs, Rachel Muers, and Simeon Zahl, eds., *The Vocation of Theology Today: A Festschrift for David Ford* (Eugene, OR: Cascade, 2013).

20. This biographical material is based on personal information and various public sources, including John Macquarrie, "A Sketch of David Brown," *Anglican Theological Review* 84 (2002): 767–70.

his doctorate in moral philosophy from Cambridge, where he was cosupervised by Elizabeth Anscombe (1919–2001) and Bernard Williams (1929–2003). After training for ordained ministry at Westcott House, Cambridge, he returned to Oxford as chaplain and fellow of Oriel College in 1976 and was also appointed as university lecturer in philosophical theology and ethics. In 1990 Brown took up the joint appointment of residentiary canon of Durham Cathedral and Van Mildert Professor of Divinity at Durham University.[21] During his seventeen years at Durham he was deeply involved in various artistic and musical projects related to the life of the Cathedral, and served as canon librarian from 1998 to 2007. A former member of the Doctrine Commission of the Church of England, in 2002 he was made a fellow of the British Academy, and in 2007 he returned to Scotland as Wardlaw Professor of Theology, Aesthetics, and Culture at the University of St. Andrews. He retired from this position in 2015.

For the majority of his career, Brown has thus followed the traditional Anglican model of combining academic teaching and research with pastoral, homiletic, and sacramental responsibilities.[22] His scholarly work has been characterized by four broad themes. The first, associated mostly with his period at Oxford, is the interaction between philosophy and theology. Two early books represent this dialogue, with *The Divine Trinity* defending a social doctrine of the Trinity against a strongly deistic and unitarian trend in twentieth-century English theology, and with *Continental Philosophy and Modern Theology* offering more of a synoptic survey of classic and contemporary figures.[23] At this point, Brown was primarily associated with a circle of Anglo-American analytic philosophers of religion, such as Basil Mitchell and Richard Swinburne, and

---

21. The oldest professorship at Durham, and one of the great chairs of Anglican theology: previous occupants include O. C. Quick (1885–1944), Michael Ramsey (1904–1988), Stephen Sykes (1939–2014), and Daniel W. Hardy (1930–2007). Brown's immediate successor was Mark McIntosh (1960–2021), who sadly died from ALS at the age of sixty-one, and the current occupant of the chair is Simon Oliver (1971–).

22. Two of his books for a popular audience are largely based upon sermons delivered at Durham: *The Word to Set You Free: Living Faith and Biblical Criticism* (London: SPCK, 1995) and *Through the Eyes of the Saints: A Pilgrimage through History* (London: Continuum, 2005).

23. See David Brown, *The Divine Trinity* (London: Duckworth; La Salle, IL: Open Court, 1985), and David Brown, *Continental Philosophy and Modern Theology: An Engagement* (Oxford: Blackwell, 1987). The argument of *The Divine Trinity* was directed largely against the work of scholars such as Geoffrey Lampe and Maurice Wiles, as well as the essay collection edited by John Hick, *The Myth of God Incarnate* (London: SCM, 1977).

published various essays in this genre. However, even at this early stage he was already pushing against the confines of strictly analytic and empirical thought toward a more open and nuanced approach.[24]

The second theme is sacramental theology, particularly as this was renewed and expanded in the last decades of the twentieth century to view all material reality in sacramental terms. Brown's work here has been both collaborative and interdisciplinary. Along with his colleague Ann Loades at Durham, he coedited two essay collections in this area,[25] and with David Fuller of Durham's English Department, he coauthored a volume that offered commentary on selections from a wide range of literary classics.[26] Against what he views as the dangerously instrumental and utilitarian tendency of contemporary Christianity—perhaps most obvious in many prevalent approaches to worship, liturgy, and church architecture—Brown sees sacramental theology as a plea "for the material world of divine and human creation alike to be seen as capable of mediating experience of God, a sacramental reality to be valued in its own right irrespective of what further benefits it may bring."[27]

This statement provides a natural segue to the third theme, reflected in Brown's professorship at St. Andrews, which deals with the relation between theology and the arts, as well as human culture more broadly. Brown's interests in philosophy, theology, sacramentality, the arts, and human culture led him to publish five major volumes with Oxford University Press that explore these topics in great depth and detail over an enormous canvas: *Tradition and Imagination: Revelation and Change* (1999), *Discipleship and Imagination: Christian Tradition and Truth* (2000), *God and Enchantment of Place: Reclaiming Human Experience* (2004), *God and Grace of Body: Sacrament in Ordinary* (2007), and *God and Mystery in Words: Experience through Metaphor and Drama* (2008).

24. For a representative collection of his essays in philosophical theology, see David Brown, *God in a Single Vision: Integrating Philosophy and Theology*, ed. Christopher R. Brewer and Robert MacSwain (London: Routledge, 2016).

25. See David Brown and Ann Loades, eds., *The Sense of the Sacramental: Movement and Measure in Art and Music, Place and Time* (London: SPCK, 1995), and David Brown and Ann Loades, eds., *Christ: The Sacramental Word* (London: SPCK, 1996).

26. See David Brown and David Fuller, *Signs of Grace: The Sacraments in Poetry and Prose* (London: Cassell; Harrisburg, PA: Morehouse, 1995); republished by Continuum in 2000.

27. David Brown, "Re-conceiving the Sacramental," in *The Gestures of God: Explorations in Sacramentality*, ed. Geoffrey Rowell and Christine Hall (London: Continuum, 2004), 34.

Each of these volumes has been individually reviewed in *Anglican Theological Review* (among many other journals), and, collectively weighing in at almost two thousand pages, it is impossible to do them full justice here.[28]

Overarching and unifying the whole series are Brown's firm convictions, implicit in his earlier work but now articulated more clearly and impressively, that human imagination no less than reason is essential to the theological enterprise; that Scripture is not a fixed text but a manifestation of a living and moving tradition; that revelation is a culturally enmeshed, fallibly mediated, and progressively grasped phenomenon; and that divine action, grace, and truth are to be found outside the Christian church as well as within, in secular philosophy and other religions no less than through the work of painters, sculptors, writers, composers, musicians, dancers, filmmakers, architects, town planners, landscape gardeners, and so forth. In addition to being a signal example of Anglican "hospitality," this series is one of the most ambitious projects of contemporary theology and represents a substantial challenge to currently dominant perspectives across a range of important issues.[29]

The fourth and final theme has been Brown's scholarly engagement with the Anglican tradition itself. Aside from Stephen Sykes and Rowan Williams,

---

28. For *Tradition and Imagination* and *Discipleship and Imagination*, see Margaret R. Miles, *Anglican Theological Review* 83 (2001): 925–28; for *God and Enchantment of Place*, see Lizette Larson-Miller, *Anglican Theological Review* 89 (2007): 296–97; for *God and Grace of Body*, see Vaughn S. Roberts, *Anglican Theological Review* 90 (2008): 807–8; and for *God and Mystery of Words*, see Vaughn S. Roberts, *Anglican Theological Review* 91 (2009): 301–2. For a wide range of substantial engagements with these five books, see also Robert MacSwain and Taylor Worley, eds., *Theology, Aesthetics, and Culture: Responses to the Work of David Brown* (Oxford: Oxford University Press, 2012). Some sentences of this section are drawn from my introduction, 1–12.

29. For additional work in this broad area, see David Brown, *Divine Generosity and Human Creativity: Theology through Symbol, Painting, and Architecture*, ed. Christopher R. Brewer and Robert MacSwain (London: Routledge, 2017), and David Brown and Gavin Hopps, *The Extravagance of Music* (Cham, Switzerland: Palgrave Macmillan, 2018). A potential fifth theme to add to this survey is Brown's engagement with biblical interpretation, although this has been pursued largely in conversation with the arts: see David Brown, *Gospel as Work of Art: Imaginative Truth and the Open Text* (Grand Rapids: Eerdmans, 2024), and Garrick V. Allen, Christopher R. Brewer, and Denny Kinlaw, eds., *The Moving Text: Interdisciplinary Perspectives on David Brown and the Bible* (London: SCM, 2018). Brown's work in this area is interestingly different from conventional historical-critical scholarship and the kind of Scriptural Reasoning practiced by David Ford, and thus worth further investigation. For more detail, see chapter 10 in this current volume.

Brown is one of the very few contemporary Anglican *theologians* (as opposed to historians) who explicitly interacts with and draws upon earlier Anglican figures. For example, he has written on Joseph Butler, John Henry Newman, Edward Bouverie Pusey, Michael Ramsey, and Austin Farrer. He has also written more thematically on Anglican moral theology, ecclesiology, and Christology.[30]

In terms of his Anglican predecessors, Brown stands in the apologetic tradition of Butler, the philosophical tradition of Farrer and Mitchell, and the liberal Catholic tradition of Gore and Ramsey. In a classically Anglican manner, he rejects any sharp distinction between natural and revealed theology, emphasizes the essential goodness of creation over the effects of the Fall, and upholds the priority of the incarnation over the atonement.[31] Along with Newman he maintains that "revealed religion builds on natural religion rather than wholly subverts it."[32] More controversially and distinctively, Brown denies the fundamental distinction between Scripture and tradition, holds that later tradition

---

30. On Butler: "Butler and Deism," in *Joseph Butler's Moral and Religious Thought*, ed. Christopher Cunliffe (Oxford: Clarendon, 1992), 7–28, and "Butler, Joseph (1692–1752)," in *The SPCK Handbook of Anglican Theologians*, ed. Alister E. McGrath (London: SPCK, 1998), 99–102. On Newman, see his introduction to *Newman: A Man for Our Time*, ed. David Brown (London: SPCK, 1990), 1–18. On Pusey: "Pusey as Consistent and Wise: Some Comparisons with Newman," *Anglican and Episcopal History* 71 (2002): 328–49. On Ramsey: "God in the Landscape: Michael Ramsey's Theological Vision," *Anglican Theological Review* 83 (Fall 2001): 775–92. On Farrer: "God and Symbolic Action," in *Divine Action: Studies Inspired by the Philosophical Theology of Austin Farrer*, ed. Brian Hebblethwaite and Edward Henderson (Edinburgh: T&T Clark, 1990), 103–22, and "The Role of Images in Theological Reflection," in *The Human Person in God's World: Studies to Commemorate the Austin Farrer Centenary*, ed. Douglas Hedley and Brian Hebblethwaite (London: SCM, 2006), 85–105. For more thematic work in ethics and ecclesiology, see chapter 2, "The Catholic and Anglican Answer," in David Brown, *Choices: Ethics and the Christian* (Oxford: Blackwell, 1983), 25–55, and chapter 6, "Apostolicity and Conflict: Peter and Paul," in David Brown, *Discipleship and Imagination: Christian Tradition and Truth* (Oxford: Oxford University Press, 2000), 293–342, especially 327–30 and 334–35. For Christology, see the note below.

31. For a monograph on the incarnation that includes an engagement with Sarah Coakley, as well as earlier Anglican theologians such as Charles Gore and Frank Weston, see David Brown, *Divine Humanity: Kenosis and the Construction of a Christian Theology* (Waco, TX: Baylor University Press, 2011).

32. David Brown, *God and Mystery in Words: Experience through Metaphor and Drama* (Oxford: Oxford University Press, 2008), 1. Compare with Newman's Oxford University Sermon II, paragraph 24.

can improve upon and "correct" the teaching of scriptural texts, and insists that God's generous presence can be found everywhere, including "secular" culture and other religions. He is convinced that Christians worship "a God of mystery who has disclosed something of that divinity to humanity but with an inexhaustible richness that means that . . . there remains always something more to discover, something more to delight the senses and the intellect."[33]

III. Sarah Coakley: A Review by Benjamin J. King

Sarah Coakley was born in England in 1951. She studied theology at the University of Cambridge, where David Ford was in the year above her (and Rowan Williams two years above), and there she wrote her doctoral thesis under the supervision of Maurice Wiles (1923–2005) on the German liberal theologian Ernst Troeltsch.[34] Between her undergraduate and graduate degrees from Cambridge, she earned a master's in theology at Harvard Divinity School. Coakley's commitment to feminism and her education in the liberal theology of both Cambridges during the 1970s provided a critical edge against which she cuts at any theology unengaged with life in the world. However, this critical edge did not diminish her deep sense of meeting God in prayer.[35]

It has been the practice of prayer, described in Pauline terms as a conversation between God the Father and the Holy Spirit into which the practitioner is incorporated "in Christ," that guided Coakley to what could be called *critical* orthodoxy.[36] As she puts it in the first volume of a proposed four-volume

33. Brown, *God and Mystery in Words*, 278. See also Brown's *Learning from Other Religions* (Cambridge: Cambridge University Press, 2024). Brown's work has been celebrated in Christopher R. Brewer, ed., *Christian Theology and the Transformation of Natural Religion: From Incarnation to Sacramentality—Essays in Honour of David Brown* (Leuven: Peeters, 2018).

34. Sarah Coakley, *Christ without Absolutes: A Study of the Christology of Ernst Troeltsch* (Oxford: Clarendon, 1988), is a version of her doctoral thesis.

35. See the interview in Rupert Shortt, ed., *God's Advocates: Christian Thinkers in Conversation* (London: Darton, Longman & Todd, 2005), 67–85. See also Sarah Coakley, "Prayer as Crucible: How My Mind Has Changed," *Christian Century* 128, no. 6 (March 9, 2011): 32–40.

36. For her comparison of a prayer-based "incorporative model" and the doctrinal "linear" model, see her contribution to the Church of England Doctrine Commission Report of 1987, *We Believe in God* (London: Church House Publishing, 1987), 104–21, and "Why Three? Some Further Reflections on the Origins of the Doctrine of the Trinity," in *The Making and*

systematic theology, one dare not assume "that the achievement of classical orthodoxy is the arrival at some stable place of spiritual safety. 'Orthodoxy' as mere propositional assent needs to be carefully distinguished from 'orthodoxy' as a demanding, and ongoing, spiritual *project*, in which the language of the creeds is personally and progressively assimilated."[37] In what follows, five themes of this critical orthodoxy will be examined as they found expression at the four places in which she taught.

Of the many themes of Coakley's writings to emerge from fifteen years' teaching at Lancaster University in the United Kingdom, two are central to her ongoing work.[38] First is her view that the theologian is in service to the church, and second is her use of the social sciences in theology. For some theologians today these two themes would be seen as contradictory, with the social sciences being more appropriate to a school-of-religions approach rather than an ecclesial understanding of theology. But at Lancaster from 1976, Coakley recalled, she "first learnt the richness of the social science approaches to religion, *when non-reductively construed*, and how these disciplines could be turned back on Christian theology."[39] For instance, she used the methodology of sociology in the service of the Church of England's Doctrine Commission, making field studies of two groups of charismatic Christians—an Anglican parish ("church-sect" hybrid) and a group ("sect") that had just split from it. Coakley compared these groups' self-described experiences of prayer, not only with each other but also (and here was her ecclesial thrust) with the writings of various church fathers. She concluded: "*All* prayer is prayer 'in the Spirit,'" but warned of the "danger of associating particular *sorts* of experience with the Spirit . . . [which] may lead either to an implicit tritheism (a belief in three different gods), or else a sporadic, instrumentalist, and possibly impersonal, vision of the Spirit."[40] Here one sees the influence of her two most frequently quoted

Remaking of Christian Doctrine: Essays in Honour of Maurice Wiles, ed. Sarah Coakley and David. A. Pailin (Oxford: Clarendon, 1993), 29–56.

37. Sarah Coakley, "Prelude," in *God, Sexuality, and the Self: An Essay "On the Trinity"* (Cambridge: Cambridge University Press, 2013), 5.

38. Another theme from these years was a conference that eventually led to the volume *Religion and the Body*, ed. Sarah Coakley (Cambridge: Cambridge University Press, 1997).

39. Sarah Coakley, *Sacrifice Regained: Reconsidering the Rationality of Religious Belief* (Cambridge: Cambridge University Press, 2012), 4.

40. Sarah Coakley, in the Church of England Doctrine Committee, *We Believe in the Holy Spirit* (London: Church House Publishing, 1991), 17–36, at 34.

authorities and ongoing dialogue partners, the Roman Catholic anthropologist Mary Douglas and the church father Gregory of Nyssa.[41]

A third theme is Coakley's use of the Anglophone tradition of empirical reason and her awareness of its limits when talking about God. At Oriel College, Oxford, where she taught briefly, Coakley learned the analytic philosophy that Richard Swinburne and David Brown also used there (although she arrived just after Brown left for Durham). But she reminded its proponents to be aware of concerns raised by feminism.[42] At this time Coakley also delivered the Hulsean Lectures, which took an apophatic approach to God-talk, recognizing for instance the essentially metaphorical use of "Father" when applied to the first person of the Trinity.[43] As she put it later (opposing Brown's and others' "social" image for the Trinity): "What the overlapping and bombarding images of [Gregory of Nyssa's] *Song* commentary remind us is that the 'persons' of the Trinity are always being reconfigured and reconstrued as the soul advances to more dizzying intimacy with the divine."[44] Coakley also questioned the usefulness of ordinary language in Christology, interpreting the Chalcedonian "definition" (*horos* in Greek) as a horizon beyond which it is unsafe to venture in talking about Christ.[45] Yet her fluency in Anglophone philosophy enabled a joint re-

41. For Gregory, see part 3 of Sarah Coakley, *Powers and Submissions: Spirituality, Philosophy, and Gender* (Oxford: Blackwell, 2002), and her "Introduction—Gender, Trinitarian Analogies, and the Pedagogy of *The Song*," in *Re-thinking Gregory of Nyssa*, ed. Sarah Coakley (Oxford: Blackwell, 2003), 1–14.

42. See, for example, Coakley, *Powers and Submissions*, chapter 6: "Analytic Philosophy of Religion in Feminist Perspective: Some Questions," 98–106.

43. Sarah Coakley, "Three-Personed God: The Primacy of Divine Desire, and the 'Apophatic Turn,'" Hulsean Lecture 6, Cambridge University, 1992. These unpublished lectures are reviewed in Jason Byassee, "Closer Than Kissing: Sarah Coakley's Early Work," *Anglican Theological Review* 90 (2008): 139–55.

44. Coakley, *Powers and Submissions*, 129.

45. Sarah Coakley, "What Does Chalcedon Solve and What Does It Not? Some Reflections on the Status and Meaning of the Chalcedonian 'Definition,'" in *The Incarnation*, ed. Stephen T. Davis, Daniel Kendall, SJ, and Gerald O'Collins, SJ (Oxford: Clarendon, 2002), 143–63. On the linguistic problems involved in the doctrine of Christ's resurrection, see Sarah Coakley, "Response to William P. Alston: 'Biblical Criticism and the Resurrection,'" in *The Resurrection*, ed. Stephen T. Davis, Daniel Kendall, SJ, and Gerald O'Collins, SJ (Oxford: Clarendon, 1997), 184–90, and Coakley, *Powers and Submissions*, chap. 8: "The Resurrection and the 'Spiritual Senses': On Wittgenstein, Epistemology, and the Risen Christ," 130–52.

search project at Harvard with evolutionary biologist Martin Nowak, who himself shifted into theological metaphor to explain the cooperation (rather than simply selfishness) within species as "sacrifice."[46] In opposition to theologians who employ Continental philosophy to claim that Christian theology has its own untranslatable grammar, Coakley's use of analytic philosophy to talk to natural scientists has led to the employment of Christian idioms in biology.

Such use of multiple disciplines (which, she says, adds up to what she calls *théologie totale*) flourished during fourteen years' teaching at Harvard, from which comes the fourth theme: her work at the "borders." She identifies these "borderland raid[s] . . . into secular philosophy and science" with her teacher at Cambridge, Donald MacKinnon,[47] but it was in Cambridge, Massachusetts (living on the borderland between North America and Europe, between empirical/pragmatic and Continental philosophy), that "liminality" became such a theme of her theology. Her work at Harvard took place on the threshold of many disciplines, enabling her discernment that humans are liminal creatures, living on thresholds as well as crossing them. For instance, in the Pain Seminar (an off-putting name!), she worked at the threshold of neuroscience, ritual and music theory, and religious studies. Coakley also suggested theology should cross the threshold of business schools.[48] Ordination as an Anglican priest in 2001 gave her insight into the liminal life of the priesthood. She gained renewed awareness of the parish church as a "thin" place, as well as noting the Church of England's liminal role as an established church in a secular society.[49] She also meditated on the liminality of the eucharistic celebrant, specifically as a woman standing on the threshold that is the altar.[50]

---

46. For a brief description, see Coakley, *Sacrifice Regained*, 22–24 and note 45 on pages 34–35. For the papers resulting from their joint project, see Martin A. Nowak and Sarah Coakley, eds., *Evolution, Games, and God: The Principle of Cooperation* (Cambridge, MA: Harvard University Press, 2013).

47. Coakley, *Sacrifice Regained*, 3.

48. Sarah Coakley, "Shaping the Field: A Transatlantic Perspective," in *Fields of Faith: A Festschrift for Nicholas Lash*, ed. David Ford, Ben Quash, and Janet Soskice (Cambridge: Cambridge University Press, 2005), 39–55.

49. Sarah Coakley, "Introduction: Prayer, Place and the Poor," in *Praying for England: Priestly Presence in Contemporary Culture*, ed. Samuel Wells and Sarah Coakley (London: Continuum, 2008), 1–20.

50. Sarah Coakley, "The Woman at the Altar: Cosmological Disturbance or Gender Subversion?" *Anglican Theological Review* 86 (2004): 75–93. This article was later reprinted in Sarah

Coakley's greatest contribution to contemporary theology is perhaps her consideration of the liminality of human gender and sexuality from a doctrinal perspective. She argues that, in prayer, a human's desire for God leads to a "porous" selfhood to which gender binaries do not apply.[51] Neither difference between human persons nor their sexuality can be reduced to binaries, and, for Coakley, this is the case for humans because it is *first* true of God. This is the fifth theme of Coakley's work, and it was the topic of the first volume of her systematics published at Cambridge, where from 2007 to 2018 she was Norris-Hulse Professor of Divinity. As she wrote in the preface, the existence of the Spirit means that God cannot be reduced to a Father-Son binary or to some undifferentiated unity; rather, "its love presses not only outwards to include others, but also inwards (and protectively) sustains the difference between the persons, thus preserving a perfect and harmonious balance between union and distinction."[52] Notice the Spirit is called "it" in accordance with the Greek of the Nicene Creed, not, as has become fashionable, "she." Coakley is clear about the dangers of, on the one hand, projecting gender stereotypes onto the divine persons, but also, on the other, of negating difference within the Trinity by ignoring questions of sexuality and desire when speaking of God's inner life.[53] Human desire for God brings us to the threshold of divinity, as we submit to God in prayer and are thus empowered. Indeed, through prayer we heighten both our attention to God and neighbor, with our senses slowly being purged of our gender and racial biases.[54] The topic of race promises to feature prominently in the next volume of her systematics.[55]

Coakley, *The New Asceticism: Sexuality, Gender, and the Quest for God* (London: Bloomsbury, 2015), 55–84.

51. She makes this point with reference to two other favorite authorities, Pseudo-Dionysius and Teresa of Ávila, in her introduction to *Re-thinking Dionysius the Areopagite*, ed. Sarah Coakley and Charles M. Stang (Oxford: Wiley-Blackwell, 2009), 1–10, at 6–7.

52. Coakley, "Prelude," in *God, Sexuality, and the Self*, 24. Although published while at Cambridge, the book incorporates much of her previous material on these topics.

53. These, she says, are the mistakes of two other Anglican theologians: Sarah Coakley, "Why Gift? Gift, Gender and Trinitarian Relations in Milbank and Tanner," *Scottish Journal of Theology* 16 (2008): 224–35. For a critique of Coakley on these issues, see Linn M. Tonstad, *God and Difference: The Trinity, Sexuality, and the Transformation of Finitude* (London: Routledge, 2017).

54. See her Père Marquette lecture, *Sensing God? Reconsidering the Patristic Tradition of "Spiritual Sensation" for Contemporary Theological Ethics* (Milwaukee: Marquette University Press, 2022).

55. Coakley's work has been celebrated in Janice McRandal, ed., *Sarah Coakley and the*

IV. Conclusion

Much more could be said about the work of these three contemporary Anglican theologians, both individually and collectively, but our task has not been to analyze and evaluate but rather to introduce and describe. However, after comparing our sections, we noticed that whereas Fout and King spent as much time describing the contextual character of their subjects' thought as they devoted to content, MacSwain focused primarily on Brown's thematic concerns. In reflecting on this difference, we concluded that it was not accidental. Although Brown has written insightfully on postmodernism and Continental philosophy, it is probably fair to say that, of the three figures considered here, he has maintained the most conventionally "self-effacing" scholarly voice, and this may well have to do with his commitment to the British empirical tradition noted earlier. To varying degrees and for differing reasons, Ford and Coakley are more critical of this native British approach, and supplement it accordingly from various other sources. We raise this issue here not to settle the debate but to indicate where the fault lines still lie. That is to say, questions of the nature of reason and the relation between reason and faith, theory and practice, remain as live for contemporary Anglican theologians as they were for the writers of *Essays Catholic and Critical*. However, the border crossing exhibited in these three suggests that, although they are writing from England and Scotland, their Anglicanism is less insular than in earlier generations.[56]

Future of Systematic Theology (Minneapolis: Fortress, 2016). A new collection of her essays that appeared as this current volume was being prepared for publication is titled *The Broken Body: Israel, Christ, and Fragmentation* (Hoboken, NJ: Wiley-Blackwell, 2024).

56. The authors are grateful to Timothy F. Sedgwick and Charles M. Stang for comments on earlier versions of this article, which has been updated by the three authors for inclusion in this current volume.

CHAPTER 9

The Tradition of Reason:
David Brown, Joseph Butler, and Divine Hiddenness

In the autumn of 1999 I wrote to David Brown to inquire about possibly pursuing doctoral research under his supervision, focusing on either Austin Farrer (1904–1968) or Joseph Butler (1662–1752). When I wrote this letter, I was immersed in a year of Anglican studies at Virginia Theological Seminary; Brown was Van Mildert Canon Professor at Durham University and Cathedral; and my scholarly goal was to fuse philosophical theology, historical theology, and Anglican studies. I had first encountered Brown through Eleonore Stump's review of his book *The Divine Trinity*,[1] and then again a few years later through his essay "God and Symbolic Action."[2] As this essay was published in a volume on the philosophical theology of Austin Farrer, it was clear that Brown could supervise a Farrer-related project, but on arriving at Virginia Seminary I also read his entry on Butler in *The SPCK Handbook*

1. Eleonore Stump, review of *The Divine Trinity*, by David Brown, *Faith and Philosophy* 3 (1986): 463–68. For an analysis of Brown's and Stump's respective approaches to interpreting scriptural narrative, see Robert MacSwain, "Moving Texts and Mirror Neurons: David Brown and Eleonore Stump on Biblical Interpretation," in *The Moving Text: Interdisciplinary Perspectives on David Brown and the Bible*, ed. Garrick Allen, Christopher Brewer, and Denny Kinlaw (London: SCM, 2018), 51–69, now reprinted as chapter 10 of this volume.

2. David Brown, "God and Symbolic Action," in *Divine Action: Studies Inspired by the Philosophical Theology of Austin Farrer*, ed. Brian Hebblethwaite and Edward Henderson (Edinburgh: T&T Clark, 1990), 103–22, now reprinted in Robert MacSwain, ed., *Scripture, Metaphysics, and Poetry: Austin Farrer's* The Glass of Vision *with Critical Commentary* (Farnham, UK: Ashgate, 2013), 133–47.

Originally published in *Christian Theology and the Transformation of Natural Religion: From Incarnation to Sacramentality—Essays in Honour of David Brown*, ed. Christopher R. Brewer (Leuven: Peeters, 2018), 21–35.

of Anglican Theologians.[3] A picture was thus beginning to emerge: Brown was a philosophical priest-theologian with a strong interest in the Anglican tradition—exactly what I was looking for in a PhD supervisor!

Brown wrote back to say that he would be happy to direct a thesis on either Farrer or Butler, but he thought that Farrer might be the more fruitful option, not least because the centenary of his birth was approaching in 2004. My doctorate thus serendipitously commenced in September 2004 when I attended the Farrer centenary conference in Oxford, to which Brown was one of the primary contributors.[4] The research began with Brown at Durham, was completed with him at St. Andrews, and was ultimately published by Peeters as *Solved by Sacrifice: Austin Farrer, Fideism, and the Evidence of Faith*.[5]

However, after a sustained period of research on Farrer, my interest in Butler was eventually rekindled, and given Brown's significant work on this neglected figure (along with their joint Oxford and Durham associations), Butler seemed to be a fitting topic for this Festschrift chapter. In the following section I will describe Brown's Butlerian bona fides; in the subsequent section I will look at an important philosophical conversation in which Butler has been recently invoked and implicated in, namely, the problem of divine hiddenness; and finally I will conclude with some brief reflections on the regrettable neglect of Butler in contemporary Anglican theology.[6]

---

3. David Brown, "Joseph Butler (1662–1752)," in *The SPCK Handbook of Anglican Theologians*, ed. Alister E. McGrath (London: SPCK, 1998), 99–102.

4. Held at Oriel College from September 6 to 9, the conference proceedings were published as Douglas Hedley and Brian Hebblethwaite, eds., *The Human Person in God's World: Studies to Commemorate the Austin Farrer Centenary* (London: SCM, 2006), and Brown's paper was included as "The Role of Images in Theological Reflection," 85–105.

5. Robert MacSwain, *Solved by Sacrifice: Austin Farrer, Fideism, and the Evidence of Faith* (Leuven: Peeters, 2013). Brown's Durham colleague Ann Loades wrote the entry on Farrer in the *SPCK Handbook* cited in note 3 above (120–23); discussions with her were significant as my research on Farrer developed, and we coedited an anthology of his work: Ann Loades and Robert MacSwain, eds., *The Truth-Seeking Heart: Austin Farrer and His Writings* (Norwich, UK: Canterbury, 2006).

6. In my contribution to the coauthored essay "Contemporary Anglican Systematic Theology: Three Examples in David Brown, Sarah Coakley, and David F. Ford" (now chapter 8 in this book), I note that Brown's work has been characterized by four broad themes: (i) philosophical theology, (ii) sacramental theology, (iii) theology and the arts, and (iv) Anglican studies. This current chapter engages with both (i) and (iv).

I. Joseph Butler and David Brown

As alluded to above, Butler and Brown both studied at Oriel College, Oxford (Butler in 1715–1718, Brown in 1970–1972) and later served in the Diocese of Durham (Butler as bishop, 1751–1752, Brown as canon professor, 1990–2007). But in addition to these biographical similarities, Brown has also written significant studies both on and inspired by Joseph Butler.

I have already mentioned his entry on Butler in *The SPCK Handbook of Anglican Theologians*. Although only a six-paragraph reference article, in this short span Brown clearly and carefully presents Butler's biography, moral philosophy, Christian apologetics, and influence on subsequent figures such as John Henry Newman, William Gladstone, J. B. Lightfoot, Hastings Rashdall, A. E. Taylor, and Basil Mitchell. Brown also contributed an address on Butler to a series celebrating the 900th anniversary of Durham Cathedral, in which he emphasized that against rationalist deism and fideist enthusiasm Butler insisted that "both factions were wrong, that Christianity is not only a reasonable faith but one which builds [through divine revelation] upon what we already know about God from the world around us"—characteristic claims that Brown sees as "two fundamental marks of classical Anglicanism."[7]

A more substantial contribution to Butler studies is "Butler and Deism," the first chapter in the Christopher Cunliffe-edited *Joseph Butler's Moral and Religious Thought: Tercentenary Essays*—coincidentally published soon after Brown's move from Oriel as chaplain-fellow to Durham as canon-professor.[8] Here Brown focuses on Butler's major apologetic work, *The Analogy of Religion, Natural and Revealed, to the Constitution and Course of Nature* (1736), and argues—against a strong consensus to the contrary—that "it is far from clear

---

7. David Brown, "Butler—the Apologist," in *A Christian Heritage: A Collection of Addresses in Honour of the 900th Anniversary of Durham Cathedral*, ed. Charles Yeats (Bangor, UK: Headstart History, 1993), 51–57, citing from 53 and 57. A slightly revised version of this address was later published in David Brown, *Through the Eyes of the Saints: A Pilgrimage through History* (London: Continuum, 2005), as "Joseph Butler: Reason and Nature as Sacramental," 125–29, with the parallel citations on 126 and 129.

8. David Brown, "Butler and Deism," in *Joseph Butler's Moral and Religious Thought: Tercentenary Essays*, ed. Christopher Cunliffe (Oxford: Clarendon, 1992), 7–28. After his doctoral studies and ordination training in Cambridge, Brown returned to Oriel as chaplain from 1976 until his move to Durham in 1990.

that *The Analogy of Religion* is without relevance to theological problems of our own day."[9] In particular, Brown emphasizes that, despite Butler's relative confidence in the power of reason, he nevertheless advocates a "retreat from proof to probability" and likewise "expresses scepticism about how much can be known." Ironically then, the Enlightenment Butler represents "an early anticipation of the move away from reason toward experience and feeling that characterized both Methodism and more generally the Romantic movement."[10]

Bravely acknowledging the strength of deist arguments against revealed Christian doctrines such as the Trinity, Brown nevertheless upholds Butler's claim that, however limited, "reason must be our final court of appeal" and yet also Butler's equal insistence that reason does not in fact preclude "anything new being disclosed by revelation."[11] Brown says that Butler's commitment to the finality of reason—properly understood—is "unequivocally expressed in several places" and as an example cites A.II.I.28, in which Butler writes: "if in revelation there be found any passages, the seeming meaning of which is contrary to natural Religion; we may most certainly conclude, such seeming meaning not to be the real one."[12] Another example is A.II.III.1, in which Butler boldly states that reason "is the only faculty we have wherewith to judge concerning anything, even revelation itself." Admitting that the "details of his specific arguments lost their relevance once evolution established a much more remote relation between God and the natural order," Brown concludes that Butler "still offers the best strategy of response to deism" in both its historical and contemporary forms.[13]

9. Brown, "Butler and Deism," 28. Butler citations will be from *The Works of Joseph Butler*, ed. J. H. Bernard, vols. 1 and 2 (New York: Macmillan, 1900), using the standard system of referring to Butler's works in this edition by title, part, chapter, and paragraph rather than by volume or page numbers, and with *The Analogy of Religion* abbreviated as "A." However, note that David McNaughton has recently published critical editions of both Butler's *Fifteen Sermons* (2017) and *The Analogy of Religion* (2021) with Oxford University Press. Readers are thus encouraged to consult these editions as well.

10. All citations from Brown, "Butler and Deism," 8. Note that Brown comments on Butler's skepticism regarding the *extent* of our knowledge, not skepticism regarding our knowledge *as such*.

11. Brown, "Butler and Deism," 17.

12. See Brown, "Butler and Deism," 17n32.

13. Brown, "Butler and Deism," 27. Bob Tennant says that in this chapter Brown finds "the possibility of continuing relevance to modern Christian apologetics in Butler's account of doubt," but asserts that Brown's interpretation does "scant justice either to Butler or to the

These three essays establish Brown's credentials as a Butler scholar, but it is his own constructive use of Butlerian strategies against twentieth-century deists such as Maurice Wiles (1923–2005) that justifies David E. White's claim that Brown "may be singled out as a leader in the use of Butler's methods in theology today."[14] White is referring to *The Divine Trinity*, where Brown explicitly says that Butler's "earlier refutation of deism has helped inspire [his] own," and concludes that, if theism is to be defended against deism, Butler's position "remains just as valid today as in the eighteenth century."[15] Brown does not simply repeat Butler's arguments, however, but rather seeks to develop and strengthen their contemporary relevance.[16] Thus, in the final paragraph of his important monograph on Butler, Terence Penelhum writes that in *The Divine Trinity* Brown

> examines the work of some contemporary Christian theologians who wish, for various reasons, to re-present Christianity without the interventionist view of God, and in consequence without the doctrines of Incarnation and Trinity that presuppose it. He points out that their views are very close to those of the deists whom Butler criticised, and claims that in arguing that interventionist theism is more probable than mere deism, Butler is making a case that applies with undiminished force against them also. [Brown] also recognises that the reasons that would prompt anyone to prefer deism to theism should lead them in consistency to atheism or agnosticism.[17]

---

modern communities of scientists and theologians." However, neither here nor in his own subsequent interpretation of Butler does Tennant give any specific reason why he finds Brown's analysis so unsatisfying. See Bob Tennant, *Conscience, Consciousness, and Ethics in Joseph Butler's Philosophy and Ministry* (Woodbridge, UK, and Rochester, NY: Boydell, 2011), 14 and 14n49. I suspect that Tennant has overemphasized and thus misunderstood Brown's demotion of the role and power of reason in Butler.

14. David E. White, introduction to his edition of *The Works of Joseph Butler* (Rochester, NY: University of Rochester Press, 2006), 6.

15. David Brown, *The Divine Trinity* (London: Duckworth; La Salle, IL: Open Court, 1985), vii and 51.

16. Brown, *The Divine Trinity*, 9: see 10–51 for the detailed discussion.

17. Terence Penelhum, *Butler* (London: Routledge & Kegan Paul, 1985), 207. For the view that Brown's *The Divine Trinity* is directed against Wiles in particular, see Basil Mitchell, "Revelation Revisited," in *The Making and Remaking of Christian Doctrine: Essays in Honour of Maurice Wiles*, ed. Sarah Coakley and David A. Pailin (Oxford: Clarendon, 1993), 177–91. Mitchell

As a philosopher rather than a theologian, Penelhum demurs from entering further into this controversy, although he makes it clear that his sympathies lie entirely with Brown, and concludes his book by writing that "it is always pleasing to find one's subject relevant to other debates, even if this means that [Butler's] influence has been less than it should have been."[18] I will return to this thought in my conclusion.

II. Joseph Butler and Divine Hiddenness

When Penelhum discusses *The Divine Trinity* in *Butler*, he notes that Brown's volume was "shortly to appear at the time" he was writing, so Penelhum had clearly read the text in manuscript.[19] It is thus a nice coincidence that in his own contribution to *Joseph Butler's Moral and Religious Thought*, published seven years later, Penelhum also refers to another book that had not yet been published at the time of his writing, namely, J. L. Schellenberg's *Divine Hiddenness and Human Reason*.[20] Although it took a while for the conversation to gather speed, Schellenberg's book was eventually to become one of the most widely debated texts in contemporary philosophy of religion, launching numerous responses, both pro and con.[21] Schellenberg is a Canadian philosopher who received his DPhil from Oxford "studying with Richard Swinburne, David

---

also contributed a chapter to Cunliffe's Butler volume from which I have benefited: "Butler as a Christian Apologist," in Cunliffe, *Joseph Butler's Moral and Religious Thought*, 97–116.

18. Penelhum, *Butler*, 207.

19. Penelhum, *Butler*, 207. Both books were published in 1985. Brown reviewed Penelhum's *Butler* in *Journal of Theological Studies* 38 (1987): 251–53.

20. J. L. Schellenberg, *Divine Hiddenness and Human Reason* (Ithaca, NY: Cornell University Press, 1993), subsequently *DHHR* in footnotes. A paperback edition with a new preface was issued in 2006, as I discuss briefly in note 44 below.

21. See, for just two examples out of many, Daniel Howard-Snyder and Paul K. Moser, eds., *Divine Hiddenness: New Essays* (Cambridge: Cambridge University Press, 2002)—the first volume in response to Schellenberg, although almost a decade after his book was published—and Adam Green and Eleonore Stump, eds., *Hidden Divinity and Religious Belief: New Perspectives* (Cambridge: Cambridge University Press, 2015). See also Schellenberg's new introduction to the argument and the discussion around it, *The Hiddenness Argument: Philosophy's New Challenge to Belief in God* (Oxford: Oxford University Press, 2015), subsequently *HA* in footnotes, with a seven-page bibliography of specific primary and secondary literature on 133–39.

Brown, Maurice Wiles, and Anthony Kenny," and his book "introduced a new argument for atheism now known as the hiddenness argument"[22]—or what Schellenberg also describes as the argument from *reasonable nonbelief.* As he puts it, "the weakness of evidence for theism . . . is itself evidence against it," and so "we can argue from the reasonableness of nonbelief to the nonexistence of God."[23] Particularly interesting in this current context—aside from Schellenberg being one of Brown's students—is (i) apparently the very first published mention of Schellenberg's argument occurred in the context of a discussion of Butler, (ii) Schellenberg appeals explicitly to Butler in developing one aspect of his argument, and yet (iii) the Butler/Schellenberg connection has so far been largely ignored. This present essay is thus an opportune moment to rectify this deficiency.

Penelhum introduces Schellenberg's argument in the final section of an essay on Butler and human ignorance.[24] Why is God's existence not more clearly evident? In one of the sermons he preached at the Rolls Chapel, "Upon the Ignorance of Man," Butler considers this question and says (in Penelhum's summary) that "God may deliberately hide himself from us, even if his workings are not beyond our intellectual capacities to understand, for purposes that we cannot now grasp, but which relate to our probationary state."[25] In A.II.VI, "Of the Want of Universality in Revelation; and of the Supposed Deficiency in the Proof of It," Butler further suggests that the specific reason God may hide Godself from some human searchers is to provide a special test to those "who do not experience the common forms of temptation to neglect duties that are clear to them."[26] Penelhum calls this form of testing *intellectual probation* and says that this theory "is not the same as the view found in Pascal, John Hick, and others that God hides himself from those who do not sincerely seek him, so his hiddenness is the divine response to the corruption of their minds. It is rather the theory that those disposed to seek the truth with full seriousness might have to be presented with obstacles to test their moral determination."[27]

22. Citations from http://www.jlschellenberg.com.

23. *DHHR*, 2–3; see also *HA*, 15.

24. Terence Penelhum, "Butler and Human Ignorance," in Cunliffe, *Joseph Butler's Moral and Religious Thought*, 117–39.

25. Penelhum, "Butler and Human Ignorance," 137.

26. Penelhum, "Butler and Human Ignorance," 137.

27. Penelhum, "Butler and Human Ignorance," 137.

Penelhum originally introduced the term "intellectual probation" on page 193 of *Butler* in his earlier discussion of this same material (193–97), where he also compared Butler to Pascal and Hick. But in the footnote to the previous citation from "Butler and Human Ignorance" he says, "I owe the recognition of this difference [between divine hiddenness in response to noetic corruption and divine hiddenness as intellectual probation] to John Schellenberg, who discusses both forms of response to the problem of divine hiddenness in *Divine Hiddenness and Human Reason* (Ithaca, forthcoming). This is an important work which carries forward the understanding of this fundamental but neglected issue in a major way."[28] Penelhum continues in the main text that Butler's argument here is weak, "partly, as John Schellenberg has made clear, because these seem a particularly inappropriate group of persons to present with *this* hurdle to surmount, and partly because any unsuspected reluctance or frivolity could as well be brought to the surface by strong evidences as by weak and obscure ones."[29] This second reason had already been discussed by Penelhum in *Butler* on page 197, so the specific insights he has since gained from Schellenberg are (i) the *contrast* rather than parallel between Pascal and Hick on one hand and Butler on the other, and (ii) the *inappropriateness* of divine hiddenness as intellectual probation for the scrupulous rather than the frivolous. Thus, "Butler is inevitably in difficulty if he wants to argue that weak evidence is a deliberate divine test of our doxastic conscientiousness, for it is generally a sign of such conscientiousness that weak evidence is rejected."[30]

Penelhum considers various ways in which Butler's argument for intellectual probation could be strengthened, but he remains troubled by the problem already identified in his volume on Butler but now intensified and formalized by Schellenberg, namely, that "if Christianity is true, why is this not unambiguously clear?"[31] Schellenberg's own focus is less on Christianity and more on theism, and he thus argues that "the weakness of our evidence for God is not a sign that God is hidden; it is a revelation that God does not exist."[32]

28. Penelhum, "Butler and Human Ignorance," 137n22.
29. Penelhum, "Butler and Human Ignorance," 138.
30. Penelhum, "Butler and Human Ignorance," 139.
31. Penelhum, "Butler and Human Ignorance," 139, and see also Penelhum, *Butler*, 197.
32. *DHHR*, 1.

Aside from the nuances mentioned above, Schellenberg's interpretation of Butler in *Divine Hiddenness and Human Reason* closely follows Penelhum's in *Butler*.[33] In his more recent volume, *The Hiddenness Argument*, Schellenberg returns to Butler, citing A.II.VI.1: "If the evidence of revelation appears doubtful, this itself turns into a positive argument against it: because it cannot be supposed that, if it were true, it would be left to subsist upon doubtful evidence."[34] This statement, Schellenberg says, is "a tantalizing suggestion of something like hiddenness reasoning." He acknowledges that Butler himself was convinced of the existence of God and the truth of Christianity, so it takes some creative adaptation to apply his concerns about the doubtful evidence for revelation to theism itself, but "trade his focus for that of the hiddenness argument and you have an intriguing suggestion of how to argue against the existence of God: when the evidence for God is inconclusive [*contra* Butler, but now widely admitted], this itself should be taken as a conclusive reason for disbelief, because God would never allow the evidence to be thus inconclusive."[35] Indeed, Schellenberg continues, in an autobiographical vein:

> What Butler says here is, as far as I know, the earliest clear case of such reasoning in the history of philosophy. The very same sort of reasoning occurred to me when, in my twenties and studying at the University of Calgary in Alberta, Canada [with, as he makes clear elsewhere, Penelhum, and under his influence] I began thinking about hiddenness issues. This experience started a train of thought that, while doing a doctorate in philosophy at Oxford [studying with Swinburne, Brown, Wiles, and Kenny], brought me finally to the hiddenness argument. It was while investigating this experience that I discovered Butler had reached the germ of my thinking before me. But neither he nor anyone else had developed the idea, and neither in its

33. For Schellenberg's own development of these claims vis-à-vis Butler, see *DHHR*, "Butler on Intellectual Probation," 168–80, but for my purposes in this essay it seemed more illuminating to hear them mediated in advance through Penelhum. The influence was reciprocal: in *DHHR* Schellenberg describes Penelhum as "my first teacher in the philosophy of religion," the one who "provided the impetus for my thinking about Divine hiddenness," and indeed the source of the book's title (ix; see also *HA*, 15, 28, and 127); and in *DHHR*, 168-80, he appeals to Penelhum's discussion in *Butler*, 195–97.

34. Cited in *HA*, 25; see also *DHHR*, 169.

35. Both citations from *HA*, 25.

Christian form nor in the more general form that spoke to my concerns had it ever made so much as a dent on philosophical discussion.[36]

That is, while the hiddenness of God is a familiar topic in theology and philosophy, it was not developed into an argument for atheism until Schellenberg, and yet Butler was an essential part of its genealogy.[37]

In both of these books Schellenberg acknowledges openly that he is developing and adapting Butler's "germ" of hiddenness reasoning in a way that Butler himself would not approve, applying to generic theism what Butler only applied to Christian revelation. But as a point of historical and textual accuracy, it is important to state that Butler would be even less sympathetic to Schellenberg's argument than Schellenberg admits. In both books Schellenberg cites Butler's claim in A.II.VI.1 as if it straightforwardly begins, "If the evidence for revelation appears doubtful . . . ," and thus as if Butler accepted the conditional claim himself. But if one turns to the text, one finds that the paragraph actually begins: "It has been thought by some persons, that if the evidence for revelation appears doubtful . . ." While the paragraph then continues as cited by Schellenberg, it concludes with the additional sentence: "And the objection against revelation from its not being universal is often insisted upon as of great weight." However, in the very next paragraph Butler replies:

> Now the weakness of these opinions may be shewn by observing the suppositions on which they are founded: which are really such as these; that it cannot be thought God would have bestowed any favour at all upon us, unless in that degree, which we think, He might, and which, we imagine, would be most to our particular advantage; and also that it cannot be thought He would bestow a favour upon any, unless He bestowed the same upon all: suppositions, which we find contradicted, not by a few instances in God's natural government of the world, but by the general analogy of Nature altogether. (A.II.VI.2)

36. *HA*, 26.

37. For another essay in *Joseph Butler's Moral and Religious Thought* dealing with this topic, but from a different, nonatheistic angle and without reference to Schellenberg, see Albino Babolin, "*Deus Absconditus*: Some Notes on the Bearing of the Hiddenness of God upon Butler's and Pascal's Criticism of Deism," 29–35.

Butler thus does not endorse even the validity of the conditional claim in A.II.I.1 against revelation, as Schellenberg says, but is simply citing it as an objection, and indeed as a weak objection, that he intends to refute in the remainder of part II, chapter VI, which is after all titled "Of the Want of Universality in Revelation: and of the *Supposed* Deficiency in the Proof of It" (emphasis added).

Let me be clear that I am not accusing Schellenberg of deliberately misrepresenting Butler's views, but rather of being an analytic philosopher. Schellenberg indeed found the germ of the hiddenness argument in those lines as previously cited, because the germ is there, albeit propositionally rather than intentionally. That Butler himself did not accept even what Schellenberg thought he accepted is almost beside the point, especially as Schellenberg explicitly states that he is interested in "possible" arguments *suggested* by a given figure, not primarily with historical accuracy.[38] My deeper concern is that Schellenberg's whole *method* of philosophy is incompatible with Butler's, at least as exemplified in *The Analogy of Religion*, and this may itself present a challenge to the hiddenness argument.

To see this, first consider the full deductive argument from reasonable nonbelief currently defended by Schellenberg:

1. If a perfectly loving God exists, then there exists a God who is always open to a personal relationship with any finite person.
2. If there exists a God who is always open to a personal relationship with any finite person, then no finite person is ever nonresistantly in a state of nonbelief in relation to the proposition that God exists.
3. If a perfectly loving God exists, then no finite person is ever nonresistantly in a state of nonbelief in relation to the proposition that God exists (from 1 and 2).
4. Some finite persons are or have been nonresistantly in a state of nonbelief in relation to the proposition that God exists.
5. No perfectly loving God exists (from 3 and 4).
6. If no perfectly loving God exists, then God does not exist.
7. God does not exist (from 5 and 6).[39]

---

38. *DHHR*, 95–96, 96n1.

39. *HA*, 103; cf. the "classic" five-step argument in *DHHR*, 83. A slightly different and more formal version of the new seven-step argument is also provided in *HA*, 130–31, cited from

My concern at present is not with the formal validity or invalidity of the argument itself, but with Schellenberg's *a priori* assumption that a propositional deductive argument can *logically* prove that it is *necessarily* the case that God's existence is incompatible with nonresistant reasonable nonbelief. In making this *a priori* assumption about propositional deductive arguments of logical necessity regarding metaphysical reality, Schellenberg is in good company, and many contemporary philosophers of religion (both theists and atheists) would concur, but this is not the method of philosophy endorsed by Butler in the *Analogy*, and for at least two reasons.

First, recall David Brown's point stated earlier that in the *Analogy* Butler initiates an epistemic "retreat from proof to probability" and likewise "expresses scepticism about how much can be known." It is important to stress that this retreat is not just in relation to contested religious beliefs, but to human knowledge more generally—that is, to our actual character as epistemic agents. Thus, as Butler famously wrote: "Probable evidence, in its very nature, affords but an imperfect kind of information; and is to be considered as relative only to beings of limited capacities. For nothing which is the possible object of knowledge, whether past, present, or future, can be probable to an infinite Intelligence; since it cannot but be discerned absolutely as it is in itself, certainly true, or certainly false. But to Us, probability is the very guide of life" (A.Intro.3). It is crucial to see that Butler's probabilistic approach in *The Analogy of Religion* is not simply the general conviction that—in the words of the equally-famous opening sentence—"Probable evidence is essentially distinguished from demonstrative by this, that it admits of degrees" (A.Intro.1), but also that throughout this text Butler is concerned with the *practical* rather than the *theoretical* implications of such evidence *for us*, with probability as a *guide to life*. Butler thus prefers inductive and practical probabilistic reasoning to deductive and theoretical propositional reasoning.[40]

Second, Butler's method in the *Analogy* is *a posteriori* rather than *a priori*, and *analogical* rather than *logical*. That is, scrupulously avoiding all metaphysical speculation, *The Analogy of Religion* is a vast thought experiment exploring, in

---

Schellenberg's "Divine Hiddenness and Human Philosophy," in Green and Stump, *Hidden Divinity and Religious Belief*, 13–32, on 24–25.

40. Contrast this with Schellenberg's overt statement in *HA* that he takes a deductive approach and that inductive arguments, "which aim only at some measure of probability, . . . are ignored here" (3–4).

the full words of the title, the analogy of both natural *and* revealed religion, not to *themselves*, but "*to the Constitution and Course of Nature.*"[41] It is precisely such empirical natural reality as known through practical probability that both grounds and limits Butler's reasoning in this text. He thus contrasts explicitly his approach with that of Descartes, whose method he characterizes as follows: "Forming our notions of the constitution and government of the world upon reasoning, without foundation for the principles which we assume, whether from the attributes of God, or any thing else, is building a world upon hypothesis" (A.Intro.7).[42] But this description of Descartes is also arguably true of Schellenberg, whose argument is based on a counterfactual hypothesis, eventually designated as $P2'$ and expressed formally as: "If God exists and is perfectly loving, then for any human subject S and time t, if S is at t capable of relating personally to God, S at t believes that G ['God exists'] on the basis of evidence that renders G probable, except insofar as S is culpably in a contrary position at t."[43]

I say "arguably" because admittedly, unlike Descartes, Schellenberg does indeed base his argument on a specific attribute of God, namely, that God is "perfectly loving." Thus, in a new preface for the 2006 paperback edition of *Divine Hiddenness and Human Reason*, Schellenberg says that, rather than beginning with reasonable nonbelief, "I begin with reflection on Divine love and allow the problematic phenomenon to receive its shape therefrom."[44] And several years later, in *The Hiddenness Argument*, he describes his approach by saying that he starts "'from above' (with abstract reflection on the concept of God) rather than 'from below' (with reference to ordinary human experience and common ideas)."[45] But beginning with such abstract reflection on divine love or indeed anything at all is not to reason like Butler from analogy to "the constitution and course of nature." Butler does not start "from above," he starts "from below." And so Schellenberg's approach is more Cartesian than Butlerian, even though he incorporates an attribute of God into his reasoning, because his concept of God is so abstract and *a priori*.

---

41. On this point, see Penelhum, *Butler*, 96, and on these general matters, 89–95.

42. For more on Butler's anti-Cartesianism, see Tennant, *Conscience, Consciousness, and Ethics*, 86–87 and 121–22.

43. *DHHR*, 38.

44. J. L. Schellenberg, *Divine Hiddenness and Human Reason*, with a new preface (Ithaca, NY: Cornell University Press, 2006), viii.

45. *HA*, 17.

Thus, protests to the contrary notwithstanding, when it comes to *P2'* Schellenberg knows in advance that this counterfactual conditional does not obtain, and he thus reasons from what is *not the case* to what *should be the case* to arrive at what *is the case*. Formally valid or not, Butler rejects such an approach, saying, "Let us then, instead of that idle and not very innocent employment of forming imaginary models of a world, and schemes of governing it, turn our thoughts to what we experience to be the conduct of Nature with respect to intelligent creatures.... And let us compare the known constitution and course of things with what is said to be the moral system of Nature; the acknowledged dispensations of Providence, or that government which we find ourselves under, with what religion teaches us to believe and expect; and see whether they are not analogous and of a piece" (A.Intro.11).

Finally, David Brown has not engaged directly with Schellenberg or commented on the divine hiddenness debate. However, in a recent essay on Brown's *God and Enchantment of Place: Reclaiming Human Experience*, Charles Taliaferro astutely makes the connection by observing that

> if Brown is right about the capaciousness and graciousness of God's bounteous revelation [in natural religion as well as revealed], this would constitute a direct reply to the "hiddenness of God" objection as developed by John Schellenberg. Schellenberg argues that a necessary/essential property of any divine personal being is perfect love, and perfect love would entail that God would always seek a relationship with creatures: that is, God would be maximally available to creatures. Schellenberg argues that if there is a loving God, God's existence would be more evident. If Brown is right, God is more evident than Schellenberg and others grant. From Brown's point of view, our failure to see and encounter God in the world is largely due to bad theology and a failure of imagination.[46]

Although he does not appeal specifically to Butler in this volume, in *God and Enchantment of Place* Brown does indeed argue for the return of the category

---

46. Charles Taliaferro, "Transcending Place and Time: A Response to David Brown on Enchantment, Epistemology, and Experience," in *Theology, Aesthetics, and Culture: Responses to the Work of David Brown*, ed. Robert MacSwain and Taylor Worley (Oxford: Oxford University Press, 2012), 109–10.

of "natural religion" as contrasted with "natural theology" as it is commonly practiced, and this is an implicitly Butlerian move.[47] Thus, with both theists such as Swinburne and atheists such as Schellenberg in view, Brown writes that analytic philosophy of religion

> is currently flourishing, and I would not wish to decry its concerns. But from my perspective its present conventions and practice are symptomatic of a malaise that affects theology in general, and that is the assumption of very limited horizons as its domain which are in fact the product merely of the Western world's more recent history. . . . Sport, drama, humour, dance, architecture, place and home, the natural world are all part of a long list of activities and forms of experience that have been relegated to the periphery of religious reflection, but which once made invaluable contributions to a human perception that this world is where God can be encountered, and encountered often. The reduction of the relevance of such areas to the moral, political, or philosophical is what I want to resist as I seek to expand and transform what used to be called "natural religion."[48]

For example, in another Butlerian move, Brown questions the value of logical arguments for God's existence and asks "why proof should be seen as the only way of experiencing the divine impact on our world. Instead of always functioning as an inference, there was [once] the possibility that a divine structure is already implicit in certain forms of experience of the natural world, whether these be of majesty, beauty, or whatever."[49] And Brown is cautiously optimistic that such noninferential, implicit, mediated ways of experiencing the divine presence in natural religion might yet return within our culture.[50]

---

47. See David Brown, *God and Enchantment of Place: Reclaiming Human Experience* (Oxford: Oxford University Press, 2004), 8–9.

48. Brown, *God and Enchantment of Place*, 9; see also 410–12.

49. Brown, *God and Enchantment of Place*, 21–22. For further discussion and development of this passage, see Mark Wynn, "Re-enchanting the World: The Possibility of Materially-Mediated Religious Experience," in MacSwain and Worley, *Theology, Aesthetics, and Culture*, 115–27.

50. For more on this prospect, see Robert MacSwain, "'A Generous God': The Sacramental Vision of David Brown," *International Journal for the Study of the Christian Church* 15 (2015): 139–50, now reprinted as chapter 11 of this volume.

III. Conclusion

Even though Schellenberg's appeal to Butler as an indirect progenitor of the hiddenness argument is more problematic than he perhaps thought, it is still ironic that one of the most significant and widely read discussions of Joseph Butler in recent scholarship has come from an atheist philosopher rather than an Anglican theologian.[51] For a number of complex social, historical, intellectual, and religious reasons, Butler's once-dominant influence in Anglican theology faded gradually at the end of the nineteenth century and was then practically extinguished over the course of the twentieth. As Brown notes, this was partly due to the rise of evolutionary theory and biblical criticism, but again ironically Butler's analogical/probabilistic method was actually more able to cope with those challenges than his historical positions on providence and scriptural authority might suggest.[52] Had his defenders focused more on his method and less on his conclusions, Butler's influence might have lasted longer. More recently, the strong influence of so-called "Yale School" Barthianism and Radical Orthodoxy in Anglican circles has made any appeal to Butlerian natural religion and apologetics seem not just misguided but either quaint or dangerous or both. White's claim that David Brown "may be singled out as a leader in the use of Butler's methods in theology today" thus seems valid, if only because most contemporary theologians have quit the field!

But this suspicion and reticence seem to be a mistake, especially for Brown's fellow Anglicans, as Butler is indeed a defining figure of that tradition. Whether or not White is correct in claiming that "to learn to think theologically one must apply oneself to the works of Bishop Butler," that should at least be true for Anglican theologians.[53] In particular, as Brown has argued, Butler's appeal

51. An interesting exception that proves the rule is Ellen Charry's chapter on Butler in *God and the Art of Happiness*, but even here her concern is with his moral philosophy in the *Fifteen Sermons* rather than his natural religion in the *Analogy*. See Ellen T. Charry, *God and the Art of Happiness* (Grand Rapids: Eerdmans, 2010), 132–53. See also Timothy F. Sedgwick's discussion of Butler's ethics in "The Anglican Exemplary Tradition," *Anglican Theological Review* 94 (2012): 207–31, at 221–23.

52. See Brown, "Butler and Deism," 8 and 20–21.

53. White, introduction to *The Works of Bishop Butler*, 1. But see also Brown's interesting claim that Butler's very success in securing Christian England for the Enlightenment, an apparent victory for reasonable faith, nevertheless meant that "English thought was diverted

to the authority of reason in relation to both nature and revelation is strong yet nuanced, culturally conditioned but still relevant for today. I would contend that it is also necessary. As Brown says in regard to the famous confrontation between Butler and John Wesley, "enthusiasm ceases to make much sense once a climate is created in which Christianity is no longer seen as a reasonable or viable option" and so therefore the church needs both "the reasonableness of Butler and the enthusiasm of Wesley."[54] This seems exactly right, and worth emphasizing. The Anglican tradition is often divided into "Catholic," "Evangelical," and "Liberal" strands, but Timothy Sedgwick reminds us that there is also a small but important *philosophical* strand that can neither be ignored nor simply assimilated into liberalism, and which includes figures such as Locke and Butler. What we may call the "tradition of reason" is an essential aspect of Anglican identity and one that we neglect at our peril, opening the doors to self-deception and obscurantism.[55] For indeed, as Butler says, reason (again, properly understood as probabilistic, analogical, implicit, and contextual) "is the only faculty we have wherewith to judge concerning anything, even revelation itself."[56]

---

from considering some of the more substantial issues that were being raised on the continent, particularly by Voltaire": David Brown, *Tradition and Imagination: Revelation and Change* (Oxford: Oxford University Press, 1999), 14–15.

54. See Brown, "Butler—the Apologist," 55; *Through the Eyes of the Saints*, 127–28.

55. See Timothy F. Sedgwick, *The Christian Moral Life: Practices of Piety* (New York: Seabury, 2008; original Eerdmans, 1999), 47–49, and also Charles Hefling, "On Being Reasonably Theological," in *A New Conversation: Essays on the Future of Theology and the Episcopal Church*, ed. Robert Boak Slocum (New York: Church Publishing, 1999), 48–59. Although I do not develop it further in this essay, in referring to the Anglican "tradition" of reason I am gesturing toward Alasdair MacIntyre's influential understanding of human rationality as "tradition-constituted," in the sense that arguments always take place within specific historical, cultural, institutional, linguistic, and textual contexts. The point of this essay is not to endorse uncritically either Butler's own understanding of reason or his convictions about the relationship between "natural religion" and "revelation," but to ask what a broadly Butlerian vision would consist of in the contemporary context, and I take Brown's work to be an example of that project.

56. Primary thanks go to David Brown for inspiring this essay with his scholarship, supervision, conversation, and friendship. Second, to my colleague Ben King, a church historian with whom I have team-taught a seminar at Sewanee titled "The Anglican Tradition of Reason: Butler, Newman, and Farrer": teaching that seminar and discussing these topics with him have been extremely helpful. I am also grateful to Chris Brewer, the late Ann Loades, and Eleonore Stump for comments on earlier versions of this paper. And I am very grateful to Gladstone's Library in Wales for a residential scholarship in July 2013 to pursue Butler research in that wonderful and ideal setting.

Moving Texts and Mirror Neurons:
David Brown and Eleonore Stump on Biblical Interpretation

I first encountered David Brown through the philosopher Eleonore Stump's substantial review of his book *The Divine Trinity*.[1] She began by stating that it was "an important book which I hope will influence the direction of certain work in contemporary philosophy of religion. It is an attempt to stimulate a dialogue between philosophers of religion and biblical scholars, a dialogue I think is long overdue, in order to combine the studies of the historical basis for and philosophical credibility of Christian doctrines."[2]

I. Introduction: Philosophy and Biblical Studies

Stump observes that according to Brown, the Jewish and Christian Scriptures are "a fallible record of a progressive dialogue between God and human beings in which God's nature is increasingly revealed but often enough misunderstood and misreported by Scriptural authors."[3] After noting Brown's various arguments regarding continuing divine action, Chalcedonian and kenotic models of the incarnation, the full personhood of the Holy Spirit, and the social nature

---

1. Eleonore Stump, review of *The Divine Trinity*, by David Brown, *Faith and Philosophy* 3 (1986): 463–68. *The Divine Trinity* was published in 1985 by Duckworth in the UK and Open Court in the USA.

2. Stump, review of *The Divine Trinity*, 463.

3. Stump, review of *The Divine Trinity*, 463.

Originally published in *The Moving Text: Interdisciplinary Perspectives on David Brown and the Bible*, ed. Garrick V. Allen, Christopher R. Brewer, and Dennis F. Kinlaw III (London: SCM, 2018), 51–69.

of Trinitarian relations, she registers specific points of agreement and disagreement. In one of her commendatory passages Stump says that Brown

> moves easily from discussions of the historical conditions surrounding the Old Testament exile of the Jews to [David] Wiggins's view on identity. He is familiar with the complexities of Patristic theology and scholastic philosophy and yet clearly is able to address contemporary theology in its own terms. And, most importantly for the overall purpose of this book, he comprehends the historical concerns of the biblical critic, but he is also familiar with the methods and the literature of current philosophy of religion. In consequence, his book is itself an example of the sort of dialogue between biblical exegetes and philosophers Brown is urging; and in my view the importance of his beginning such a dialogue far outweighs his book's flaws.[4]

Stump's review of *The Divine Trinity* appeared at a time when philosophers of religion were indeed beginning to take up this particular interdisciplinary dialogue. Focusing on Stump's contribution, in addition to some essays dealing with medieval biblical commentary,[5] she coedited *Hermes and Athena: Biblical Exegesis and Philosophical Theology*, bringing together philosophers and New Testament scholars, to which she also contributed a chapter responding to Wayne A. Meeks.[6] A much later volume focused on the Hebrew Bible is

---

4. Stump, review of *The Divine Trinity*, 464. Some of this review is also included in Eleonore Stump, "Modern Biblical Scholarship, Philosophy of Religion, and Traditional Christianity," *Aletheia* 1 (1985): 75–80.

5. See Eleonore Stump, "Visits to the Sepulcher and Biblical Exegesis," *Faith and Philosophy* 6 (1989): 353–77; Eleonore Stump, "Biblical Commentary and Philosophy," in *The Cambridge Companion to Aquinas*, ed. Norman Kretzmann and Eleonore Stump (Cambridge: Cambridge University Press, 1993), 252–68; Eleonore Stump, "Aquinas on the Sufferings of Job," in *Reasoned Faith: Essays in Philosophical Theology in Honor of Norman Kretzmann*, ed. Eleonore Stump (Ithaca, NY: Cornell University Press, 1993), 328–57; and Eleonore Stump, "Revelation and Biblical Exegesis: Augustine, Aquinas, and Swinburne," in *Reason and the Christian Religion: Essays in Honour of Richard Swinburne*, ed. Alan G. Padgett (Oxford: Clarendon, 1994), 161–97. Brown also contributed an essay to the Swinburne Festschrift: "Did Revelation Cease?," 121–41.

6. See *Hermes and Athena: Biblical Exegesis and Philosophical Theology*, ed. Eleonore Stump and Thomas P. Flint (Notre Dame: University of Notre Dame Press, 1993). Meeks's chapter is "'To Walk Worthily of the Lord': Moral Formation in the Pauline School Exemplified by

Divine Evil? The Moral Character of the God of Abraham, to which Stump made three contributions.[7] And in 2010 Stump published *Wandering in Darkness: Narrative and the Problem of Suffering*, a massive volume dealing with both the methodology and practice of biblical exegesis in the context of a larger argument about theodicy, which I will discuss further below.[8] The dialogue between philosophers and biblical scholars that Stump saw beginning in *The Divine Trinity* has now become a lively conversation, and Stump has been one of the major voices promoting and contributing to it.[9]

What then of Brown? Fourteen years after *The Divine Trinity*, Brown returned to the theme and task of biblical interpretation with *Tradition and Imagination: Revelation and Change* and *Discipleship and Imagination: Christian Tradition and Truth*.[10] A trilogy on religious experience mediated through culture and the arts followed: *God and Enchantment of Place: Reclaiming Human Experience*, *God and Grace of Body: Sacrament in Ordinary*, and *God and Mystery in Words: Experience through Metaphor and Drama*.[11] As I have written elsewhere, the five volumes inaugurated by *Tradition and Imagination*

---

the Letter to Colossians," 37–58, and Stump's reply is, "Moral Authority and Pseudonymity: Comments on the Paper of Wayne A. Meeks," 59–70. Meeks followed up with "Response to Stump," 71–74.

7. See *Divine Evil? The Moral Character of the God of Abraham*, ed. Michael Bergmann, Michael J. Murray, and Michael C. Rea (Oxford: Oxford University Press, 2011). Stump's three contributions are (i) "Comments on 'Does God Love Us?,'" 47–53—a response to Louise Antony's "Does God Love Us?," 29–46, and see also Antony's "Reply to Stump," 54–57; (ii) "The Problem of Evil and the History of Peoples: Think Amalek," 179–97, and see also Paul Draper's "Comments on 'The Problem of Evil and the History of Peoples,'" 198–203; and (iii) Stump's "Reply to Draper," 204–7.

8. Eleonore Stump, *Wandering in Darkness: Narrative and the Problem of Suffering* (Oxford: Oxford University Press, 2010). Brown reviewed *Wandering in Darkness* in the *Church Times* (November 8, 2011)—available online at https://tinyurl.com/3h9ta8tk—and engaged with both Swinburne and Stump in "Present Revelation and Past 'Problematic' Texts," in David Brown, *God in a Single Vision: Integrating Philosophy and Theology*, ed. Christopher R. Brewer and Robert MacSwain (London: Routledge, 2016), 73–85, on 78–81. For my joint review of *Wandering in Darkness* and *Divine Evil?*, see *Sewanee Theological Review* 57 (2014): 582–86.

9. Other philosophers of religion who turned substantial attention to biblical interpretation during this general period include William Abraham, Stephen T. Davis, C. Stephen Evans, Richard Swinburne, and Nicholas Wolterstorff.

10. Both Oxford University Press, 1999 and 2000, respectively.

11. All three Oxford University Press, 2004, 2007, and 2008, respectively.

present many detailed arguments across a vast canvas through a sophisticated blend of philosophy, theology, biblical studies, classical studies, church
history, comparative religion, comparative literature, and a wide range of
other disciplines and cultural studies, particularly those related to the fine
and performing arts, up to and including pop culture in its various manifestations and media. The primarily analytic and empirical approach of *The
Divine Trinity* was not totally abandoned, but has now been thoroughly
integrated into a much deeper and richer context, one that more faithfully
represents the genuine complexity of the Christian tradition and which is
thus more fruitful in interpreting, assessing, and defending it.[12]

Both Brown and Stump have developed their respective understandings of
biblical interpretation in different ways since 1985. Neither is a professional biblical scholar as the guild defines such matters. Yet their work in this area surely
deserves more attention than it has so far received. It is especially interesting to
note how they independently focus on some of the same narratives—Abraham,
Job, and Mary Magdalene/Mary of Bethany—and yet again with different concerns and conclusions. Brown engages with the hermeneutical philosophical
tradition and traces the reception exegesis of these narratives, showing how they
have been "rewritten" through the centuries in Judaism, Christianity, and Islam
in order to address different contexts, mediating divine revelation in the process.[13] Stump, by contrast, situates herself in the analytic philosophical tradition,
current discussions of philosophy and literature, and contemporary neuroscience, and offers original interpretations that often bear little relation to more
common readings of these texts, while sometimes intentionally bracketing the

12. Robert MacSwain, "Introduction: Theology, Aesthetics, and Culture," in *Theology, Aesthetics, and Culture: Responses to the Work of David Brown*, ed. Robert MacSwain and Taylor
Worley (Oxford: Oxford University Press, 2012), 1–10, citation from 5. See also my review of
these five volumes in *Faith and Philosophy* 29 (2012): 362–66.

13. Brown expresses his interest in the newer project of "reception exegesis," rather than the
older approach of "reception history," because of the former's concern with "possible meanings
for today": see "From Past Meaning to Present Revelation: Evaluating Three Approaches," in
Brown, *God in a Single Vision*, 73–85, esp. on 81–83, where he lifts up the work of Paul M. Joyce,
Diana Lipton, Judith Kovacs, and Christopher Rowland as examples of the sort of biblical
scholarship he has in mind. I am grateful to David Brown and Chris Brewer for clarifying
comments on this point.

question of their revelatory status. The following sections will compare Brown's *Tradition and Imagination* and *Discipleship and Imagination* with Stump's *Wandering in Darkness* to bring their respective approaches to biblical interpretation into conversation with one another.[14]

II. Methodology: Hermeneutics and Neuroscience

Before comparing their interpretations of selected biblical narratives, it is illuminating to consider their divergent methodological starting points. Ever since *Continental Philosophy and Modern Theology*, published two years after *The Divine Trinity*, Brown has been identified as an analytic philosopher in dialogue with the Continental tradition.[15] It is thus not surprising that in *Tradition and Imagination* he positions himself between modernism and postmodernism;[16] and in *Discipleship and Imagination* he says that he wants to locate himself "on both sides at once, as it were, of the modernist-postmodernist debate."[17]

From modernism's Enlightenment inheritance Brown retrieves an insistence on "properly researched history" that is not simply the reiteration of a communal tradition's prejudices and self-understanding, immune from external criticism or confirmation.[18] Brown rejects both extreme confidence and extreme

14. In my contribution to the coauthored essay "Contemporary Anglican Systematic Theology: Three Examples in David Brown, Sarah Coakley, and David F. Ford" (now chapter 8 in this book), I noted that Brown's work has been characterized by four broad themes: (i) philosophical theology, (ii) sacramental theology, (iii) theology and the arts, and (iv) Anglican studies. I also noted that a fifth theme might well be biblical interpretation, but that Brown has often pursued this topic by engagement with the arts. We will see that tendency in this chapter, which in various ways also engages with philosophical theology. For a more recent major example, see David Brown, *Gospel as Work of Art: Imaginative Truth and the Open Text* (Grand Rapids: Eerdmans, 2024).

15. See David Brown, *Continental Philosophy and Modern Theology: An Engagement* (Oxford: Blackwell, 1987).

16. See David Brown, *Tradition and Imagination: Revelation and Change* (Oxford: Oxford University Press, 1999), chapter 1, "Narrative and Enlightenment: The Challenge of Postmodernism," 9–59.

17. David Brown, *Discipleship and Imagination: Christian Tradition and Truth* (Oxford: Oxford University Press, 2000), 390.

18. Brown, *Tradition and Imagination*, 11.

skepticism about our knowledge of the past. Complete historical knowledge is impossible, but "provisional judgements" can "make some claim to truth," and such truth claims exhibit "vast differences in degrees of plausibility even if these are often difficult or even impossible to quantify."[19] Advocating "plausibility as the norm" is Brown's Anglican epistemological *via media* between cognitive certainty and ignorance.[20] When it comes to the Jewish and Christian Scriptures, this means that many canonical narratives must be judged nonhistorical and the theological implications faced squarely, although those implications vary greatly and are often difficult to predict in advance.[21]

From postmodernism Brown retrieves an emphasis on tradition, narrative, community, multivalence, and the cultural conditioning (although not determinism) of human thought.[22] Unusually for an analytic philosopher, this leads to a critical but sympathetic conversation with Continental hermeneutics, engaging with Schleiermacher, Dilthey, Bultmann, Ricoeur, and Gadamer, among others.[23] For example, Brown cites approvingly Gadamer's claim that history "does not belong to us, but we belong to it. Long before we understand ourselves through the process of self-examination, we understand ourselves in a self-evident way in the family, society and state in which we live."[24] However, Brown faults Gadamer for not recognizing that there are more than "just two dialogue partners, the present community and its prejudices and the past text. For, in so far as we are aware of its history, each stage of the transmission of the tradition, including those aspects that were jettisoned, has the potential to act as a critique of our present concerns and obsessions."[25] This emphasis

19. Brown, *Tradition and Imagination*, 22.

20. Brown, *Tradition and Imagination*, 32. For further discussion of appeals to probability as a distinctively "Anglican epistemology," see William J. Abraham, *Canon and Criterion in Christian Theology: From the Fathers to Feminism* (Oxford: Oxford University Press, 1998), 188–214, especially 212n50, and Robert MacSwain, *Solved by Sacrifice: Austin Farrer, Fideism, and the Evidence of Faith* (Leuven: Peeters, 2013), 65–69.

21. See, for example, his discussion of historical and empirical criteria in *Discipleship and Imagination*, 390–95.

22. See Brown, *Tradition and Imagination*, 6, 9–10, 32, and then 32–44 for a more detailed engagement.

23. Brown, *Tradition and Imagination*, 44–54.

24. Brown, *Tradition and Imagination*, 51, citing Hans-Georg Gadamer, *Truth and Method* (London: Sheed & Ward, 1979), 245.

25. Brown, *Tradition and Imagination*, 51.

on the "staged-process" of a developing tradition where each individual stage has its own intrinsic value is important and will return in due course.[26] Equally important is Brown's conviction that seeking authorial intention and original meaning is legitimate and indeed necessary, but that such intentions and meanings are not final. Indeed, when it comes to certain biblical texts—such as Galatians 3:28—it is appropriate that we should now interpret them in ways that differ from the authors' original intentions, just so long as we know that we are doing so.[27]

Having endorsed the modernist project of "properly researched history," Brown also insists with postmodernism that "nonhistorical" does not automatically equal "untrue." Metaphor and fiction can convey truth just as well as literal or historical discourse "by conveying significance and values rather than one to one correspondence with historical fact."[28] The truth-value of fiction and metaphor leads to perhaps Brown's most distinctive methodological/theological points, namely, (i) that "tradition, so far from being something secondary or reactionary, is the motor that sustains revelation both within Scripture and beyond,"[29] and (ii) one "of the principal ways in which God speaks to humanity is through the imagination, and, as we might have expected, the human imagination has not stood still."[30] Despite his training in analytic philosophy with its emphasis on empiricism, logic, propositions, and conceptual analysis, Brown now makes the crucial Romantic move that doctrines are in fact "secondary and parasitic on the stories and images that give religious belief its shape and vitality."[31] Indeed, toward the end of *Tradition and Imagination* he says that his "most important claim" in the volume is that "imagination is absolutely integral to the flourishing of any religion, Christianity included."[32]

---

26. Brown, *Tradition and Imagination*, 50.

27. Brown, *Tradition and Imagination*, 41–43, 55, and Brown, *Discipleship and Imagination*, 26, where he says it is highly improbable that Paul held to the equal status of men and women in either church or society, as this verse is often now interpreted to mean.

28. Brown, *Tradition and Imagination*, 56.

29. Brown, *Tradition and Imagination*, 1.

30. Brown, *Tradition and Imagination*, 6.

31. Brown, *Tradition and Imagination*, 2.

32. Brown, *Tradition and Imagination*, 366. For engagements with Brown that expand on these various themes, see William J. Abraham, "Scripture, Tradition, and Revelation: An Appreciative Critique of David Brown," in MacSwain and Worley, *Theology, Aesthetics, and*

In Stump's *Wandering in Darkness* we encounter a different set of methodological assumptions, but with some interesting parallels. Even more than Brown, Stump is known for her commitment to the Anglo-American tradition of philosophy, a tradition that "prizes lucidity, analysis, careful distinction, and rigorous argument."[33] Without disavowing her commitment to this approach in its proper context, Stump admits that its considerable strengths can mask profound weaknesses, particularly when engaging with literary texts and personal relations. The characteristic practices of Anglo-American philosophy are ("to use amateur but accurate neurobiological concepts") left-brain skills, but there is "no reason to suppose that left-brain skills alone will reveal to us all that is philosophically interesting about the world" (24). We also need right-brain skills such as breadth of focus, the capacity to understand stories and poems as well as arguments, and an appreciation "for that part of reality that includes the complex, nuanced thought, behavior, and relations of persons" (25).

To employ such right-brain skills, Stump appeals to the interdisciplinary field of philosophy and literature. Stump holds that "there are things that can be known through narrative but which cannot be known as well, if at all, through the methods of analytic philosophy" (26). She advocates an "antiphonal" interaction between philosophy and literature, in which a narrative "is considered in its disorderly richness. But once it has been allowed into the discussion on its own [right-brain] terms, philosophical reflection enlightened by the narrative can proceed in its customary [left-brain] way" (27). Stump characterizes her method in *Wandering in Darkness* as combining "the techniques of philosophy and literary criticism in order to achieve something neither set of techniques would accomplish on its own" (29).

Stump's approach to philosophy and literature could be applied to any narrative whatsoever, but in *Wandering in Darkness* her focus is on biblical narratives, specifically those of Job, Samson, Abraham, and Mary of Bethany. Any treatment of biblical texts raises at least implicit questions regarding history and revelation, but Stump brackets those questions for this particular project. She

---

Culture, 13–28; Douglas Hedley, "Revelation Imagined: Fiction, Truth, and Transformation," in MacSwain and Worley, *Theology, Aesthetics, and Culture*, 79–90; and Nicholas Wolterstorff, review of *Theology, Aesthetics, and Culture*, *International Journal of Systematic Theology* 17 (2015): 73–75.

33. Stump, *Wandering in Darkness*, 23. Hereafter, page references from this work will be given in parentheses in the text.

acknowledges that her approach to these texts is not historical, and thus mostly not in dialogue with historical-critical scholarship, although she does engage with some standard treatments as a foil to her own. She is more in dialogue with literary approaches such as Robert Alter's (30).[34] Likewise, she says, "for my purposes here I am treating the biblical narratives only as stories, not as history or as revelation; and nothing in this project presupposes the truth of belief in God" (37). As other work of Stump's makes clear, questions of the historicity and revelatory character of the biblical texts are indeed important to her, but not in terms of the interpretations she offers in *Wandering in Darkness*.[35]

As a final piece of her methodological assumptions, Stump links narrative and the knowledge of persons and joins them under an account of so-called second-person experience. Drawing on recent studies in neuroscience and cognitive psychology, Stump notes that autism consists of "a severe impairment in the cognitive capacities necessary for . . . the knowledge of persons and their mental states."[36] Acknowledging that autism remains mysterious, Stump reports that since the 1990s a major theory has involved so-called mirror neurons—that is, those that "fire in the brain both when one does some action oneself *and also* when one sees that same action performed by someone else"—and says that it now seems that "the mirror neuron system is the foundation for the capacity of all fully functional human beings at any age to know the mind of another person."[37] In contemporary philosophy such knowledge is known as "second-person experience." The autistic lack or have difficulty with second-person experience, arguably due to a defect in their mirror-neuron system.

How does this neuroscience connect to narrative? Stump argues that genuine second-person experiences can be conveyed to others via "second-person accounts," and that such accounts are most effective when expressed through detailed stories rather than plain expository prose.[38] A second-person account is not identical to *real* second-person experience, but it is the closest approximation to it, and Stump sees mirror neurons as the crucial explanation of this as well. Why do we respond to fiction as though it were real? Perhaps because

34. See 29–35 for the full discussion.

35. See, for example, her substantial essay "Revelation and Biblical Exegesis: Augustine, Aquinas, and Swinburne," in Padgett, *Reason and the Christian Religion*, 161–97.

36. Stump, *Wandering in Darkness*, 65.

37. Stump, *Wandering in Darkness*, 68. See 67–75 for the full discussion.

38. Stump, *Wandering in Darkness*, 78.

"when we engage with fiction, we also employ the mirror neuron system" to give us access to second-person accounts of human experience.[39] This is likewise true of the biblical narratives Stump interprets in *Wandering in Darkness*, not because they are necessarily fiction but because they are complex and profound stories regardless of their authorship or historicity.[40]

To compare the interpretive methodologies of Brown and Stump shows interesting similarities and differences. Despite their shared background in analytic philosophy, they both now appeal (although in different ways) to the power of imagination and narrative in opening crucial aspects of reality to us and granting us access to those aspects. Both are thus seeking (again in different ways) to break out of a single "Enlightenment" approach to the biblical texts, exemplified by the dominance of historical-critical method. But the differences are perhaps more striking than the similarities. Although fully aware of the need for "properly researched history," Brown's emphasis on the "staged process" of the developing biblical tradition and its interpretive history, combined with his insistence on imagination, leads to a reception exegesis approach to the biblical texts in conversation with hermeneutical theory. Moreover, his method is explicitly open to the questions of both historical accuracy and divine revelation through these texts, to the point where these questions drive his project—for example, in his view that certain biblical narratives may be nonhistorical yet still "true" and even revelatory. By contrast, and fascinatingly, Stump completely avoids any engagement with the hermeneutical tradition and its historic concern for knowing the minds of others through texts and replaces it with contemporary neuroscience. Likewise, despite her known theological commitments, in *Wandering in Darkness* she adopts a secular stance to the biblical narratives, bracketing their historicity and potentially revelatory character, and treating them simply as stories that can be incorporated into a philosophical argument

39. Stump, *Wandering in Darkness*, 79. See 75–80 for the full discussion. In comments on an earlier version of this paper, Chris Bryan pointed out that such second-person experience is also mediated through theater, and one could add film as well.

40. Although I focused above on Stump's *avoidance* of historical-critical method in *Wandering in Darkness*, in the context of her other work in this area, it is clear that she is also highly *critical* of it, and that criticism emerges here as well. For a response from a biblical scholar, addressing both Stump and Alvin Plantinga, see C. L. Brinks, "On Nail Scissors and Toothbrushes: Responding to the Philosophers' Critiques of Historical Biblical Criticism," *Religious Studies* 49 (2013): 357–76.

via her "antiphonal" approach to philosophy and literature. That they are *biblical* stories seems largely irrelevant to this project—what matters is the specific content of their respective narratives.

III. Interpreting Scripture: Tradition and Originality

Although I have focused thus far on their respective methodologies, both Brown and Stump spend much more time in rich, detailed, and interesting engagements with selected biblical narratives. As it happens, both offer interpretations of the stories of Abraham, Job, and Mary Magdalene/Mary of Bethany.[41] In this section I offer the barest summary of their respective readings, simply to demonstrate further similarities and differences in their practice of biblical interpretation. Readers are directed to the full and lengthy treatments in their work for the regrettably missing nuances in this section.

A. Abraham

Brown argues that the long and complex tradition of biblical exegesis is best described as a *moving text*. He admits that (once the canon has been fixed) "the words on the page do not alter," but nevertheless insists that in the interpretative process "content, focus and themes are so restructured . . . that effectively a wholly new grid has been imposed, with what is most important often seen as hidden, as it were, in the interstices of the text."[42] A key example is offered in the Akedah, or "binding" of Isaac by Abraham (Gen. 22:1–19). Brown explores the reception exegesis of this famously disturbing story in Christianity, Judaism, and Islam, including within the New Testament itself. The Letter to the Hebrews, for example, "sought to defuse the tension by giving Abraham

---

41. As indicated above, Stump also engages with the story of Samson, but as Brown does not, I will omit it here. See Stump, *Wandering in Darkness*, 227–57. Stump also treats the shared stories in the order of Job, Abraham, and Mary of Bethany, but I will follow their canonical sequence and start with Abraham. Brown deals with Abraham in *Tradition and Imagination*, and with Job and Mary Magdalene/Mary of Bethany (I explain the conflation below) in *Discipleship and Imagination*.

42. Brown, *Tradition and Imagination*, 208–9.

grounds for continued trust" in the hope of raising Isaac from the dead (Heb. 11:19), and Philo takes the similar line that "to God all things are possible."[43] Perhaps the most influential interpretation among general readers is Kierkegaard's in *Fear and Trembling* (1843), where religious faith supersedes ethical norms. But Brown rejects Kierkegaard's reading on theological grounds, for if "we are forced to say that God is the source of two distinct demands (the moral and the religious) that can conflict, then we seem to end up with a God divided against himself."[44]

Brown thus lifts up an important but now largely neglected thread of Jewish and Christian tradition in which, unlike in Hebrews, Philo, or Kierkegaard, the primary moral agent of the story is not Abraham but Isaac.[45] The age of Isaac is unspecified in the biblical narrative, but despite common assumptions that he was still a young boy, Josephus identifies him as an adult of twenty-five, and the midrash Genesis Rabbah reckons him to be thirty-seven based on the age of Sarah at her death.[46] The details cannot detain us, but the point is that in this thread Isaac is now seen as an adult and thus as a full participant in Abraham's test, perhaps even initiating it himself against the cavils of Ishmael. The offered sacrifice was not Abraham's but Isaac's. Thus, in Judaism Isaac "was to become the norm for life understood as self-sacrificial dedication to God,"[47] and in Christianity he was even seen as a type of Christ.[48] Brown acknowledges that such readings depart from the original meaning of the text, and even from the canonical Christian interpretation of it offered in Hebrews, but insists that the focus on self-sacrifice is morally, religiously, and imaginatively superior to the sacrifice of another (however understood), and this superiority can be discerned in various paintings of the story as well as written interpretations.[49]

43. Brown, *Tradition and Imagination*, 239, citing Philo's *De Abrahamo* 32.

44. Brown, *Tradition and Imagination*, 242.

45. Brown, *Tradition and Imagination*, 247.

46. Brown, *Tradition and Imagination*, 249.

47. Brown, *Tradition and Imagination*, 251. See 247–54 for details.

48. Brown, *Tradition and Imagination*, 257. See 254–57 for details.

49. Brown, *Tradition and Imagination*, 256–60, discussing the work of G. D. Tiepolo, Ghiberti, and Rembrandt, among others. Caravaggio, for example, shows what is "so profoundly wrong with the biblical version: Abraham is shown pinning down his victim, a squirming and screaming son" (258). Of course, such graphic details are not in the biblical text itself, but Brown's point is that they are imaginatively implied by it if Isaac is a mere child without any self-determination.

Stump agrees with Brown in rejecting Kierkegaard's interpretation of Genesis 22, and for similar moral/theological reasons, but she follows Hebrews, Philo, Kierkegaard, and others in identifying Abraham as the primary agent rather than Isaac. For Stump, the story is about discerning the true desires of Abraham's heart and purifying them from misdirection. Rather than surrender the desires of his heart, Abraham must learn to "trust in the goodness of God to fulfill those desires."[50] Stump places the binding of Isaac in the context of the entire story of Abraham's life up to this point, with detailed discussions of Abraham's encounters with God, God's promises to Abraham, and Abraham's complicated relationships with Lot, Sarah, Hagar, Ishmael, Isaac, and his six other sons by Keturah.[51] The gist of this narrative is that Abraham has benefited from God's blessings thus far but has also demonstrated a troubling double-mindedness when it comes to trusting God to fulfill God's promises. How can God (and we) know if Abraham now truly trusts God to keep God's promise that, through Isaac, he will have many descendants? Only through a test—and God thus tells Abraham to sacrifice Isaac.[52]

Noting that the narrative does not specify Isaac's age, Stump says that "the only way to mark time is by the description of Isaac. He is still young enough to be diffident and deferential toward his father. On the other hand, he is old enough to carry some distance up a mountain a load of wood big enough for him to lie down on."[53] Stump thus proposes that Isaac is an adolescent in the story, about the same age as Ishmael when he was sent out into the desert with Hagar at God's command (another, but more ambiguous, sacrifice). Abraham's dilemma, as Stump sees it, is whether he will trust God to provide him descendants through Isaac even if Abraham obeys God's command to perform an act that would (all things being equal) make that impossible: "Abraham passes this test not in case he is willing to give up Isaac, as most commentators assume, but just in case he believes that, if he obeys God's command to sacrifice Isaac, he will *not* be ending Isaac's life."[54] Stump acknowledges that, as an adolescent, Isaac could have resisted his aged father's test, and thus must have cooperated in it,

50. Stump, *Wandering in Darkness*, 259. For her discussion of Kierkegaard, see 260–63, 302–4.

51. Stump, *Wandering in Darkness*, 263–93.

52. Stump, *Wandering in Darkness*, 293.

53. Stump, *Wandering in Darkness*, 295.

54. Stump, *Wandering in Darkness*, 300.

but the central figure whose faith is tested and commended remains Abraham.[55] Abraham passes the test, and the desires of his heart are refined, but "what is praiseworthy about Abraham is not his readiness to kill his son in obedience to God" (à la Kierkegaard), but rather "Abraham's willingness to believe in God's goodness, even against strong temptations to the contrary."[56]

B. Job

Brown begins his chapter on Job by stating that his concern here is "not so much with the so-called problem of evil and its more technical philosophical or theological resolution, as with religious attitudes, with how believers have chosen to face the onslaught of unmerited suffering, and in particular with what the practice of discipleship has meant in such a context."[57] Rather than look for a "presumed original intention" and end the discussion there, Brown is more interested in seeing how Jews and Christians have applied the narrative over the years to cope with specific situations. He thus takes a historical approach, moving from the canonical text to the Testament of Job, Gregory the Great, Aquinas, Calvin, and Blake. He argues that "these later and often much despised interpretations" at least sometimes "constitute significant advances on the canonical text," and concludes that "the Christian community today is the poorer if in its response to innocent suffering it is not allowed to build upon these rewritings of Job's story."[58]

Turning to the canonical text, Brown first notes possible antecedents in Egyptian and Babylonian documents and observes that "questions do not arise out of thin air, but from specific cultural contexts" such as belief or not in an

---

55. See Stump, *Wandering in Darkness*, 593n133. In 592n121, Stump acknowledges the midrash discussed by Brown that derives Isaac's age of thirty-seven from Sarah's age at her death, but says that "there is no tangible evidence for it, and in my view it assigns an age to Isaac at the time of the binding that is improbable as the narrative portrays him in that episode."

56. Stump, *Wandering in Darkness*, 302.

57. Brown, *Discipleship and Imagination*, 177. For a more formal philosophical and theological approach, see his essay "The Problem of Pain," originally published in 1989 and now reprinted in Brown, *God in a Single Vision*, 28–40.

58. Brown, *Discipleship and Imagination*, 177. Hereafter, page references from this work will be given in parentheses in the text.

afterlife (183). God's decisive reply to Job from the whirlwind (chapters 38–41) is normally thought to provide one or more of three possible answers to Job's accusation: "that it was intended to put an end to further debate; that it spoke of a type of God of whom such questions were inappropriate; and that a specific answer was after all given, in a particular type of reassuring experience" (183). Brown has varying degrees of unhappiness with all three, both as answers to the perceived problem and as readings of the text, and he thus engages in a substantial survey of contemporary studies on Job supplemented with a critical engagement with Girard (182–94). In regard to each proposed answer, Brown concludes that the "final shape of the book as a whole argues for a quite different conclusion: the legitimacy of continuing exploration" (187).

In this short essay I cannot begin to do justice to the remainder of Brown's chapter that looks at postcanonical trajectories of interpretation in Judaism and Christianity (194–225). He maintains that later tradition often improves on Job by moving the questions from an externalist to an internalist perspective, "stimulating deeper reflection in response to such questions as these: What is it to be good? What are the proper limits of anger? and, What resources are required for one to be good?" (198). For example, in the midst of detailed and occasionally critical expositions, Brown endorses the expanded role the Testament of Job provides for Job's wife, Gregory the Great's internalization of Job's ethics, and Aquinas's discussion of competing value systems.[59] And the chapter concludes with an analysis of William Blake's illustrations of the book of Job as "indicative of perhaps the most important way of coming to terms with suffering in this new [i.e., post-eighteenth-century] understanding of experience as no longer directly engineered by God" (220). In the art of Blake we find "a much more complete integration of ethics and internalization in that the 'solution' to suffering is seen to lie not just in attitudes (patience, faith, and so forth) but also in our capacity to change those attitudes in light of such experiences. Our freedom now plays an integral part" (223).

Stump's interpretation of Job differs from Brown's in many respects, and perhaps the best way in is by noting their contrasting appeals to the instigating conversations between God and *ha-satan*, "the Accuser," in chapters 1–2. Brown does not dwell on this exchange at length but simply notes that "Job's

59. In Brown's discussion of Aquinas he cites Stump's chapter on Aquinas's biblical commentaries but not her essay "Aquinas on the Sufferings of Job," both cited in note 5 above.

complaints would lack the power of specificity without the opening prose section; so we can be sure that, even if from a different author, the poetry was intended to expand upon the basic prose plot" (183). For Stump, by contrast, what she calls the "framing story"—both the prologue and the conclusion—is essential to understanding the book, which on her reading is as much about "Satan" as Job himself.[60] In addition to the prologue and conclusion, she focuses on the "dramatic episode when God intervenes to talk to Job, which is the culmination of the dialogues among Job and his comforters," rather than on those dialogues themselves, although she acknowledges that they contain much material of interest.[61]

As with Abraham, Stump reads the story of Job as about losing and regaining the desires of his heart, but her distinctive take on this story is to also probe the inner life of "Satan" as revealed by his conversations with God about Job. In a *tour de force* of psychological subtlety, Stump draws a detailed character analysis out of "Satan's" incongruous arrival among the "sons of God," God's greeting to him, and their subsequent exchanges leading on to Job's trials. On Stump's reading, God is motivated by care and love for "Satan," and yet "Satan" is an internally divided self not integrated around the good and thus cynically out of fellowship with God and everything else.[62] As Stump reads the book of Job, the framing story "is a complicated second-person account within which the nested second-person accounts comprising the story of Job's relations with God are embedded."[63]

Again, as with Brown's chapter, I cannot here do justice to the remaining twenty-five pages of detailed analysis in which, as Stump sees it, God tests Job in order to provide "Satan" an exemplar of a self truly integrated around the good, but also to make Job into a greater person than he had been before his trials began. "Because of Satan's second attack and Job's endurance under it, in

---

60. Stump, *Wandering in Darkness*, 179. I place Satan's name in scare quotes to indicate Stump's decision to read *ha-satan* as a proper noun and thus as the devil of Christian tradition rather than as "the adversary" or "the accuser" among the "sons of God" more naturally suggested by the Hebrew text: on this point, see Brinks, "On Nail Scissors and Toothbrushes," 372.

61. Stump, *Wandering in Darkness*, 179. For rather different earlier interpretations of Job, see Stump's essays "Aquinas on the Sufferings of Job" and "Revelation and Biblical Exegesis: Augustine, Aquinas, and Swinburne," cited in note 5 above.

62. Stump, *Wandering in Darkness*, 197–203.

63. Stump, *Wandering in Darkness*, 197.

the story Job becomes the sort of person whose life captures the imagination of anyone who learns of it. Job stood up to the ruler of the universe, and in response God came to talk to him in one of the longest conversations between God and human beings in any of the biblical stories."[64] In resisting the arguments of his friends, Job "takes his stand with the goodness of God, rather than with the office of God as ruler of the universe," and in so doing Job chooses "to be on the side of goodness rather than on the side of power, even if the side of power should be God's side."[65]

Perhaps most distinctively, Stump sees the book of Job as "fractal" vision of divine-human reality in which "tucked within the overarching story of Satan's relations with God is the story that is focused on Job. In regard to *that* story, considered not as a detail in Satan's story (which it is) but as its own whole story—namely, the story of Job's life (which it also is)—*Job* is the primary beneficiary of the events involving his suffering."[66] Thus, in Stump's reading, Job is not "a pawn heartlessly used in a wager between God and Satan. On the contrary, the nested stories of Satan and Job show us God's providence operating in a fractal way, to deal with each of God's creatures as an end in himself, even while interweaving all the individual stories into one larger narrative."[67]

C. Mary Magdalene/Mary of Bethany

This final comparison must be extremely compressed, but in the service of completeness it is essential to include, both because it takes us into the New Testa-

---

64. Stump, *Wandering in Darkness*, 217.

65. Stump, *Wandering in Darkness*, 217. Although Stump does not mention him, Mark Twain's Huck Finn comes inevitably to mind. When choosing to help the escaped slave Jim because his conscience tells him it is the right thing to do, even though his religious authorities tell him it is a damnable offense, Huck famously says, "All right, then, I'll go to hell."

66. Stump, *Wandering in Darkness*, 219. "In my view, the book of Job is to second-person accounts what a fractal is to mathematics. A fractal is a set of points with this peculiar feature: when it is graphed, the shape of each part of the whole resembles the shape of the whole; and the shape of each of the parts of any one part also resembles that of the whole, indefinitely. . . . A graphed fractal is thus a picture within a picture within a picture, and so on, each picture of which is similar to the picture of the whole, only reduced in scale" (220).

67. Stump, *Wandering in Darkness*, 225.

ment and because Brown's and Stump's respective interpretations of this figure are among their most interesting and provocative. Fortunately, in both cases their conclusions can be summarized briefly, if regrettably shorn of nuance.

Acknowledging that it is almost certainly a historical and exegetical error, Brown nevertheless endorses the literary, theological, and moral value of Gregory the Great's influential conflation of Mary Magdalene, Mary of Bethany, and the unnamed penitent sinner who washes Jesus's feet with her tears.[68] Here we see Brown's penchant for splitting the difference between modernism and postmodernism. He argues that, "though what emerged was less than loyal to history, it embodied the more important truth, one which has very effectively engaged the imagination of believers over the centuries in establishing and deepening their relation with Christ and one which we will now lose at our peril: what is involved in the dialectics of discipleship, in the growth of the disciple from sin and misunderstanding through forgiveness to intimacy and empowerment."[69] Against both historical-critical and feminist "rehabilitations," Brown thus defends the traditional figure of Mary Magdalene/Mary of Bethany as the reformed prostitute who becomes the Apostle to the Apostles, contemplative exemplar, and missionary preacher. As with Abraham and Job, Brown supports his case with artistic examples, drawing from painting, poetry, sculpture, and film. Although this composite figure is almost completely imaginary, in the Christian tradition she has become "the primary symbol for understanding what our own discipleship and commitment entail."[70]

By contrast, although Stump is well aware of the patristic and medieval tradition of conflating Mary Magdalene, Mary of Bethany, and the penitent sinner, and is even personally inclined to accept it, she deliberately avoids arguing for such conflation in *Wandering in Darkness*.[71] She rather proposes that the motivation of Mary of Bethany's anointing of Jesus in John 12 may be found, not in a life of notorious sin imported from Luke 7, but from the previous chapter of John's Gospel. When Martha and Mary informed Jesus that his friend and their brother Lazarus was ill, Jesus deliberately waited until Lazarus was dead

68. Brown, *Discipleship and Imagination*, 32–33.

69. Brown, *Discipleship and Imagination*, 32.

70. Brown, *Discipleship and Imagination*, 54. For details, see the whole chapter, "Prostituting and Valuing Women: Equality and Mary Magdalene," 31–61.

71. Stump, *Wandering in Darkness*, 605–6n121.

before making his way to Bethany (John 11). Although he knew that he would restore their brother to them alive in a glorious miracle, in different ways the sisters responded in anger when Jesus finally arrived, and Stump contends that he made a human (but not divine) error of judgment in not informing them of his plan. Martha confronts Jesus directly, whereas Mary withdraws and only comes when told by Martha (truthfully or not) that Jesus was asking for her. Stump reads Mary's subsequent anointing of Jesus (John 12) as an act of gratitude for the restoration of her brother, but also as an act of repentance and reconciliation. According to Stump, Mary thought that Jesus had betrayed her trust in him, but belatedly came to see that, if there was a betrayal of trust here, through her anger and grief she had betrayed his trust in her rather than the other way around. But, whatever the motivation, this image of Mary of Bethany has come down to us as the paradigm of Christian devotion and discipleship: "Even images of that fervent disciple Peter at his most generous are no match for this picture of Mary, with her hair down, heedless, anointing [Jesus's] feet in an outpouring of love."[72]

IV. Conclusion: Left Brain/Right Brain

As with their interpretive methodologies, comparing Brown and Stump on these biblical narratives reveals many interesting similarities and differences that cry out for further analysis, commentary, and critique. Note, for example, that despite highly divergent interpretations, their evaluations of Mary Magdalene and Mary of Bethany arrive at precisely the same point. Collectively weighing in at 1,500 pages, I have barely scratched the surface of *Tradition and Imagination*, *Discipleship and Imagination*, and *Wandering in Darkness* and their implications for biblical studies, philosophy, and theology, nor begun to do justice to the subtleties of their respective arguments. For this essay my concern is more

---

72. Stump, *Wandering in Darkness*, 353. For details see the whole chapter: "The Story of Mary of Bethany: Heartbrokenness and Shame," 308–68. Although she does not explore further the conflation between Mary Magdalene and Mary of Bethany, later in the chapter Stump does consider the possibility that Mary of Bethany is the woman in Luke 7, but the main aspect of her argument does not depend on that potential identification. The above paragraph in the main text is adapted from my "Sermon for 13 March: 5th Sunday in Lent," *Expository Times* 127 (2016): 235–36.

expository than critical, but having summarized their methodological positions and exegetical offerings, I must now offer some brief interim conclusions.

To begin with, even when Brown and Stump engage in biblical interpretation, they clearly do so with an eye for the theological and philosophical significance of these texts, although I have resisted engaging with them on these normative matters, either pro or con. For example, Brown and Stump disagree regarding the nature of an adequate defense for the theistic problem of human suffering, and I contend that their disagreement turns first on their views of particular providence and only secondarily on their readings of Job.[73] While I cannot adjudicate this debate here, it is indeed fascinating that Stump offers a mathematical example to explain the narrative of Job while Brown points to aesthetic considerations. Hence Stump's "fractal" reading, where God interweaves all the individual stories into one larger narrative in which each story has its place in the whole while maintaining the integrity of each character as an end in herself; and hence Brown's preference for Blake's illustrations of a world in which the minute details of our experience are enabled but not engineered by God. This generic difference—mathematics versus art—correlates with Stump's methodological appeal to neuroscience and mirror neurons against Brown's preference for hermeneutics and a fluid reception exegesis of moving texts. When it comes to method, Stump's approach to the biblical texts is thus still more "left brain" than she may have desired or intended, and is more likely to appeal to philosophers and scientists, whereas Brown's more "right-brain" approach is more likely to appeal to readers in the arts and humanities.

When it comes to their interpretations of the compared biblical narratives, Brown typically lifts up a neglected stage of a traditional reading discerned through the written and artistic record, explains why it was abandoned as a result of various critiques, and then argues for its continuing value for contemporary audiences. Stump, by contrast, while familiar with those traditional readings and historical-critical demolitions of them, typically offers an original and highly creative reading unprecedented in the history of interpretation. Stump is thus more "right brain" in practice than in method, and has indeed been accused by historical-critical scholars of "rewriting" the biblical narratives

---

73. For details see "The Problem of Pain: Why Philosophers and Theologians Need Each Other," in Brown, *God in a Single Vision*, 28–40, especially 34, and the theodicy section of Stump, *Wandering in Darkness*, 371–481.

to suit her purposes.[74] Ironically, whether this is a fair characterization of her interpretations or not, this is precisely what Brown claims that other interpreters have done as well, including canonical authors and editors, namely, rewritten the biblical narratives in order to address specific social and religious concerns.[75] Also ironically, Brown now seems more "left brain" in practice than in method, at least in comparison with Stump, as he has identified the creative process at work in interpretation but draws his own understanding of the narratives from the various stages of rewriting through commentary, art, and literature rather than—à la Stump—contributing a "moving text" of his own. Unless, that is, one reads *Tradition and Imagination* and *Discipleship and Imagination* as intentional palimpsests of such "moving texts" and thus as intellectually imaginative acts in their own right.[76]

74. See, for example, Brinks, "On Nail Scissors and Toothbrushes," 373.

75. Brown, *Discipleship and Imagination*, 177.

76. Although I came up with this literary analogy to describe creative scholarship such as Brown's on my own, I eventually realized that others had used it as well and that it has indeed become a significant concept in a number of fields: see, for example, Sarah Dillon, "Reinscribing De Quincey's Palimpsest: The Significance of the Palimpsest in Contemporary Literary and Cultural Studies," *Textual Practice* 19 (2005): 243–63. Dillon's discussion of Foucault on 253–54 suggests that while historical-critical biblical scholars are archaeological "palimpsest readers," only interested in recovering the original text, Brown's reading is genealogically "palimpsestuous," interested in the layered rewritings and their interactions. I am grateful to Chris Brewer, David Brown, Chris Bryan, and Eleonore Stump for helpful comments on earlier versions of this essay, and to Corey Stewart for pointing me toward Dillon's article.

CHAPTER 11

"A Generous God": The Sacramental Vision of David Brown

In 2014, John Hoffmeyer, sometime president of the Society of Anglican and Lutheran Theologians (SALT), kindly invited me to participate in their annual meeting on the general theme "Sacramental Theology." However, it was not the theme itself but his specific description of it that caught my attention: he wrote that "we do not intend to limit presenters to a focus on ritual practice. We are interested in broad and creative thinking on the sacramental presence of the divine." And that phrase, "broad and creative thinking on the sacramental presence of the divine," sounded like an excellent summary of the sacramental theology of David Brown, who retired in 2015 as Wardlaw Professor of Theology, Aesthetics, and Culture at the University of St. Andrews. As we will see, it is difficult to think of a better extended example of such "broad and creative thinking," but in addition to introducing and summarizing Brown's work in this area I will also consider critiques of it from both philosophical and theological angles.[1]

Before assuming his position at St. Andrews in 2007, Brown had been fellow and chaplain at Oriel College, Oxford, and then Van Mildert Professor of Divinity at the University of Durham and residentiary canon at Durham Cathedral. It was during his early years in Durham that Brown first engaged

1. In my contribution to the coauthored essay "Contemporary Anglican Systematic Theology: Three Examples in David Brown, Sarah Coakley, and David F. Ford" (now chapter 8 in this book), I note that Brown's work has been characterized by four broad themes: (i) philosophical theology, (ii) sacramental theology, (iii) theology and the arts, and (iv) Anglican studies. In this current chapter I am focusing on (ii) but touching on (iii) as well.

Originally published in *International Journal for the Study of the Christian Church* 15, no. 2 (2015): 139–50.

with sacramental theology in a substantial way, and these initial forays were both collaborative and interdisciplinary in nature. In 1993, Brown and Ann Loades—then professor of divinity at Durham—organized a series of lectures in sacramental theology to mark the 900th anniversary of the founding of Durham Cathedral. This series resulted in two volumes of essays by theologians, philosophers, historians, musicians, biblical scholars, and literary critics, edited by Brown and Loades.[2] While they did not contribute chapters of their own to these two volumes, the respective editorial introductions—"The Dance of Grace" and "The Divine Poet"—express their contemporary Anglo-Catholic sacramental convictions, which are occasionally at variance with some of their contributors', especially those of a more Reformed background.[3] In addition, with David Fuller—then senior lecturer in English literature at Durham— Brown coauthored a commentary on selections from a wide range of literary classics dealing directly or indirectly with the traditional seven sacraments.[4] These collaborations with Fuller and Loades, and the engagements with the various contributors to the edited volumes, ultimately led to three substantial and wide-ranging volumes by Brown unified by their joint concern with sacramental theology and religious experience, beginning in 2004 with *God and Enchantment of Place: Reclaiming Human Experience*.

I. Manifesto: "Re-conceiving the Sacramental"

However, before getting to those volumes, I will engage directly with Brown's constructive sacramental theology by first looking at an essay he contributed to *The Gestures of God: Explorations in Sacramentality*—itself the result of another major ecumenical and international forum on sacramental theology, this time organized by Geoffrey Rowell and Christine Hall in Windsor, England,

2. David Brown and Ann Loades, eds., *The Sense of the Sacramental: Movement and Measure in Art and Music, Place and Time* (London: SPCK, 1995), and David Brown and Ann Loades, eds., *Christ: The Sacramental Word: Incarnation, Sacrament, and Poetry* (London: SPCK, 1996).

3. For a summary of their joint position, see Brian Douglas, *A Companion to Anglican Eucharistic Theology*, vol. 2, *The 20th Century to the Present* (Leiden: Brill, 2012), 313–18.

4. David Brown and David Fuller, *Signs of Grace: Sacraments in Poetry and Prose* (London: Cassell, 1995).

in 2003. Brown's chapter was published the same year as *God and Enchantment of Place* and is basically a précis of that book and its sequels, so this essay forms a convenient manifesto of his particular sacramental convictions. The essay, "Re-conceiving the Sacramental," begins as follows:

> In talking of the need to re-conceive the sacramental I want to stake out my claim that the Church and its theologians have made a very serious error in withdrawing from theological engagement with large areas of experience that were once the Church's concern. Topics like body and food, music and dance, landscape art and town planning, architecture and gardening were all once integral to a religious conception of the world, whereas, if they are discussed in theological context at all these days, the tendency is to treat them as merely illustrative of questions more appropriately raised elsewhere rather than as raising issues and challenges in their own right. The result is that both in its practice and in its theology Christianity has become a very inward looking religion with its perceived external relevance almost wholly confined to ethics and politics.[5]

Brown's description of Christianity having become a more "inward look-ing religion" than (in his view) it used to be finds an interesting parallel in a critical comment by the American environmental activist and author Edward Abbey. In a journal entry dated December 15, 1988, Abbey dismissed existen-tialism, jazz, and Christianity as, respectively, "indoor" philosophy, "indoor" music, and "indoor" religion.[6] For Abbey, a devotee of wilderness and desert, no description could be more damning. Brown thus finds a surprising ally here, but whereas Abbey thinks that Christianity is irredeemably and essentially an "indoor" affair, Brown sees this as a relatively new and potentially redeemable circumstance. Thus, he says that it is "partly in the hope of reversing that trend" that he embarked on the trilogy that we will get to in due course: *God and Enchantment of Place: Reclaiming Human Experience* (2004), *God and Grace of Body: Sacrament in Ordinary* (2007), and *God and Mystery in Words: Expe-*

5. David Brown, "Re-conceiving the Sacramental," in *The Gestures of God: Explorations in Sacramentality*, ed. Geoffrey Rowell and Christine Hall (London: Continuum, 2004), 21.

6. Edward Abbey, *Confessions of a Barbarian: Selections from the Journals of Edward Abbey*, ed. David Peterson (Boulder, CO: Johnson Books, 2003), 373.

rience through Metaphor and Drama (2008). Here, however, Brown says that although "the argument need not be conducted in the terms of sacramental theology, it does in [his] view provide one helpful avenue in,"[7] and in the remainder of the essay he pursues that possibility under three headings: "a more comprehensive notion of sacrament, objections to such a revised understanding, and finally some specific applications."[8]

In regard to "a more comprehensive notion of sacrament," far from arguing about whether the number of Christian sacraments is properly limited to either two or seven, Brown wants us to return to a pre-Lombardian world where a vast number of objects and practices can be described legitimately as sacraments.[9] According to Brown, "Augustine, for example, includes among his list of sacraments the Lord's Prayer, the Creed, the sign of the cross, ashes of penitence, oil of anointing, and even the Easter liturgy itself. All of these signs offer a foretaste or anticipation of a larger reality. It is this notion of mediated participation that, I think, leads Augustine to concede that essentially the same phenomenon can occur outside Christianity."[10] Far from seeing such interfaith implications as a problem, Brown embraces them. For example, he points out that the parallels between the traditional seven Catholic sacraments and "the sixteen rituals that mark the chief phases of a Hindu's life" are so strong that "the most commonly used textbooks introducing English children to Hinduism now translate the related term *samskara* simply as 'sacrament.'" Again, however, Brown accepts this development and argues:

> It is not that everything labeled sacramental in this way must therefore now necessarily be endorsed by the Christian but rather that thereby the potential for a more positive estimate is indicated. Taking the doctrine of creation seriously generates an expectation that God will address his creation through its material reality, and that must surely mean all humanity and not just those who are explicitly Christian. The use of *mysterion* in the New Testament commits the Christian to the existence of "sacraments" al-

7. Brown, "Re-conceiving the Sacramental," 21.
8. Brown, "Re-conceiving the Sacramental," 21–22.
9. The seven Catholic sacraments were not fixed until Peter Lombard's *Sentences* in the twelfth century.
10. Brown, "Re-conceiving the Sacramental," 24–25.

ready in the Old Testament, and so this might seem a natural extension of such a way of thinking. At all events, this wider conception for which I am appealing has been gaining pace throughout the twentieth century. Significant names in Anglicanism would include Charles Gore, Oliver Quick and William Temple, while since the Second Vatican Council it has become commonplace within Roman Catholicism to set discussion of the specific sacraments within the wider frame of Christ as the "primordial sacrament" and the Church as the "fundamental sacrament."[11]

When he turns to consider objections to this broader notion of sacrament and sacramental presence, Brown makes a concession that within some influential circles of contemporary theology would be sufficient to dismiss his project without further ado. He says: "In effect what I am pleading for is a new form of natural religion, taking seriously religious experiences within the Church that are not closely tied to any specific aspect of biblical revelation and [that] parallel experience outside the Church of the many who lay claim to some form of encounter with God but yet seldom, if ever, darken a church's door."[12] What precisely he means by "natural religion" requires some further discussion to understand properly, which he provides in *God and Enchantment of Place* and its sequels.[13] But in this essay Brown then engages directly with two currently prominent theologians who would dissent strongly from such an approach, namely, Karl Barth and Hans Urs von Balthasar. Brown responds to them as follows:

> [A] puzzling paradox, if not contradiction, lies at the heart of both theologians' writings. On the one hand, we have God portrayed as marvelously generous in the way he has disclosed himself through the biblical revelation and in the Church; on the other, he speaks outside that revelation faintly and only then in a manner that acquires proper legitimacy and intelligibility when set in the context of the Christian faith. But if God is truly generous, would we not expect to find him at work everywhere and in such a way that

11. Brown, "Re-conceiving the Sacramental," 25.
12. Brown, "Re-conceiving the Sacramental," 26.
13. See, for example, David Brown, *God and Enchantment of Place: Reclaiming Human Experience* (Oxford: Oxford University Press, 2004), 5–10.

all human beings could not only respond to him, however implicitly, but also develop insights from which even Christians could learn?[14]

This contested question of the extent of God's "generosity" lies at the heart of Brown's sacramental project. As we will see in due course, it is also a question that some of Brown's critics focus upon. Brown develops this thought further in a related passage in *God and Enchantment of Place* from whence this article derives its title: "Basic to Christian conviction is belief in a generous God. In his life, death and resurrection Jesus Christ revealed a loving and merciful God who, while calling human beings back from sin, none the less fully endorsed our material world by himself becoming part of it."[15] This comment reveals that Brown's sacramental theology is indeed grounded not only in the doctrine of creation but also Christologically in the doctrine of the incarnation, understood in a strongly kenotic sense—although again, as we will see, there is some debate as to which comes first in his view: sacrament or incarnation, incarnation or sacrament.

Brown's third goal in this essay is to consider specific applications of his expanded sacramental theology, and he looks briefly at athletics and architecture. Rather than interact further with this essay, however, I now turn to the trilogy of books where Brown's manifesto is worked out in remarkable detail and a wealth of often surprising examples.

II. Examples and Implications

As Brown himself admits in "Re-conceiving the Sacramental," while he may be pushing this expanded notion of the sacrament rather more forcefully than many of his contemporaries, the notion itself is not unique to him, but is at least officially in some Roman Catholic and Anglican circles the "new normal," however abstractly conceived and articulated. Thus, for example, what gives the Eucharist its basic meaning is the universal human practice of sharing meals, as well as the natural symbolism of bread and wine, flesh and blood, all of which is

14. Brown, "Re-conceiving the Sacramental," 26–27. For a later volume on this theme, see David Brown, *Learning from Other Religions* (Cambridge: Cambridge University Press, 2024).
15. Brown, *God and Enchantment of Place*, 6.

then given additional significance by association with the institution narratives of the Last Supper, and so on. Furthermore, Brown accepts the classic Augustinian and catechetical definition of a sacrament as "an outward and visible sign of an inward and spiritual grace," although, as we will see, he expands it further to include the audible as well as the visible. What thus sets Brown's sacramental theology apart from that of most other contemporary theologians is rather how he has developed and applied it in the three books I mentioned earlier: *God and Enchantment of Place*, *God and Grace of Body*, and *God and Mystery in Words*. While only the second volume has the word "sacrament" in the title, with its subtitle of *Sacrament in Ordinary*, all three engage both explicitly and implicitly with sacramental theology. The explicit engagement is found primarily in the opening chapter of the first volume, which develops in more detail the ideas expressed in "Re-conceiving the Sacramental"; in part 3 of the second volume, titled "The Eucharistic Body"; and in a brief section of the third volume, dealing with sacramental language.[16]

But it is the implicit engagement I wish to focus on, as Brown makes good on his argument that theologians need to reengage with aspects of human experience that were once central to religious reflection but which have now become peripheral: art and architecture, place and pilgrimage, gardens and athletics, food and drink, music and dance, metaphor and drama. Brown thus seeks to reconfigure theology so that these matters are once again central to the discipline. He is convinced that—to return to John Hoffmeyer's inviting phrase—"the sacramental presence of the divine," and hence *grace* as well, is indeed already everywhere, mediated to us through these manifold quotidian forms, if only we have eyes to see and ears to hear. Such sacramental presence of the divine and its accompanying grace may even be found in the most unlikely corners of our culture, such as film, television, and popular music. Because these volumes are long and cover a wide range of arts and genres, I can only barely scratch the

16. For two subsequent and more thematic treatments of sacramental theology, see Brown's chapter "Sacramentality," in *The Oxford Handbook of Theology and Modern European Thought*, ed. Nicholas Adams, George Pattison, and Graham Ward (Oxford: Oxford University Press, 2013), 613–31, and "A Sacramental World: Why It Matters," in *The Oxford Handbook of Sacramental Theology*, ed. Hans Boersma and Matthew Levering (Oxford: Oxford University Press, 2015), 603–15. For a recent study that draws appreciatively on Brown's work, see Lizette Larson-Miller, *Sacramentality Renewed: Contemporary Conversations in Sacramental Theology* (Collegeville, MN: Liturgical Press, 2016).

surface of each one, but perhaps enough to give a taste of their contents, with some representative examples.[17]

As noted earlier, *God and Enchantment of Place* begins with a more detailed argument for Brown's expanded notion of sacramentality, as well as a defense of what he means by "natural religion." His sustained discussion of examples begins in the next chapter, in which he defends the realism of representational Renaissance and later Western art against the more stylized conventions of Eastern Orthodox iconography. Although not at all wishing to disparage the significant spiritual and artistic achievement of the iconic tradition, Brown is concerned that the current popularity of icons in the West fails to take seriously the inherent limitations of the form and ignores the strong Eastern polemic *against* Western art from whence icons emerge. In Brown's view, icons emphasize transcendence at the expense of immanence, so much so that they can make "the divine world seem totally set apart from this world rather than integrating with it and so transforming it."[18] To that extent, icons are inadequately sacramental. Likewise, by traditionally refusing to set their scenes and subjects in contemporary contexts and clothing, icons "draw attention to a world that is gone, and so [for example] place Mary firmly in the past rather than as part of our world" (47).

By contrast, Brown finds great religious and spiritual value in precisely those aspects of Renaissance and later Western art that are rejected by the iconic tradition and its theological advocates, such as its realism and its attempts to make the gospel events contemporary to the painting's original viewers. Rather than a conflict between transcendence and immanence, Brown argues that both are necessary, and so "for God to have impact on every aspect of us immanence must also be claimed: God involved with matter. Christians believe that this happened at the deepest and most profound level in the incarnation, but if there is to be a continuing effect this cannot have happened just once, but must relate to all material existence. It is this insight that the Renaissance takes up and defends in its art" (81–82). Such art is therefore, in Brown's view, properly described as sacramental: "an outward and visible sign of an inward and spiritual grace."

---

17. The following treatment of these three volumes was enhanced in the original lecture by projected images of the discussed art and architecture, which is also partly why each volume is treated in decreasing length, given the significant visual focus of *God and Enchantment of Place*.

18. Brown, *God and Enchantment of Place*, 44. Hereafter, page references from this work will be given in parentheses in the text.

The next chapter deals with the natural world and depictions of it in landscape paintings: that is to say, works of art that are not necessarily explicitly religious in having a biblical theme and so forth. For example, among many instances, Brown discusses nineteenth-century painters such as Caspar David Friedrich, John Constable, and the American Hudson River School. In such art Brown often finds a similar evocation of transcendence or immanence or both as is conveyed by explicitly religious art, and so finds a similar value in it as mediating a potential sacramental experience of the divine presence in creation. After discussing Van Gogh and Cézanne, Brown then considers twentieth-century abstractionist or expressionist artists such as Mondrian, Kandinsky, and Klee, arguing that all three are "religious painters" who "assert that the underlying reality of the world is spiritual, not purely material" (150 and 140). Despite often being nonrepresentational in any conventional sense, such art may also be sacramental in both intent and effect.

Due to limits of length, I will pass over the next chapter, on place and pilgrimage, which deals among other issues with the symbolic and spiritual implications of town planning and city life, and move to the following chapter, on architecture. One of Brown's distinctive claims is that we should recover a sense of buildings as themselves sacramental in design and impact, independently of what happens within them and whether or not they are intended for a religious purpose. As Brown puts it: "architecture can be seen as having a [sacramental] role, provided the intention or result still reflects something of what God is believed to be doing anyway through his presence in our world. In other words, architecture has the power to imitate or mimic God's actions elsewhere in the natural and human world; so through that imitation it can open up the possibility of God himself using such means to communicate with humankind" (245). Thus the "indoor" both reflects and interprets the "outdoor," helping us to understand it better as a manifestation of divine creativity.

Against what he sees as the prevalent utilitarian and instrumentalist mindset of our contemporary age, Brown appeals to the symbolic power of classical or neoclassical buildings to convey a sense of rationality, of Romanesque buildings to convey immanence, of Gothic buildings to convey transcendence, of Baroque buildings to convey playfulness, of modern buildings to convey simplicity, and of postmodern buildings to eclectically convey all five of these properties. As these are also divine attributes or activities, to the extent that such buildings evoke these aspects of divine presence, however implicitly or subliminally, they may be described as at least latently sacramental. When such buildings are also churches, their sacramental potentiality is intensified, again even if the clergy and people are unaware of it or formally opposed to the building's inherent meaning.[19]

The remainder of the book widens the perspective to take account of Hindu and Muslim examples, as well as gardens as symbolic representations of paradise or the entire universe, and concludes with the religious implications of athletics, particularly as interpreted through popular films such as *Enter the Dragon*, *Rocky*, *Field of Dreams*, *The Legend of Bagger Vance*, and *He Got Game*. I turn now, more briefly, to the second volume, *God and Grace of Body*, and will conclude this section with a mere glancing mention of the third, *God and Mystery in Words*.

As noted earlier, the second volume's subtitle is *Sacrament in Ordinary*, and so Brown's sacramental intentions are more overt. The book is divided into three parts, "Finding God in Bodies," "Ethereal and Material" (which deals with music), and "The Eucharistic Body." While this is all germane to our topic, I will focus on the second part, which has three chapters, "Classical Music," "Pop Music," and "Blues, Musicals, and Opera."[20] This is where Brown expands the classical definition of the sacrament to include the audible as well as the visible. Brown writes in the book's introduction that God may be "found in every as-

---

19. For further engagement with these various arguments from *God and Enchantment of Place*, see Gordon Graham, "Enchantment and Transcendence: David Brown on Art and Architecture," in *Theology, Aesthetics, and Culture: Responses to the Work of David Brown*, ed. Robert MacSwain and Taylor Worley (Oxford: Oxford University Press, 2012), 91–102. (Subsequent references to this volume in the notes will be as *TA&C*.) For further discussion of the religious significance of architecture in particular, see Brown's chapter in *The Routledge Companion to Theism*, ed. Charles Taliaferro, Victoria S. Harrison, and Stewart Goetz (New York: Routledge, 2013), 555–63, now reprinted as "Architecture and Theism," in David Brown, *Divine Generosity and Human Creativity: Theology through Symbol, Painting, and Architecture*, ed. Christopher R. Brewer and Robert MacSwain (London: Routledge, 2017), 156–66, as well as the other chapters in part 4 of this volume.

20. In *God and Grace of Body*, the chapter "Food and Drink," 120–84, and the two-chapter section "The Eucharistic Body," 389–428, directly address more conventional discussions in sacramental theology, but my assigned task was to highlight "broad and creative thinking on the sacramental presence of the divine." I am therefore here looking at the less conventional applications of Brown's work rather than his engagements with familiar debates about eucharistic presence, etc. These are still worth considering, but not now.

pect of human experience,"[21] and that, when it comes to music, as "a deliberate challenge to the reader, I try to indicate how God might be experienced through musical forms as varied as opera and jazz, Schubert and Led Zeppelin."[22] Asserting the sacramental power of sacred and some forms of secular classical music is perhaps less controversial today than in the past, at least in some circles, although it is explicitly denied by others, and indeed Brown charts a strong and pervasive suspicion of music as such in the Christian tradition. However, given that popular music is normally completely disparaged or ignored by both church and academy, let me focus even more specifically on that chapter.[23]

Brown is concerned by the elitism inherent in such contempt or neglect, and observes that popular music "is often the only form of non-visual culture to penetrate the modern home."[24] His claim is supported by a statement from Bruce Springsteen, who grew up in a working-class Roman Catholic family in New Jersey, and for whom rock music arrived with the transformative power of a revelation: as Springsteen said, "Rock and roll reached into all those homes where there was no music or books or anything. . . . That's what happened in my house."[25] In this chapter Brown considers multiple genres and dozens of ostensibly "secular" musicians and bands, ranging from pop to rock to heavy metal to grunge to rap to soul to hip-hop, and in a subsequent chapter considers blues and country in addition to musicals and opera. What he appreciates about such popular music is the way it often raises spiritual issues implicitly or indirectly, but in his view thus potentially more effectively than either conventional hymnody or contemporary Christian music.

His treatment of Springsteen is a case in point, tracing the story of his negative experiences in a Catholic parochial school as a child to his eventual return to some form of faith. This return is exemplified powerfully in Springsteen's

---

21. David Brown, *God and Grace of Body: Sacrament in Ordinary* (Oxford: Oxford University Press, 2007), 2.

22. Brown, *God and Grace of Body*, 3.

23. For a discussion of Brown's view of classical music, see Jeremy S. Begbie, "Openness and Specificity: A Conversation with David Brown on Theology and Classical Music," in *TA&C*, 145–56. For Begbie's own proposals about the sacramental character of music, see his "Music, Mystery and Sacrament," in Rowell and Hall, *The Gestures of God*, 173–91.

24. Brown, *God and Grace of Body*, 296.

25. From Dave Marsh, *Born to Run: The Bruce Springsteen Story* (New York: Dell, 1981), cited by Brown, *God and Grace of Body*, 296.

2002 album *The Rising*, dealing with the aftermath of 9/11 by exploring themes of self-sacrifice, resurrection, and even ascension. Brown writes that the cover song's "catchy chorus, 'Come on up for the rising,' is thus about much more than merely transcending human difficulties. Implicitly, it can also be seen to be about Christ's own resurrection and the possibilities for new life that this offers to us."[26] Again, sacramental encounter with divine presence mediated through music, in this case a rock song.[27]

Finally, and far more briefly, the third volume, *God and Mystery in Words*, deals with the potential for words themselves to function sacramentally, partly through the power of metaphor to make integrating connections between disparate objects, and partly through the power of poetic beauty and verbal rhetoric to move us closer to God. Brown thus rejects the conventional sharp distinction between "word" and "sacrament" and writes: "Words, I shall contend, are not just a medium for conveying something else but sometimes themselves an essential constituent in the experience. Put concisely, God is himself sometimes to be found in and through the words."[28] As the Roman Catholic Australian poet Les Murray (1938–2019) writes: "God is the poetry caught in any religion, / Caught, not imprisoned."[29] In addition to poems, sermons, and hymn lyrics, Brown also considers drama as a place of sacramental encounter, including but not limited to the drama of the liturgy.[30]

26. Brown, *God and Grace of Body*, 314. Cf. Bruce Springsteen, *The Rising* (New York: Columbia Records, 2002).

27. Brown's engagement with contemporary popular music is considered (positively) in Gavin Hopps, "Infinite Hospitality and the Redemption of Kitsch," 157–68, and (more critically) in Judith S. Casselberry, "Were We Ever Secular? Interrogating David Brown on Gospel, Blues, and Pop Music," 169–83, both in *TA&C*. Brown and Hopps later coauthored a book dealing with religious experience mediated through both classical and popular musical forms: *The Extravagance of Music* (Cham, Switzerland: Palgrave Macmillan, 2018).

28. David Brown, *God and Mystery in Words: Experience through Metaphor and Drama* (Oxford: Oxford University Press, 2008), 17.

29. From "Poetry and Religion," in Les Murray, *Collected Poems* (Manchester: Carcanet, 1991), cited by Brown, *God and Mystery in Words*, 60. Brown's use of this poem, and his view of the sacramental capacity of poetry, is discussed in David Fuller, "'A Sensibility for the Infinite': Metaphor, Symbol, Form, and the Sublime," in *TA&C*, 213–25.

30. Brown's various arguments here are subjected to scrutiny in Ben Quash, "The Density of Divine Address: Liturgy, Drama, and Human Transformation," in *TA&C*, 241–51. As noted

III. Critique and Conclusion

So, what are we to make of all this? Obviously many objections could be raised against Brown's sacramental vision at any number of points along the way, and from multiple angles. For example, one may question Brown's assumption that Christ's incarnation entails a general divine endorsement of material reality as such, and likewise whether simply affirming the "spiritual" nature of things is sufficient for a truly *sacramental* insight or encounter. Let me conclude by considering briefly just two external critiques, one more philosophical and one more theological, both of which were raised at a conference on Brown's work that I coorganized with Taylor Worley at the University of St. Andrews in 2010.

In "Presence without Absence? A Critique of David Brown's Ontology of Divine Generosity," Jonathan Mackenzie argues that Brown's sacramental theology, particularly as expressed in *God and Enchantment of Place*, is "founded upon a 'metaphysics of presence'" that is unsustainable in our contemporary and specifically post-Heideggerian philosophical context.[31] Because of this context, Mackenzie says, "it has become untenable to simply content oneself as a theologian with the claim, 'God is present in the world.' . . . To speak of 'the presence of God,' therefore, requires explanation of what exactly this might mean. That is to say, a return to a universal account of sacramentality in our own world appears not only naïve . . . but also kitsch to the sensibilities of a world which has learned to live 'without God.'"[32] Furthermore, Mackenzie argues that, ironically, Brown's ontology of divine generosity inadvertently evacuates the material world of significance in its own right, as it seems valuable only to the extent that it becomes a site of divine presence.[33]

Mackenzie's critique needs to be taken seriously, but it is perhaps an example of overreading Brown's position and applying a Continental and specifically Heideggerian analysis to Brown's avowedly more British and empirical methodology. As Brown says in the introduction to *God and Enchantment of*

---

above, for a brief discussion of formal sacramental theology in this book, see Brown, *God and Mystery in Words*, 38–43.

31. I am grateful to Mackenzie for making the manuscript of his paper available to me. This citation is from page 5 of the manuscript.

32. Mackenzie, "Presence without Absence?," 6.

33. Mackenzie, "Presence without Absence?"

Place, "British thought is often contrasted with Continental as more naturally empirical in approach. I believe that to be not only true but also right. Criteria set in advance can all too easily read like alien impositions that have failed to grapple sufficiently with the way the world is."[34] Brown thus takes a more inductive approach to these matters than Mackenzie seems to require of him. Furthermore, Mackenzie thinks that Brown is talking about "presence"—that is, "the metaphysics of . . ."—whereas, without being flippant or glib, I think that Brown is talking about *presence*. That is, it is not the philosophical *concept* of "presence" and its metaphysical implications that Brown is dealing with, but the actual presence of actual objects in our midst, and our actual presence in actual places, and what we believe to be God's actual presence to us in and through these objects and places—whatever that might ultimately be taken to mean.[35]

I of course realize that this reading of Brown could be accused of begging the question, and I am neither seeking to avoid a legitimate critique of his thought nor naïvely implying that our perception of the world is innocent of conceptual schemes and lenses. But I am suggesting that, recalling the citation from Edward Abbey, there is a three-dimensional "outdoor" element to Brown's work that moves beyond the conventionally textual-and-conceptual "indoor" world in which most philosophy and theology operate. Brown is at least inviting us to consider presence *without* metaphysics, rather than the metaphysics *of* pres-

---

34. Brown, *God and Enchantment of Place*, 3.

35. In the original version of this essay, I did not say that in the back of my mind while making these perhaps dark sayings was Fergus Kerr's appreciative discussion of Victor Preller's provocative claim:

> From God's point of view there is undoubtedly an "analogy of being"; from our point of view, however, there is only an "analogy of 'being.'"

See Fergus Kerr, "'Real Knowledge' or 'Enlightened Ignorance': Eric Mascall on the Apophatic Thomisms of Victor Preller and Victor White," in *Grammar and Grace: Reformulations of Aquinas and Wittgenstein*, ed. Jeffrey Stout and Robert MacSwain (London: SCM, 2004), 106–7, quoting from Victor Preller, *Divine Science and the Science of God: A Reformulation of Thomas Aquinas* (Princeton: Princeton University Press, 1967), 170. My point in response to Mackenzie here is not to endorse Preller's precise reading of Aquinas, but rather to acknowledge that, like the concept of "being" in that medieval context, Mackenzie was using the term "presence" in a metaphysically loaded way, and just as Preller distinguished between an "analogy of being" and an "analogy of 'being,'" I was asking if we could make a similar distinction between "a metaphysics of presence" and a "metaphysics of 'presence.'"

ence: to look at the painting, to inhabit the building, to listen to the song, and thus open ourselves to the independent reality of these things. Or, put differently, if not less problematically, by "presence" Brown means (alleged) "experienced presence," not (supposed) "metaphysical presence." Rather than (just) an *ontology* of divine generosity, Brown (also) has an *epistemology* of divine generosity, and that's what I think is the main point of dispute here. This shift of focus from ontology to epistemology may only exacerbate Mackenzie's concerns about Brown's work, but I think it more accurately depicts Brown's self-understanding.[36]

From a more doctrinal perspective, Trevor Hart argues that Brown's use of sacramental theology as the overarching framework through which to interpret alleged experiences of divine presence and grace comes at the expense of a more robust incarnational theology. According to Hart, although Brown does indeed acknowledge an incarnational element to his sacramental understanding of material reality, "in practice [he] makes surprisingly little of it, preferring to rely instead on the category of sacrament to provide his theological ballast (and in doing so, inclining unhelpfully in the direction of the Word's incarnational presence itself grounded in terms of a notion of 'sacrament' rather than vice versa)."[37] For Hart, incarnation precedes sacrament, both ontologically and chronologically. In the accompanying footnote, Hart explains further that his "own inclination is to suppose that, while analogies between incarnational and sacramental presence are certainly appropriate and helpful, they can also be misleading. The modes of divine presence alluded to in each case remain quite distinct, and the relevant order of priority is significant. 'Sacrament,' at least as used to refer to Christian Baptism and Eucharist, denotes something wholly secondary to and contingent on the reality of the incarnation itself, sacramental presence being a communication of Christ's humanity to the believer by faith,

36. For more thoughts along these lines, see Patrick Sherry, "The Sacramentality of Things," *New Blackfriars* 89 (2008): 575–90, and Mark Wynn, "Re-enchanting the World: The Possibility of Materially-Mediated Religious Experience," in *TA&C*, 115–27. Sherry and Wynn are more sympathetic to Brown's project than Mackenzie and thus provide examples of contemporary thinkers who do not find it either philosophically naïve or theologically demeaning of the natural world.

37. Originally published in Trevor Hart, *"Lectio Divina?"* in *TA&C*, 239; later published as "The Economy of the Flesh," in Hart's *Between the Image and the Word: Theological Engagements with Imagination, Language and Literature* (Farnham, UK: Ashgate, 2013), 88.

and only thus a sharing in his own intimate communion with the Father in the Spirit."[38]

As with Mackenzie, this is an important and serious critique. Brown responds to it in his own contribution to *Theology, Aesthetics, and Culture: Responses to the Work of David Brown*, commenting that he prefers to use sacramental terminology in these contexts for two reasons: first, "sacramental" is a more neutral term than "incarnation" and "so can more easily be used in dialogue with those of another or no religion"; and, second, "incarnation suggests a more resolved way of reading the world that admits less easily of the conflicts inherent in so much religious experience."[39] Brown then associates his understanding of sacramentality with Karl Rahner's, and it is with that association that I will close.

In his review of *Theology, Aesthetics, and Culture*, Robert Hughes responds to Hart's concern by suggesting that rather than seeing "incarnation" and "sacrament" in tension or conflict, with one necessarily prior to or dependent upon the other, we should instead engage more deeply with "Rahner's thought on the sacramental character of the Incarnation itself."[40] In other words, these are mutually interpreting terms: incarnation is sacramental and sacrament is incarnational. As that proposal opens up yet a further line of investigation, I trust that this brief tour through Brown's project has at least demonstrated that his vision does indeed exemplify "broad and creative thinking on the sacramental presence of the divine."[41]

38. Hart, "*Lectio Divina*?," 239; "The Economy of the Flesh," 88.

39. David Brown, "Experience, Symbol, and Revelation: Continuing the Conversation," in *TA&C*, 274.

40. Robert Davis Hughes, "God in Culture": a review of *TA&C* in the *Living Church*, October 5, 2014, 28. For a further comparison of Brown and Rahner, see Richard Viladesau, "Revelation, Christ, and Fundamental Theology: David Brown and Karl Rahner in Dialogue," in *TA&C*, 29–41.

41. I am grateful to John Hoffmeyer for inviting me to deliver the original version of this chapter on November 21, 2014, at the SALT meeting held at the First Lutheran Church in San Diego, California, USA. I am also grateful to David Brown, the late Ann Loades, and all those whose comments and questions before, during, and after its initial delivery have helped to improve it.

Conclusion

Whereas the first half of the twentieth century was an era of great individual Christian theologians such as Karl Barth (1886–1968), Paul Tillich (1886–1965), Karl Rahner (1904–84), the Niebuhr brothers, and so on, for the past fifty years academic theology in the English-speaking world has been dominated by a successive series of more collective movements. Emerging from the impasse of liberal and evangelical Protestantism in the 1970s, "Yale School" postliberalism drew on the work of Hans Frei and George Lindbeck and their students such as Stanley Hauerwas, David Ford, and Kathryn Tanner. While this school of thought became increasingly diffuse as the center shifted from Yale to other institutions, the historic manifesto was Lindbeck's *The Nature of Doctrine*.[1] About a decade later, the "Radical Orthodoxy" of John Milbank, Graham Ward, Catherine Pickstock, and their associates emanated boldly from Cambridge. Primarily Anglo-Catholic in origin and Augustinian in inspiration, it too developed in divergent ways, but remains a force to be reckoned with.[2] More recently, the "Analytic Theology" spearheaded by Michael Rea at the University of Notre Dame and Oliver Crisp at the University of St. Andrews has taken a provocative place at the intersection of analytic philosophy and systematic theology; and the "Canonical Theism" of William Abraham and his students at Southern Methodist University made a promising start that was

---

1. See George A. Lindbeck, *The Nature of Doctrine: Religion and Theology in a Postliberal Age* (Philadelphia: Westminster, 1984), as well as the twenty-fifth-anniversary edition with an introduction by Bruce D. Marshall and afterword by Lindbeck (Louisville: Westminster John Knox, 2009). The major influences on Yale School postliberalism are certain readings of Thomas Aquinas, Karl Barth, and Ludwig Wittgenstein.

2. See John Milbank, Catherine Pickstock, and Graham Ward, eds., *Radical Orthodoxy: A New Theology* (London: Routledge, 1999).

sadly undercut by Abraham's death in 2021.[3] During these past five decades, vital forms of liberation and contextual theology have also proliferated: Black, feminist, queer, disability, Latino, indigenous, and so on. Meanwhile, Roman Catholicism continues to grapple with the legacy of Vatican II and its contested aftermath (with Hans Urs von Balthasar [1905–1988] emerging as a major figure), both liberal and evangelical Protestantism still have their adherents, and the current disciples of the great individual figures mentioned above continue to study and develop their still-generative work.[4]

In a forthcoming monograph, I will survey and assess these movements in more detail, with special attention to their methodological aspects, but I wish to conclude this current volume by asking where Anglican philosophical theologians such as Austin Farrer and David Brown belong in the contemporary landscape. My sense is that while Farrer would—and that Brown does—find certain aspects of these various schools of thought congenial, they do not fit clearly and comfortably into any specific one of them. Hence my proposal from the introduction that "Critical Catholicism" might be the best description of Farrer, Brown, and any fellow travelers that they may have.[5] While I think that the Anglo-Catholic Farrer would be broadly sympathetic with the contours of Critical Catholicism described below, given his death in 1968 they are mostly drawn from Brown's more recent body of work. Brown himself, however, acknowledges Farrer as an inspiration.

By contrast with Yale School postliberalism, Critical Catholicism takes a somewhat different approach to biblical interpretation, being more receptive to historical-critical findings, although certainly not using that method alone. Indeed, when it comes to the scriptural texts, Critical Catholicism embraces

3. See Oliver D. Crisp and Michael C. Rea, eds., *Analytic Theology: New Essays in the Philosophy of Theology* (Oxford: Oxford University Press, 2009), and William J. Abraham, Jason E. Vickers, and Natalie B. Van Kirk, eds., *Canonical Theism: A Proposal for Theology and the Church* (Grand Rapids: Eerdmans, 2008).

4. Greek, Russian, and other forms of Eastern Orthodoxy have influenced some Western theologians, including Canonical Theists, but they have not as yet emerged as an equal conversation partner to Roman Catholicism and Protestantism. Much the same could be said about Pentecostal and charismatic theology.

5. I first proposed this category in my editor's introduction to David Brown, *God in a Single Vision: Integrating Philosophy and Theology*, ed. Christopher R. Brewer and Robert MacSwain (London: Routledge, 2016), vii–x, and I draw on some of that material here.

a variety of interpretative strategies. But it is also less narratively focused and textually oriented than postliberalism, being more open to the full range of literary genres—especially poetry—as well as visual art, music, architecture, and so on. Furthermore, unlike some forms of Protestantism, Critical Catholicism does not object to metaphysics and natural theology in principle, and sees special revelation as building upon general revelation rather than being in discontinuous tension with it.

By contrast with Radical Orthodoxy, Critical Catholicism is more receptive to British empirical and analytic modes of thought, although it also takes seriously and draws upon the Continental traditions of philosophy. Perhaps most crucially, unlike Radical Orthodoxy, Critical Catholicism does not make theology the master discipline over philosophy, history, and the social and natural sciences, but it allows these other academic discourses the freedom to be themselves and then seeks to learn what they have to teach. Therefore, rather than being tempted to isolate the Christian faith in a protected and privileged world of its own, Critical Catholicism integrates it fully with what is known in other fields of human inquiry.

By contrast with Analytic Theology, as already noted, Critical Catholicism is receptive to a wide range of philosophical methods and sources, not just one. And even within the analytic tradition, to refer back to the distinction made by William Abraham and discussed in the introduction, Critical Catholicism is very much of the strand of "St. Basil" rather than the strand of "St. Alvin." That is, it does not focus on formal and technical modes of argument, but operates "in a way that allows access to those interested in the big questions that motivate philosophical inquiry, cultivate wisdom and other informal intellectual virtues, and allow elbow room for growth in insight and spiritual perception."[6] Critical Catholicism is also more open than Analytic Theology to metaphorical and other nonliteral modes of discourse; as well as to potentially revisionist understandings of Christian doctrine, although within certain limits, as described further below.

When it comes to various forms of liberation and contextual theology, Critical Catholicism values their insights and takes seriously their urgent

---

6. William J. Abraham, "Turning Philosophical Water into Theological Wine," *Journal of Analytic Theology* 1 (2013): 1–16, quoting from 8. Available online at https://tinyurl.com /3ekjkyhr.

moral concerns. Indeed, Critical Catholicism enthusiastically welcomes new sources of knowledge whenever they can be found, and so views the expansion of perspectives as an epistemic good. There is therefore no conflict in principle between a Critically Catholic approach and these schools of thought, as long as they are not construed in a totalitarian or reductionist manner, with just one agenda, context, or identity trumping all others. Human life is simply too diverse and complex to be thus reduced, so any adequate theology must express that diversity and complexity. However, as the very meaning of the word bears witness, "catholicity" does strive to be as universal as possible, so it will emphasize the primal importance of our common humanity as well as celebrating marks of difference.[7]

In many ways, of these current methodological options, Critical Catholicism is perhaps the closest to Abraham's Canonical Theism, especially in their shared ecclesial and sacramental commitments. In an early articulation of this approach, Abraham described Canonical Theism as "that rich vision of God, creation, and redemption developed over time in the scriptures, articulated in the Nicene Creed, celebrated in the liturgy of the church, enacted in the lives of the saints, handed over and received in the sacraments, depicted in iconography, articulated by canonical teachers, mulled over in the Fathers, and treasured, preserved, and guarded by the episcopate."[8] Likewise, Critical Catholicism takes seriously the basic contours of Nicene Christianity and works as much as possible within those parameters, adjusting them only when it seems absolutely necessary in light of new knowledge. In addition to the "universal" sense of the term noted above, Critical Catholicism is also ecumenically "catholic" when it comes to institutional church structures, ordained ministry, and liturgical worship, and is thus especially hospitable to receiving from the Roman Catholic, Orthodox, and Anglican traditions. But whereas Canonical Theism is formally "restricted to the theism embodied in the canonical heritage of the church,"[9] Critical Catholicism

---

7. For a relevant philosophical exploration of this theme in conversation with current debates about racism and genocide, see Raimond Gaita, *A Common Humanity: Thinking about Love and Truth and Justice*, 2nd ed. (London: Routledge, 2000).

8. William J. Abraham, *Crossing the Threshold of Divine Revelation* (Grand Rapids: Eerdmans, 2006), 43–44.

9. Jason E. Vickers, "Canonical Theism and the Primacy of Ontology: An Essay concerning Human Understanding in Trinitarian Perspective," in Abraham, Vickers, and Van Kirk, *Canonical Theism*, 172.

is more open to also learning from outside those boundaries, including other religious traditions as well as the findings of contemporary science. Moreover, even within Christianity, other than taking its bearings from the classical creedal pronouncements on the Trinity and the incarnation of the Word of God in Jesus Christ, Critical Catholicism does not prioritize a specific period such as the patristic or medieval or Reformation era, or a particular Christian figure such as Augustine or Aquinas or Calvin, as being of decisive doctrinal significance.

In short, while not strongly revisionist in character, and by comparison with many contemporary theologies undoubtedly rather conservative in its firm commitment to a triune and incarnate deity, catholic order, formal liturgy, and sacramental realism, such Critical Catholicism is both theoretically and practically poised to learn radically new truths about God, humanity, and creation from any source whatsoever, including imaginative and artistic ones. It could thus potentially provide Christian theology a helpful way forward that avoids some of the limitations of other methodological approaches, especially in its fearlessly open stance toward general revelation and continuing progress in human understanding, along with its explicit desire to integrate information from beyond conventional sources such as Scripture and tradition, seeking expansion and insight rather than reiteration and reaction.

As indicated in the introduction, in articulating such Critical Catholicism I am not drawing simply on Austin Farrer and David Brown, but from the broader yet now largely neglected Anglican school of so-called Liberal Catholicism as expressed in essay collections such as *Lux Mundi: A Series of Studies in the Religion of the Incarnation* (1889) and *Essays Catholic and Critical* (1926), along with the report *Catholicity: A Study in the Conflict of Christian Traditions in the West* (1947), while also developing it further in a contemporary context. Other important figures in this general tradition—which contrasts with more conservative forms of Anglo-Catholicism—are Charles Gore (1853–1932), editor of *Lux Mundi*, and Michael Ramsey (1904–1988), author of *The Gospel and the Catholic Church* (1936), as well as Donald MacKinnon (1913–1994), Basil Mitchell (1917–2011), John Macquarrie (1919–2007), and Kenneth Leech (1939–2015). Ann Loades (1938–2022) would also fit within Critical Catholicism, and is a good example of a feminist version of it.[10] And while Sarah Coakley is developing her own substantial project under

---

10. Her recent essay collection *Explorations in Twentieth-Century Theology and Philoso-*

the rubric of what she calls "*théologie totale*," I think that she broadly belongs to what I call Critical Catholicism as well.[11] The leading Anglo-Catholic theologian of his generation, Rowan Williams—who among other prominent appointments was Lady Margaret Professor of Divinity at Oxford from 1986 to 1992 and archbishop of Canterbury from 2002 to 2012—would find aspects of Critical Catholicism congenial, but he is closer to Radical Orthodoxy on the philosophical side, and draws more deeply from the Greek and Russian Orthodox traditions on the doctrinal and spiritual sides. Other than Liberal Catholicism broadly construed, it is difficult to locate him within a particular contemporary school of thought or methodological stance.

All this brings us back to my twin concern in part 1 of the introduction with the contested nature of Anglicanism and the current debates about postcolonialism, race, gender, and sexual orientation. Obviously I cannot even begin to address adequately such issues here, although I will seek to do so in the forthcoming monograph mentioned above. However, when it comes to those particular concerns, some will undoubtedly view this present collection as regrettably reinscribing British "whiteness" at the heart of Anglican identity. But this is certainly not my intention! Indeed, although he was not an academic theologian, the South African Desmond Tutu (1931–2021)—recipient of the Nobel Peace Prize in 1984 and archbishop of Cape Town from 1986 to 1996—also belongs within the Liberal Catholic school, partly due to the strong influence on him of the Community of the Resurrection, an Anglo-Catholic monastic order founded by Charles Gore in 1892. Tutu is thus an important reminder not only of the vibrancy of African Anglicanism but of how the ecclesial role of "theologian" can be exercised in various ways.[12]

---

phy: *People Preoccupied with God*, ed. Stephen Burns (Melbourne: Anthem, 2023) is a helpful contribution to these titular themes.

11. See her *God, Sexuality, and the Self: An Essay "On the Trinity"* (Cambridge: Cambridge University Press, 2016), esp. xvii, 34–35 (including note 2), and 44ff. For more detail, see Ben King's section on Coakley in chapter 8 of this current volume. Ellen Charry is less concerned with philosophical issues and is probably more sympathetic with postliberalism and Canonical Theism than with the project of Critical Catholicism as I have outlined it here, but for a winsome defense of gradual spiritual development in the context of regular liturgical discipline and sacramental participation, see her "On Being an Anglo-Catholic," *Sewanee Theological Review* 47 (2003): 20–32.

12. Rather than an extended body of scholarly work, Tutu's immense contribution was

And there are also more academic theologians from other African, Asian, and Australasian contexts who derive their intellectual inspiration from a wider spectrum of the Anglican tradition than just the Catholic strand: T. C. Chau, Kwok Pui-lan, John Mbiti, Esther Mombo, John Pobee, Jenny Te Paa-Daniel, and K. H. Ting, among others.[13] Anglicanism is a diverse and lively communion of Christian churches spanning many cultures and contexts and with many different theological voices. My colleague James Tengatenga thus calls for a deeper "tri-continental" engagement that is required for "the fruition and coming into being of a more comprehensive Anglican theology." He insists, quite rightly, that "until all God's people speak, access the platforms and fora, and are heard, we have not finished doing theology."[14]

I fully agree with his claim and enthusiastically endorse this project, and as noted above, I will address these concerns more fully in the forthcoming monograph. Nevertheless, as Tengatenga also astutely observes, "contextualization does not mean the same thing in every context."[15] Given the current state of academic theology and philosophy of religion as discussed in the introduction, I am personally still confronted with a different set of problems than typical postcolonial ones, as important as they are, namely, the pervasive absence of any recognizably Anglican theology in dominant doctrinal discourses as well as an entrenched Alvinist rather than Basilian approach to philosophical theology. Aside from the specific topics of the essays themselves, these are the two broader issues that I hope this particular essay collection might help rectify, or at least generate conversation around, as a modest contribution to theology, philosophy, and Anglican studies. I am certainly not suggesting that those such as Farrer and Brown or other "Critical Catholics" provide everything we need here, only that they offer valuable but neglected perspectives for us to consider

---

made primarily through sermons, leadership, and advocacy, and yet he undoubtedly merits his chapter, written by Michael Battle, in *Twentieth Century Anglican Theologians: From Evelyn Underhill to Esther Mombo*, ed. Stephen Burns, Bryan Cones, and James Tengatenga (Chichester, UK: Wiley-Blackwell, 2021), 138–46.

13. Some of these have chapters in *Twentieth Century Anglican Theologians*, and some are mentioned in the list of additional names on p. xviii of the introduction by Stephen Burns and Bryan Cones, "Un/Usual Suspects."

14. James Tengatenga, "Afterword: God's Gift in Every Voice," in Burns, Cones, and Tengatenga, *Twentieth Century Anglican Theologians*, 237.

15. Tengatenga, "Afterword," 233.

as we seek to understand "the mystery that has been hidden throughout the ages and generations but has now been revealed to [God's] saints" (Col. 1:26 NRSV). *Now therefore to the indivisible Trinity and social Unity, one Godhead in three Persons, be ascribed as is most justly due all might, dominion, majesty and power, henceforth and for ever.*[16]

16. The closing doxology of Austin Farrer's fourth Bampton Lecture, "The Metaphysician's Image," here quoted from *Scripture, Metaphysics, and Poetry: Austin Farrer's* The Glass of Vision *with Critical Commentary*, ed. Robert MacSwain (Farnham, UK: Ashgate, 2013; London: Routledge, 2016), 69. For comments on earlier drafts of this conclusion, I am grateful to David Brown, Kelli Joyce, Ben King, Scott MacDougall, and James Tengatenga.

Index

Harris, Harriet, 150

Hart, Trevor, 239

Hartshorne, Charles, 12, 25

Hauerwas, Stanley, 16, 119, 124–27, 128, 129, 132–33

Hawk among Sparrows, A (Curtis), 14, 64

Hebblethwaite, Brian, 24–25, 35, 118, 120, 121

Hefling, Charles, 47

Hermes and Athena (Stump), 205

Heyward, Carter, 59

hiddenness argument, 193–97, 199

Hiddenness Argument, The (Schellenberg), 195, 199

Hillesum, Etty, 153

Hoffmeyer, John, 225

holiness, human, 151–53, 155–58, 164–65

Holy Spirit, 56–57

Hooper, Walter, 105

Houlden, Leslie, 40–41, 43, 59, 100

Hovey, Craig, 166

Howard-Snyder, Daniel, 25

Howatch, Susan, 36, 43

Huff, Margaret C., 59

Hughes, Robert, 240

human nature, 120–25

imago Dei, 2

"imbecile" (term), 120n7

"Imperfect Lives" (Farrer), 119–24, 128, 130, 132

incarnation, 239–40

indirection, 126, 128

"In His Image" (Farrer commemoration of Lewis), 108–11

Institute for Theology, Imagination, and the Arts (ITIA), 18

Integrity of Anglicanism (Sykes), 60

intellectual probation, 193–94

internalism, 136–37, 141

interpretation, biblical, 204, 206–8, 209–10, 211–12, 213–22, 242–43

Inwagen, Peter van, 7, 23, 153, 161

Isaac, 214, 215, 216

James, William, 160–61

Jellema, William Harry, 145

Jesus Christ, 46, 50, 58, 63

Job, 217–20

Joseph Butler's Moral and Religious Thought, 192

Keble, John, 101

Kellenberger, James, 34

Kerr, Fergus, 13

Kierkegaard, Søren, 215, 216

King, Ben, 18

knowledge, 137, 142, 149–50. *See also* belief; epistemology

Leech, Kenneth, 245

left brain/right brain, 211, 222–23

Letter to the Hebrews, 214–15

Lewis, C. S.: as Anglican, 101; "Christian Apologist" (Farrer), 105, 111–15; criticisms by Farrer, 113–15; doctrine in Farrer, 107; encouragement of Farrer, 116; Firsts, 102–3; friendship with Farrer, 15–16, 105, 116–17; "In His Image" (Farrer commemorative sermon), 108–11; meeting Farrer, 104–5; and philosophy, 113–14;